Killer Camera Rigs That You Can Build

How to build your own camera cranes, car mounts, stabilizers, dollies, and more!

Third Edition

Dan Selakovich

ELSEVIER

AMSTERDAM • BOSTON • HEIDELBERG • LONDON
NEW YORK • OXFORD • PARIS • SAN DIEGO
SAN FRANCISCO • SINGAPORE • SYDNEY • TOKYO

Focal Press is an imprint of Elsevier

Focal Press

Focal Press is an imprint of Elsevier
30 Corporate Drive, Suite 400, Burlington, MA 01803, USA
The Boulevard, Langford Lane, Kidlington, Oxford, OX5 1GB, UK

Notices
Knowledge and best practice in this field are constantly changing. As new research and experience
broaden our understanding, changes in research methods, professional practices, or medical treatment
may become necessary.
   Practitioners and researchers must always rely on their own experience and knowledge in evaluating
and using any information, methods, compounds, or experiments described herein. In using such
information or methods they should be mindful of their own safety and the safety of others, including
parties for whom they have a professional responsibility.
   To the fullest extent of the law, neither the Publisher nor the authors, contributors, or editors,
assume any liability for any injury and/or damage to persons or property as a matter of products
liability, negligence or otherwise, or from any use or operation of any methods, products, instructions,
or ideas contained in the material herein.

Library of Congress Cataloging-in-Publication Data
Selakovich, Dan, 1960-
   Killer camera rigs that you can build : how to build your own camera cranes, car mounts, stabilizers,
dollies, and more! / Dan Selakovich ; foreword by Michael Ferris.
      p. cm.
   ISBN 978-0-240-81337-0
   1. Cinematography—Equipment and supplies—Design and construction. 2. Motion picture camera
stabilization systems—Design and construction. I. Title.
   TR878.S45 2010
   778.5'30288—dc22

                                                                           2010019355

British Library Cataloguing-in-Publication Data
A catalogue record for this book is available from the British Library.

ISBN: 978-0-240-81337-0

For information on all Focal Press publications
visit our website at www.elsevierdirect.com

10 11 12 13 14 5 4 3 2 1

Printed in the United States of America

Working together to grow
libraries in developing countries

www.elsevier.com | www.bookaid.org | www.sabre.org

ELSEVIER   BOOK AID
            International   Sabre Foundation

Praise for the Previous Editions of *Killer Camera Rigs That You Can Build*

"The singular beauty of this book is that Mr. Selakovich has successfully dedicated himself to producing clarity with every page."

–Michael Ferris, Camera Operator/D.P. (Die Hard, Never Say Never Again)

"To make great shots, you need great equipment. D.W. Griffith made his greatest shots with balloons before there were cranes. Francois Truffaut made his greatest tracking shots from a wheelchair. Then the Steadicam came along. Now we have Killer Camera Rigs That You Can Build. *Buy the book, build it all, and make a great movie!"*

–Peter Medak, Director (The Ruling Class, Let Him Have It, Romeo Is Bleeding)

"For filmmakers who like to shoot their films with a mobile camera, without spending a fortune on equipment rentals, this book is a great gift indeed. I highly recommend it for its clarity and common sense."

–Kris Malkiewicz, Cinematographer/Author (Cinematography, Film Lighting)

"Dan has succeeded in making a nonintimidating how-to for camera rigs! No small feat! There are no excuses now! Even the smallest budget DV shoot can get 'that shot.' Clearly, talent is one thing, but Dan has made it easier for you to have the tools to bring out your vision. I applaud the book—whatever it takes to tell the story and make great-looking film... on a budget or otherwise!"

–Judy Marks, Cinematographer's Agent

"Sure, we'd like to shoot gorgeous panning shots like the Hollywood pros. But without expensive camera rigs, dollies, stabilizers, and other moviemaking niceties, we're often left pushing each other around in our office chairs. However, if you're handy with tools and can follow instructions, film teacher Dan Selakovich has another option: build your own rigs. In his book, Killer Camera Rigs That You Can Build, *Selakovich offers step-by-step instructions and tons of useful photos for building your own cranes, dollies, mounts, and more—all from materials you can find at your local hardware store."*

–Kelly Lunsford, MacWorld Magazine, *March 2004*

"Many times in VideoCamera *we discuss the use of tripods, dollies, booms, and other gadgets to make your shots steadier, more interesting, and even safer. But in many cases, the cost of the commercial versions of these things is prohibitive to the casual film maker or hobbyist.*

Even our own Mike Jones, who is an accomplished filmmaker, has been known to have resorted to using a skateboard to zoom through the street off Sydney's Newtown deftly holding onto his Canon XM-2 instead of hiring a dolly!

So when Killer Camera Rigs That You Can Build *was mentioned in the Sony Vegas forum of Digital Media Net (no matter what NLE you use, there will be a forum there, trust me—see www.dmnforums.com) that discussed making your own gizmos, I just had to get a copy and see for myself.*

When it turned up the following week, I was amazed. This A4 spiral bound book—it lays flat for ease of viewing when you are building these things—contains over 1300 step-by-step photographs to build everything from dollies, cranes, stabilizers, car mounts, and more, all from materials easily obtainable at your local hardware.

...The book contains over 300 pages, is a fun read as well, and highly recommended."

–David Hague, VideoCamera Australia Magazine, *July 2004*

"...I can't leave, however, without telling you about a new book written by Dan Selakovich that will save you infinite amounts of money on the production of your movie and will allow you to get some of the coolest shots you can imagine.

Killer Camera Rigs That You Can Build *is a 340-page masterpiece of build-it-yourself camera tools that are both easy on the budget and easy to build. Selakovich's instructions are fun and funny, and are accompanied by a ton of photographs that illustrate each project step by step. And what are the projects? Well, let's see...you get the 'Dark Passage Dolly,' which allows you to make the kind of amazing shots that will have your friends asking, 'How the hell did you do that?' Then there's the 'Big Combo Crane,' the 'Killer's Kiss Crane,' the 'They Drive By Night Car Mount,' 'The Touch of Evil Cam'—are you sensing a theme here? Despite the silly noir-influenced names, each one of these projects looks like a winner."*

–Rob Gregory-Browne, ScreenTalk Magazine, *May/June 2004*

*Without the unwavering support of these individuals,
my life would be in shambles. This edition is dedicated to them:*

*My mom, Beth Selakovich. My dearest friends Bo Harwood
and Paola Rauber. They have not only made my life better because
they are in it, but this book would not have been
possible without them.*

Table of Contents

About Michael Ferris

Hey, Dan, why would you get someone nobody's ever heard of to write your foreword? Who the heck is Michael Ferris, anyway?

Yes, I was asked that. Fact is, Mike is a quite famous cinematographer in certain circles. Besides, even the most removed from the film industry have seen his work. Maybe you've seen these little, lesser known films: *Die Hard, Water World, End of Days, Point of No Return, Internal Affairs, Back to the Future Part II, Colors, Never Say Never Again...* I could go on and on. His credit list is as long as my arm. Yep, he knows his stuff. There isn't a piece of filmmaking equipment he hasn't had his hands on. A pretty good person to write a foreword on film equipment, don't you think?

But the main reason for asking him to write the foreword is his long collaboration with John Cassavetes. Cassavetes is arguably the father of American Independent film. (I saw *Shadows* 15 years after its release, and it still haunts me as a film to aspire to in my own work, but I know I'll never be that good.) It's the independent filmmaker I wrote this book for. Now we don't have to compromise a shot because we couldn't afford to rent that crane—or dolly or car mount or stabilizer—now we can own these things and have them handy whenever the filmmaking mood strikes us. I can't know this for sure, but I'd like to think John would have loved a book like this. Instead of spending $500 on a dolly rental, he could have bought more film. And after hearing some of Mike's marvelous stories about his work with Cassavetes, there was almost a perpetual lack of the stuff.

I met Mike Ferris through a mutual friend, Bo Harwood (another longtime Cassavetes collaborator). I have to tell you about that first meeting: it was at a convention here in Los Angeles where film manufacturers and suppliers show their wares. Bo and I met Mike at the front entrance, and before we made it 100 feet into the place, Mike had three job offers on three major motion pictures from friends and coworkers who happened to be at the convention (It seems that Mike knows everyone!). I'm not kidding—three offers of work inside of 10 minutes! Well, I was floored. Quite the first impression.

So that's why I asked Mike. Any more stupid questions?

Foreword by Michael Ferris

When Dan Selakovich asked me to write the introduction to a book about equipment and the technology of filmmaking, I asked him, "Why me?"

We had met but a few times and I was able to think readily of many who had more aptitude regarding the subject other than myself.

It is true that I have spent many years using the technological marvels available to the modern filmmaker. During this time it has been my job to relate the desires and instincts of many to the where, how, and when to use this sophisticated machinery. Still, I thought, am I justified in writing a foreword to a book dedicated solely to the technology of filmmaking?

Then Dan answered my question. And with his answer he made me understand instantly the yes of my own qualifications. He said, "Mike, you've worked with John Cassavetes. The man that started true independent film, the man that opened the door for the rest of us. And that's what this book is truly about, not just building camera rigs, but being free to create without a studio budget."

I worked with John Cassavetes through the '70s and knew him until his death in February of 1989. I worked with him as cameraman on *A Woman Under the Influence*, *The Killing of a Chinese Bookie*, *Mikey and Nicky*, and *Opening Night*. I also worked on a film written by John and directed by his son Nick, called *She's So Lovely* (original title: *She's De Lovely*).

The man who authored this meticulous book was clearly inspired by John Cassavetes. It is a work of determined imagination, requiring perseverance and sacrifice, both common ingredients in any film John ever attempted.

As John's work continues to inspire people everywhere, Dan Selakovich has used his experience to reduce the disparity between affordable and high-cost filmmaking. This is something I think John would have deeply appreciated.

The difference between John and others was the difference between personal and professional lives. The clearly defined demarcation between work behavior and our private selves didn't exist for John. Whereas most of us leave our homes, arrive at work, and assume a public attitude, John shot his movies in his home. He used family and friends to play out the parts he wrote, and cajoled everyone in his life to help him render his ideas onto film. He was able to do this so successfully because he possessed the rarest combination of original talent and extraordinary personal humanity.

How does all this apply to the equipment used to make films?

In John's early days of picture-making, his camera platform and dolly moves were essentially limited to what his shoulders, legs, and back could withstand. His budgets limited the equipment he used. There is no question he would have enthusiastically incorporated into his projects the simple, useful techniques found in these pages. I can imagine him talking to Dan for hours (as he did with many of us) about the building and use of gear in this book for scripts he had written.

Killer Camera Rigs That You Can Build

The singular beauty of this book is that Mr. Selakovich has successfully dedicated himself to producing clarity with every page. All aspects of creating the equipment it describes has been worked out in detail. The difficulties associated with visualizing specific construction and the agonies of realizing mistakes, then remeasuring and rebuilding are gone. Anyone who desires can quickly render easily obtained, inexpensive hardware into practical, reliable, innovative filmmaking equipment. This in turn will allow greater creativity for stories less restricted by physical limitations or time constraints.

I commend Dan for his pioneering solutions to the technical dilemmas facing filmmakers. I further salute you, the reader, for caring to search for ways to overcome the many obstacles to communication that bedevil those who would entertain, illuminate, inform, or connect with the human heart.

Like John Cassavetes, who seemed to reinvent the camera to interpret his own values, who recognized no technical boundaries and generated a visual language born out of pure stubborn necessity, declare war on anything that says the filmmaker can't.

This book not only says you can, it shows you how.

Michael Ferris
Malibu, California

Introduction to the Third Edition (Hey, it's probably more important to read this than you think!)

Thank goodness for the digital video (DV) revolution. It has put filmmaking within reach of us poor folk (relatively speaking). The downside is that the things that hold and move the camera—dollies, stabilizers, cranes, and other necessities of movie making—are still darned expensive to rent. And forget purchasing (I don't know about you, but a grand for a boom arm is a little beyond my means). This book will change all that. I'm going to show you how to make this stuff. It really isn't hard. For the most part, if you can drill a hole, you can make most of the equipment in these pages. Really. And you don't even need a lot of room (for the first edition, I built everything in the book in my apartment kitchen). I've also tried to make the gear with the bits and pieces that are readily available at your local hardware store or sporting goods shop. The other great thing about DV cameras is their size. They're small and light, which means your camera rigs can be small as well. (The *Dark Passage* dolly has been used to do a dolly shot in the back seat of a car. Let's see Hollywood do that!) Smaller rigs mean more innovative shots in less time.

Most of the rigs in this book can be built for less than $100 as long as you follow my instructions! In other words, I've already made the costly mistakes for you. Not to mention the time wasted for that 100th trip back to the hardware store. Trust me, the price of this book will be saved in trial and error when you build your first crane. You may also notice that I use aluminum quite a bit in these rigs. Please don't panic! I know it's a metal, but it's a very soft one and relatively easy to work with. So don't worry, we'll be doing this step-by-step, and it's easy. Before building anything involving metal, please read the appendix, *Working with Metal*!

There are tons of new rigs in the third edition. Most are from requests of filmmakers who bought earlier editions; I do listen to you! Feel free to e-mail me about any questions, problems, rigs you'd like to see in future editions, or my favorite, praise about what a genius I am (wink, wink). You can reach me at dan@DVcameraRigs.com.

"Professional" rigs versus my rigs

First, I don't quite know what a professional rig is, but every now and then I'll hear that the rigs in these pages don't *look* professional (though they work as well or better than their professional counterparts!). In *Evil Dead 2: Dead by Dawn*, Director Sam Raimi bolted the camera to a 2×4 piece of lumber and ran through the woods with it. In *The French Connection*, cameraman Enrique Bravo was pushed around in a wheelchair used as a dolly for much of the picture. Hollywood lore is chock-full of stories like this.

I came up with my dolly design that uses in-line skate wheels around 1987. It never really caught on until the first edition of this book came out. Now you'll see some version of this dolly in use everywhere. One version I saw had six sets of wheels on each side (mine uses two sets, or rarely, three sets). When I asked the filmmaker why he decided to put so many, he answered, "this is a *professional* dolly, though he couldn't explain why so many wheels were needed on a practical matter. My guess is, well, tradition. See, there's a dolly called a Fisher dolly that is pretty standard on Hollywood pictures. Sometimes a large group of skate wheels ganged together is needed to run this dolly on track. Why so many wheels? Because a Fisher dolly has a carrying weight of 445 pounds and a maximum load capacity of 900 pounds. This is one heavy piece of machinery, so it needs a lot of support from the wheels. A small platform dolly like the ones in this book carry 400 pounds max, depending on how big your camera operator is. Twelve sets of wheels are just not needed. But hey, it's your dolly. If you want to add them go right ahead!

This example is very typical, and every time I experience it, I'm reminded of a story my dad told me as a kid: A wife was cooking a roast when her husband asked why she cut the ends off of it before popping it into the oven. She replied, "Gee, I really don't know. That's what my mother always did." Curiosity got the best of her, and she gave her mother a call. Her mother said, "I don't know. That's what *my* mother always did." So the wife calls up her grandmother and asked why she always cut the ends off of the roast. The grandmother replied, "We could never afford a new pan, and the one I had was just a bit too small for the roast, so I cut the ends off to make it fit into the pan." That's what tradition often is: a reason for something that no longer applies! The reason I'm sharing this with you is that many have used this book as a jumping off point to develop their own rigs to fit their specific needs. If you try to copy Hollywood for your 10 pound camera, you'll be overdoing it a bit, and wasting a lot of money that could be used for better sound for your movie!

"It doesn't look professional." This comment is very rare, thank goodness, but I am always surprised to hear it. I personally don't care how a rig looks. I just want it to work right. After all, where would Sam Raimi be if he said, "We can't do that shot because that 2×4 doesn't look professional." Fact is, I get about three e-mails a month from filmmakers who have purchased "professional" equipment that didn't work like it was designed to. Most often it is dolly track that created a bump in the move every time the wheels would go over a joined section of track. They ask me how to fix it. I'm always in the position of saying it can't be fixed. If a machined bit of track is wonky, it will always be wonky. My favorite track is plain ol' PVC pipe. It's cheap, it can be joined together with no bump at the joint, it's light, and it can be purchased just about anywhere. If you're in the middle of a shoot and rented only 15 feet of pro track and you need 20 feet, you're out of luck. PVC—just head for the nearest hardware store.

But as I said, I do listen to filmmakers, so you'll find "pro" versions of rigs and track in this new edition. They are harder to build, and don't work any better than the "lesser" designs, but if you want your shoot to *look* pro, have at it.

What you need to know before building anything in this book

TOOLS

Have you ever seen this really great show called *The New Yankee Workshop*? It's a PBS spin-off of *This Old House*. In it, Master Carpenter Norm Abram shows us how to build all sorts of finely crafted furniture and a plethora of other wood projects. The only bad part of the show is his amazing power tool collection.

Often I'll watch Norm work on a piece of equipment that only someone with a weekly show could afford: "Now we'll just move over to our laser cutter and glue unit...." Laser cutter? Glue unit? Dang, Norm, it's just a coffee table. And where do I get one of those laser cutter combo glue units, anyway?

You won't have that frustration in this book. Although you'll need some basic tools for these projects, I will give you cheaper options than the best option. Would it be nice to have a drill press? Yes. Do you absolutely need it? No. Mostly. The "pro" dolly track and the *Double Indemnity* crane need some specialized tools, but in the end they aren't very costly. So at the beginning of each project there will be a tools list of what you'll need to make it.

MATERIALS

As I mentioned earlier, I've gone to some great (and sometimes very frustrating) lengths to build these rigs out of materials you can find in just about any city in America. Like the tools, there will be a list of the materials you'll need at the beginning of each project. And there is also a Photo Shopping List that has pictures and measurements of what you'll need. Don't know what a lock nut is? Just look at the photo. Easy. Also, *read through the entire project* before heading to the hardware store. There are things that are left up to you that take some consideration. For example, if you're getting a different size bolt than what I'm using, you just might need a different size drill bit to match that bolt.

While we're on the subject of buying, I found that the weird little out-of-the-way hardware stores were best for finding a lot of the little odd things. As far as the big chain home centers go, they are good for only the most common materials. Orchard Supply Hardware (in California) and Ace Hardware® have a much greater selection of odd and ends, at least in the Los Angeles area. Mostly, the small indie stores will have a much better selection, and are no more costly than the big boys.

"MAKE IT GROOVY" OPTIONS

Many of the projects you'll make have what I'll call a basic construction, and then add-ons to make it really cool. For instance, the *Big Combo* crane basic camera mount is nonmovable. The Make It Groovy option adds a movable bracket so you can tilt the camera up or down.

METRIC MEASUREMENTS

We here in America are a stubborn bunch. We've held on to those inches and feet much too long in my opinion. With that in mind, in this edition you filmmakers outside our U.S. borders will appreciate the metric measurements alongside those nasty inches. I've made every effort to make sure the conversions are correct, but hey, I live in America, so the conversions might not be exact. A millimeter here or there isn't going to make any difference, but in the rarest of cases. The only thing that comes to mind is the bolt that goes through the bearing for the *Dark Passage* dolly and the *Shock Corridor* stabilizer. If you can't find an 8 mm bolt, just get one that fits through the bearing with no wiggle room. Also, some countries might have no option but to go with the "pro" versions of things in the book, as in the cradle for the *Double Indemnity* crane. I've tried my best to make these out of materials available worldwide.

READ THIS OR GO BLIND!

Please, please read the safety instructions that come with your power tools—*and follow them*! And make damn sure you buy some safety glasses. All it takes is one metal chip in your eye to end your filmmaking career.

You can't make movies if you're blind! Seriously, don't be stupid. Buy and wear the damn glasses.

ABOUT THE RIG NAMES

I know. At first glance they may seem strange. The thing is, I'm a huge fan of film noir movies. All the rigs in this book are named after film noir pictures, mostly from the 1940s. I did this for my own amusement, but it has had a very welcome result: student filmmakers are actually watching these movies. Typically, I'm very unimpressed by movies made nowadays. Filmmakers never seemed to learn, or simply ignore, basic film grammar. These old movies are steeped in lessons for the modern filmmaker, and I hope you'll search some of them out. At the end of the book you'll find a list of all the movies for which the rigs are named, with the director and year they were made.

SECTION 1: DOLLIES

The *Dark Passage* Dolly

The great thing about the *Dark Passage* dolly is its versatility. By making the dolly platform any size you choose (within reason, of course), you can adapt it for any situation for the price of a piece of plywood. And because of the unique wheel design and placement, this dolly can be mounted to run on rails overhead! And once your wheel assemblies are made, you can just move them from one size plywood to the other. No need to spend a lot of cash on extra wheels for different-sized dollies! The plans for the *Killer's Kiss Crane* later in this book makes it a perfect combination for use with this dolly. Make sure you read about all the dollies and dolly extras in the book so you can decide on the size and style of your dolly. If you want something heavy duty, double up on the plywood, making it twice as thick. Or build the *Killers dolly* in the next chapter. I use both dollies a lot!

DOI: 10.1016/B978-0-240-81337-0.00001-X

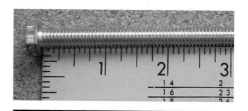

☐ (8) in-line skate wheels. It doesn't matter what size, just as long as *they're on sale!* (Make sure they have the bearings, or pick some up in a separate pack. Each wheel takes two bearings, so that's 16 in all. You'll also need some if you're building the *Shock Corridor Stabilizer*). Also, because of the design of the dolly you can use the larger Razor® scooter-type wheels. Either will work just fine.

Note: If you want to use more than four sets of wheels, you'll need two wheels for each set for each side of the dolly, and expand the number of everything that follows to build each wheel set. This will be clear once you read through the instructions.

☐ (4) ⁵⁄₁₆″ (8 mm) bolts × 3″ (76 mm) long. This goes through the wheel bearing, so make sure it's a snug fit (all the skate bearings are ⁵⁄₁₆″). I've never found a bearing that didn't have a ⁵⁄₁₆″ hole, so you should be pretty safe with any wheels you buy.

☐ (8) ⁵⁄₁₆″ (8 mm) nuts. Try to find nuts that are thinner than average. They're called jam nuts.

☐ (8) ⁵⁄₁₆″ (8 mm) washers. They don't have to have an exact ⁵⁄₁₆″ hole, but pretty close to the bolt diameter.

☐ (4) ⁵⁄₁₆″ (8 mm) lock nuts. Lock nuts have this little nylon ring that holds it tight to the bolt—important!

☐ (4) L-brackets. You won't find these with the rest of the L-brackets. These are made for deck building by Simpson Strong-Tie, model number HL-33, so check that part of the hardware store first. They are really heavy duty and take a ½″ (14 mm) bolt to attach to the dolly platform (see next page). If you don't live in earthquake or hurricane country, these might be hard to find. That's OK, simply follow the plans for the *Killers* dolly later in this section.

4

☐ (4) ½" (14 mm) bolts × 2" (50 mm) long. These hold the wheel assembly to the deck of the dolly.

☐ (8) ½" (14 mm) ID (inner diameter) or larger washers (for the ½" (14 mm) bolt).

☐ (4) ½" (14 mm) lock nuts (for the ½" bolt).

☐ ¾" (19 mm) thick plywood. This can be any size you want. I have several sizes: I use a 12" (30 cm) square a lot in tight places, a 24" square, and one big enough for a camera operator that is 26" wide × 40" long. You can make a bigger one, of course, but if you want to dolly through a standard 32" wide doorway, your dolly with its wheels must be narrower than that.

☐ ¾" (19 mm) PVC pipe. You'll find this in the plumbing section. This is used for dolly track. You can use other stuff for track depending on the situation. This stuff is good when connecting more than one length. Get ones with the *thick core* (don't panic—just look at all the PVC the hardware store offers and get the thickest stuff), as much as you need. Four 10' (3 meter) lengths is a good start. You can also use 1" (25 mm) PVC if you want. If you use 1" PVC, make sure your plumbing nipples (next) are ¾" (19 mm). We'll be going more into track in the track section, but it won't hurt to get two lengths of electrical conduit or PVC while you're at the store so you can test out your dolly.

☐ ½" (14 mm) metal pipe nipples (get one for every two sections of PVC pipe). These are good for screwing the PVC pipe together for longer sections of track. Since I wrote the first edition of this book, there are commercial connectors for PVC used as dolly track. These are expensive and don't work as well as this simple solution.

Other Options for Track

We'll be getting into all sorts of track options in individual chapters, but here are just a couple of ideas. Next time you're at a large home center, look around. I think you'll discover tons of things you can use for track! But in the meantime, grab some PVC.

Long lengths of L-shaped aluminum are a good option for dolly track where you might need a lot of strength (going overhead between two ladders, for instance).

Another option for dolly track is ¾" (19mm) electrical conduit. It comes in 10' lengths, but is difficult to string together so you don't get a bump in your camera move. I'd use it for shots of 10' (3 meters) or less.

Tools List for the *Dark Passage* Dolly

☐ A drill. Get one with variable speed ability (don't worry, most drills have this). If you're going to be building other projects that involve drilling into metal, *do not* buy a cordless drill. They just don't have enough muscle for metal. For this project, though, a cordless drill is fine.

☐ ½" (14mm) drill bit.

☐ Locking pliers. Get two pairs if you're not going to be using a socket wrench as well.

☐ A socket wrench set. Not absolutely necessary, but damned handy.

☐ An assortment of clamps. Not absolutely necessary on this project, but always handy, and very much needed on other projects in this book and for filmmaking in general.

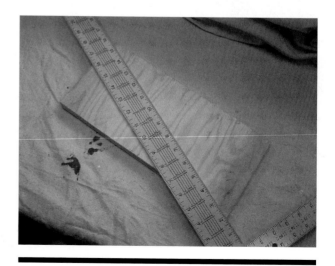

☐ Combination square. Get one, get one, get one!

☐ A big framing square. For this and other projects!

Let's Build It

1 First, we need to figure out where to put our brackets for the wheels. The plywood I'm using for this dolly measures 3' × 2' (0.60 × 1 meter), plenty big enough to hold a tripod or small boom arm.

0" to 5" (0–127 mm) from the edge seems about right. Use the framing square to make sure the placement of the bracket is square with the deck, and right on the edge of the board. If we were using a smaller piece of wood for the platform, we might want to go in only a couple of inches (50 mm). Truly, anywhere from right on the narrow edge of the dolly deck to about 5" in is just fine on a dolly this big.

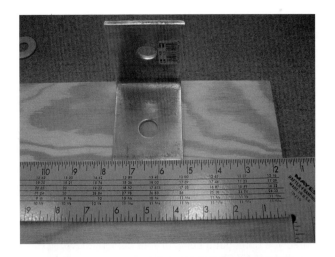

As you can see here, I'm placing the bracket flush to the edge. *Important*: Make sure all the brackets are lined up the same, or they won't fit into the track properly!

Here I'm using a piece of aluminum that runs the full length of the board as a straight edge against my framing square so I know where to place the bracket on the other end. It might be a good idea to draw a pencil line down the length of the straight edge and line both brackets against that line.

Once the bracket is in place, mark the center of the hole in the bracket. This is where we'll being drilling into our deck to attach the bracket. Do this in each corner with the remaining three brackets. In this photo, I'm using a bracket with two holes on a much smaller platform, but the principle is the same. I just want to give you the idea that you don't have to use the exact brackets in the materials list. They just need to be thick enough to hold your weight!

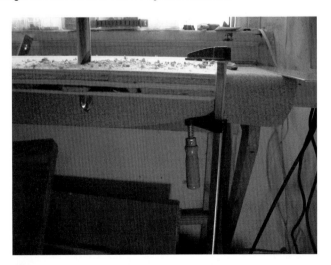

2 Let's do some drilling. Clamp the board to the table and load that big ½" (14 mm) bit into the drill. Be careful to drill the hole right on that perfect mark you made! Do this to the remaining three corners.

ATTACH THE BRACKETS

3 You're going to need that ½" (14 mm) bolt, two washers, and a lock nut (the one with the little nylon ring inside). This is pretty straightforward. Put a washer on the bolt and stick the thing up through the hole. (The head of the bolt should be on the top side of the dolly.) Thread the bracket hole over the bolt, then a washer on top of that, then tighten the whole shebang down with the lock nut.

Before you tighten that nut all the way down, grab your combo square (you did remember to get one, didn't you?) and line it up with one edge against the plywood, and the other against the edge of the bracket. Is the bracket square against the straight edge? If not, and it probably won't be, just muscle it over until it looks like the following:

Now tighten the heck out of it. Finish up the other three corners.

Hey, we're almost done. Pretty easy so far, huh?

ATTACH THE WHEELS

4 Grab your ⁵⁄₁₆" × 3" (8 mm × 76 mm) bolt, two jam nuts, two washers, one lock nut, and two skate wheels with the bearings.

Put a washer on the bolt and run it through the hole in the bracket and put a washer on the other side (see, like in the picture).

5 Screw on one of those narrow nuts and tighten the whole mess down. Hey, look at that! You just made an axle! (Make sure you put the bolt at the top of the too-big bracket hole—toward the deck—to keep it from sliding. Also, it looks like there are two washers. Nope. Just a reflection.)

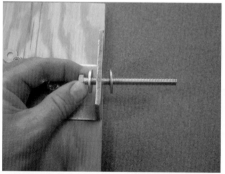

6 Put on one of your wheels and thread another nut on the other side. Not too tight, you still want the wheel to spin without being wobbly.

Hey Dan! I can't fit the wheel on the axle! What gives?

You bought the wheels with the bearings already in them, didn't you? No worries. There's a little plastic axle in there. Take a screwdriver and pop out one of the bearings, remove the plastic bit, and pop the bearing back into the wheel hub. Now you're good to go.

8

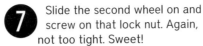 Slide the second wheel on and screw on that lock nut. Again, not too tight. Sweet!

Repeat the steps on the other three brackets and you're done.

If the hardware store didn't have the right length bolt (like you see in the picture) and you bought some longer ones, that's OK. It's best though, to use a hacksaw to chop off that extra length.

Here's what the bottom should look like when you're done.

Here's a small version with a fluid head bolted to the middle. I use this one a lot. We'll get more into that in later chapters.

When you place the finished rig on the track, make sure it fits in the groove in-between the two wheels.

Here's the dolly up off the ground using electrical conduit for track, ready to dolly though a window. There are tons of shots you can do with a small light dolly!

There you have it. Now go check out the chapter on dolly track later in this section! Because of the unique wheel design (well, not so unique nowadays!), it opens up a whole new world of what you can use for track. If you'd gone with the Hollywood regular skate wheel design, your track options would be extremely limited. You're welcome.

The *Killers* Dolly

You'll want to build this dolly if you want a really bomb-proof dolly. The wheel attachments are permanent, so you can't move them from one dolly deck to another as you can with the *Dark Passage* dolly. Once you've built this one, it's here to stay. You'll also want to make this one if you plan on using it with a small camera crane (a jib) with a camera weighing over 8 pounds. I know, 8 pounds doesn't sound like a lot, but with a jib, the heavier the camera, the more counterweight you'll need, so it can get heavy pretty fast. It's also a good idea to build this one if you'll be making a camera pedestal to go on your dolly (we'll be covering camera pedestals later, in the dolly section). And lastly, you'll want to make this one if a camera operator and assistant (focus puller) will be riding on the dolly.

I'll also be showing you how to add a handle to your dolly as well as how to mount a tripod on your dolly without a spreader. Both of these concepts will work for this dolly as well as the *Dark Passage* dolly so feel free to trick out your *Dark Passage* too!

Important: Make sure you read the appendix, *Working with Metal*, before starting this project!

Materials List for the *Killers* Dolly

Hey, wait a minute! Here's something to think about first. Is your camera over 8 pounds? And will you be using a jib or camera pedestal on this dolly? If the answer is yes, you'll need to build the deck out of two ¾" (19mm) sheets of plywood glued together. If your answer is no, you can get away with using only one sheet of ¾" (19mm) plywood for your dolly deck. The big advantage is that a lighter dolly is easier to haul around. Either dolly deck will do if all you are putting on there is an operator, a tripod, and a camera.

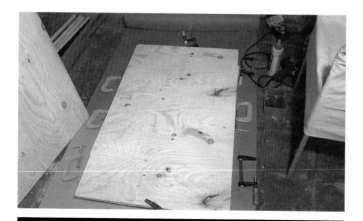

☐ (2) sheets of ¾" (19mm) thick plywood. Mine measure 26" × 40" (0.66 × 1 meter). You can make it bigger or smaller if you want. The reason mine is only 26" wide, is that someday I might want to dolly through a doorway.

☐ A big bottle of wood glue for gluing the two sheets of plywood together.

☐ (10) ¼" × 2" (7mm × 50mm) carriage bolts with a ¼" (7mm) nut for each.

Killer Camera Rigs That You Can Build

DOI: 10.1016/B978-0-240-81337-0.00002-1

☐ (2) lengths of angle aluminum or steel. I'm using ⅛" (3 mm) thick aluminum 1" (25 mm) wide on each side. This is the smallest you want to get. You can certainly get stuff that is 2" or 3" on each side. I've even taken a hacksaw to an old bed frame and used that steel angle for a dolly. The point is, there are tons of different types of angle out there you can use. It needs to be as long as your dolly. In my case, the dolly is 40" long, so my angle is also 40" long.

☐ (8) in-line skate wheels. It doesn't matter what size, just as long as *they're on sale!* (Make sure they have the bearings, or pick some up in a separate pack. Each wheel takes two bearings, so that's 16 in all. You'll also need some if you're building the *Shock Corridor* stabilizer). Also, because of the design of the dolly you can use the larger Razor® scooter-type wheels. Either will work just fine. *Note:* If you want to use more than four sets of wheels, you'll need two wheels for each set for each side of the dolly, and expand the number of everything that follows to build each wheel set. This will be clear once you read through the instructions.

☐ (4) ⁵⁄₁₆" (8 mm) bolt × 3" (76 mm) long. This goes through the wheel bearing, so make sure it's a snug fit (all the skate bearings are ⁵⁄₁₆"). I've never found a bearing that didn't have a ⁵⁄₁₆" hole, so you should be pretty safe with any wheels you buy.

☐ (8) ⁵⁄₁₆" (8 mm) nuts. Try to find nuts that are thinner than average. They're called jam nuts.

☐ (4) ⁵⁄₁₆" (8 mm) lock nuts. Lock nuts have this little nylon ring that holds it tight to the bolt—important!

Tools List for the *Killers* Dolly

☐ C-clamps. I'd get at least eight with a 3" (76 mm) mouth or bigger. You'll be using C-clamps a lot in this book, but you'll be using them even more when you shoot your movie. (Glance into any grip truck and you'll find tons of C-clamps.)

☐ A prick punch or center punch. A center punch is used to put a small dimple in metal where you're going to drill a hole. You have to have this or your drill bit will "walk" across the metal, and that's not good at all. Officially a prick punch is used for marking metal by scratching it. I've used both for making a dimple.

☐ A hammer.

☐ A variable speed drill. Try not to use a cordless drill. They just aren't great for drilling into metal. A drill you have to plug in is cheaper anyway.

☐ A tape measure.

☐ Vice grip pliers. If you're not going to use a socket wrench (next), it would really help to have two pairs of vice grips.

☐ Socket wrench set. This is super handy, but you don't *have* to have it. It really does help getting the lock nuts on better than anything though!

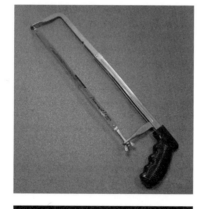

☐ A ¼" (7 mm) drill bit.

☐ A ⁵⁄₁₆" (8 mm) drill bit.

☐ A hacksaw. (You'll need this only if you need to cut the aluminum or steel angle you bought.) It's a really good idea to pick up some extra blades while you're at it.

☐ A vice. This is used for holding metal while you work on it. For this project, you could probably get away with just clamping the metal to your workbench, but if you're going to be building any of the bigger cranes in the book, go ahead and get it now! Normally, most people bolt this vice to a workbench. I bolt mine to a 12" (0.30 meter) square of plywood then use big C-clamps to attach it to my bench. I find that I move my vice around a lot, so it's handy to have it portable.

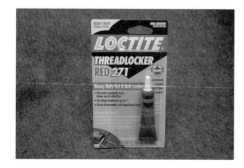

☐ Some kind of thread lock. You put this on bolt threads to keep the bolt on there for good.

☐ Thread cutting oil. When cutting into metal, you need to keep the bit well lubricated to keep the bit sharp and to keep it from jamming.

☐ A wire wheel. This goes in your drill for cleaning up metal.

Killer Camera Rigs That You Can Build

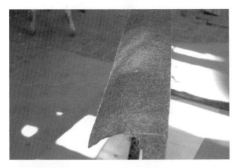

A bit of indoor/outdoor carpeting. Get this if you want to carpet your dolly. It's a good idea so the camera operator can get a good grip with his or her feet. You'll need enough to cover the top of the dolly and the sides.

Spray adhesive (to attach the carpet to the deck). This one is for vinyl because the backing on my carpet is vinyl.

A utility knife for cutting carpet.

A staple gun. This is good for tacking down the corners of the carpet if the adhesive isn't quite doing its job.

Let's Build It

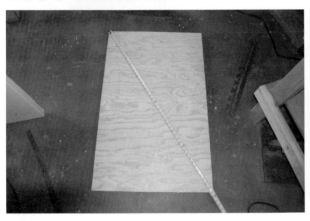
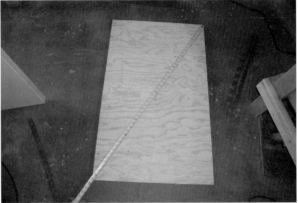

1 Make sure your plywood is square. I had these cut at the home center, and often it can be a little off. Take a look at these two photos. The easiest way to make sure a big piece like this is square is to measure from the upper-lefthand corner to the lower-righthand corner. Note the measurement, then measure from the upper-righthand corner to the lower-lefthand corner. If these measurements are exactly the same, you're good to go. If you're doubling up on the plywood, check the other one as well.

2 Have all of your clamps ready and spread a bunch of glue on one piece. You'll need to spread it out in a thin layer as if you're buttering a piece of toast, and make sure you get it right to the edges of the plywood.

3 Carefully lay your second piece of plywood on top of the first.

4 Clamp it down. Make sure that all the edges line up! Eight clamps minimum!

5 When the glue dries, we'll be attaching the angle to each side. So let's get the angle prepared while we wait for the glue to set.

First we need to drill ¼" (7 mm) holes for the ¼" (7 mm) bolts to fasten the angle to the deck. Pick five points on one side of the angle for these holes. Where you put them isn't so important, just as long as they are somewhat equally spaced.

For mine, I'm going to put the bolts on each end 1" (25 mm) in. from the edge. Set your combination square at 1" (25 mm) and mark a line there.

Since my aluminum angle is 1" (25 mm) wide on each side, I'm going to set my combo square to ½" (14 mm), so my hole will be right in the middle of the angle. If your angle is 2" (50 mm), you'd place that hole at 1" (25 mm). Get it?

Do the same on the opposite end, then three more places along the length of the angle.

Repeat the steps on the other piece of angle.

6 Take your prick punch or center punch and place the tip on your first mark and give it a good thwack with a hammer. This will put a dimple in the metal. When drilling, you put the point of the drill bit in that dimple—that way your drill bit won't "walk." This is really important when working with metal!

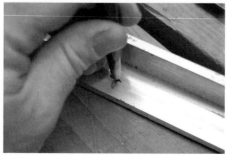

Killer Camera Rigs That You Can Build

7 Clamp your angle in the vice or clamp it to your workbench directly, but *clamp it*!

Add a little drill oil in the dimple, then drill your ¼" (7 mm) holes. You will need to add a little oil as you go. If you're drilling into steel, you'll need to add a lot of oil as you go! Do *not* pull the drill trigger all the way. You want to drill much slower through aluminum, and even slower through steel. After a few holes, you'll get a knack for bit speed.

Please make sure your bit is going straight! You don't want a crooked hole.

8 Now we need to drill the holes for the wheel axle on the second side of the angle. If you are using four wheels sets, you'll need one ⁵⁄₁₆" (8 mm) hole at each end of the angle. Mine are 2" from each end because I don't want the axle bolt getting in the way of the bolt I'm using to attach the angle to the deck. If you're going to add a third set of wheels to each side, drill another axle hole dead center of the angle. So for this 40" (1 meter) long dolly, 20" (0.50 meter) is the center. You can add as many wheel sets as you want, but anything over three is really overkill.

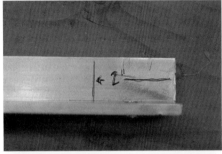

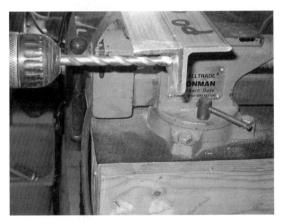

Here's what your holes should eventually look like: one side of the angle for the deck bolts and one side for the axle bolt.

Load your ⁵⁄₁₆" (8 mm) bit into the drill and repeat the preceding steps for drilling your axle holes.

To save a little time, you can drill both holes in both angle bits by clamping them together in a vice and drilling through both at the same time. Then do this on the other end too.

Warning: The holes for all the wheels *must* be the same distance from the bottom of the angle. If they are not, your dolly will wobble. Very bad indeed. Make sure you drill straight and true!

9 Clean up your drill holes. With a file, file off any bits that may be hanging on from the drilling.

To really get aluminum looking nice, put the angle in a vise and use a wire wheel to polish it up.

10 Next, we need to attach the angle to the dolly deck. Line the angle up to the edge of the plywood (you did wait for the glue to dry, right?).

If you're sure the deck is square, it's a simple matter. If your deck is not square, you're in for a world of hurt.

Clamp the angle to the edge of the deck with the ¼" (7 mm) holes against the deck.

 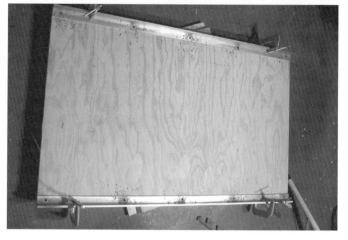

Put the ¼" (7 mm) bit back into your drill. Set the dolly deck on some scrap lumber to get it off the floor a bit. Then use the holes in the angle as a guide for drilling holes into the deck.

Drill your ¼" (7 mm) holes in the deck through all the ¼" (7 mm) holes in the angle.

11 Take your ¼" (7 mm) carriage bolts and a nut. Run the bolt through the top of the deck, through the angle, and a little thread lock to the bolt.

Add a nut and tighten the thing down tight!

Finish up the remaining holes.

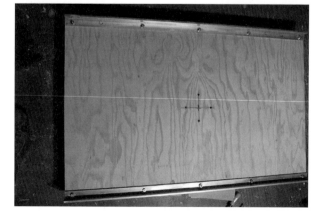 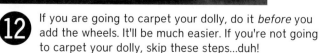

12 If you are going to carpet your dolly, do it *before* you add the wheels. It'll be much easier. If you're not going to carpet your dolly, skip these steps...duh!

There. Your angle is now attached to the deck!

Trim the carpet to a little larger than what you'll need.

Killer Camera Rigs That You Can Build

13 Lay the carpet next to the dolly and spray the adhesive on both the underside of the carpet and the dolly base (in other words, follow the directions on your adhesive can!).

14 Once the glue is tacky, tip the dolly up and over, laying it on the carpet. Pull up the sides and stick them to the edge of the dolly deck.

15 Trim the carpet straight out from the deck corner...

...and fold it up and in. Trim away the excess.

Trim the excess carpet between the aluminum and the plywood. Use acetone to clean the adhesive residue off the aluminum.

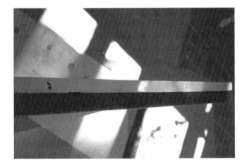

It should look something like this when you're done.

ATTACHING THE WHEEL ASSEMBLIES

Follow the directions for building your wheel assemblies in Chapter 1, *Dark Passage* Dolly, with one exception: you do not need any of the washers! Yep, you heard me. You don't need to add washers.

See. No washers.

Make It Groovy!

In this section we'll be adding a handle that folds down for easy storage from an old Razor® scooter, as well as how to mount a tripod on your dolly securely without using a spreader. The tripod in the photo is actually a surveyor's tripod that I've

adapted for film work. I have to say that I have two sets of wood sticks (wooden leg tripod—a film industry standard), and tend to use this one much more! You can learn more about adapting a low-cost surveyor's tripod later on in the book.

Adding a Handle to Your Dolly

MATERIALS

☐ Get yourself a Razor® type scooter. I've found them used at the Goodwill® store for as little as five bucks. Even new ones are not that much if they are an off brand.

☐ (3) carriage bolts. These can be anywhere from ¼" (7 mm) to ⁵⁄₁₆" (8 mm). Mine are 2" (50 mm) long, but I'm going to let you figure out what you need because different scooters can be designed a little differently. To determine your length, measure the thickness of the dolly deck, the thickness of the scooter in the middle of the foot deck, then add ½" (14 mm) to that measurement.

☐ (3) wing nuts to fit the carriage bolt. You don't have to use wing nuts, but if you need to, they make taking the handle off really easy.

Killer Camera Rigs That You Can Build

Tools

☐ A screwdriver or an Allen wrench. You'll need to take the front wheel off the scooter. Sometimes this takes a screwdriver, sometimes it takes an Allen wrench. You'll have to look at the wheel hub to see which one you'll need.

☐ A drill.

☐ A drill bit to match the size of your bolts.

☐ Some masking tape.

☐ A marker.

☐ A hacksaw, for cutting off the back of the scooter. Don't worry, these things are made from really light aluminum and are easy to cut.

☐ A vise or clamps to hold the scooter while you cut the back off.

☐ A big C-clamp with a 4" mouth or bigger. Not absolutely necessary, but very helpful.

☐ A tape measure.

Let's Build It

1 Remove the front wheel and chop off the back wheel with your hacksaw.

2 Determine the center of the scooter base, and drill three holes down the center, spaced out a bit.

It should look something like this. Don't worry about using drilling oil. These scooters are *thin!*

3 Clamp the scooter to the dolly and position it so that you can make sure the scooter handle can fold down against the dolly. Sometimes, if you mount the scooter too close to the edge of the dolly, you won't be able to fold the handle down.

Mark the foot deck of the scooter where it meets the edge of the dolly. This is just a reference point for later.

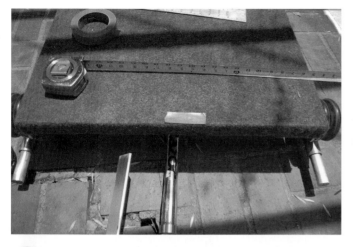

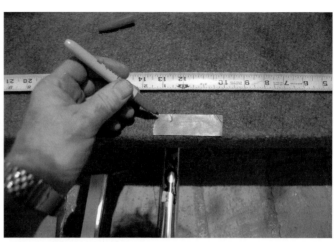

4 If you carpeted your dolly, you'll need some masking tape. Put a piece on the edge around the center.

Take your tape measure and determine the point halfway across the width of the dolly platform and mark it.

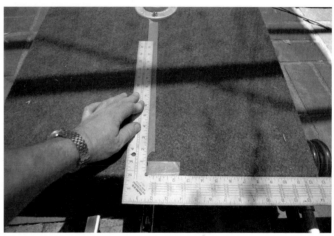

Run another long piece of masking tape up from that mark.

You can use a tape measure to determine the center point of the dolly at the top of the tape line. Or, like me, you can use a big framing square against your center mark to draw a line down the center of your dolly deck.

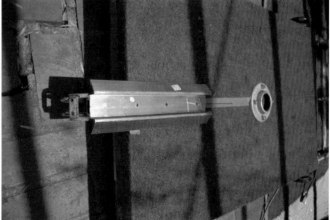

See. Like this.

5 Take your scooter and place the foot deck of the scooter on top of the dolly. Line that mark you made on the deck of the scooter to the edge of the dolly. Then line up the holes you drilled on the scooter with the line you just made on the tape.

Then mark the tape through the holes on the scooter.

You should have marks that look something like this.

6 Drill holes for the bolts on those holes.

7 Run your bolts through those holes. (I'm using long ones here just so you can see what's going on).

The top of the dolly will look like this. Carriage bolts have a nice flat head that won't get in the way.

8 Slide the scooter onto the bolts and add some nuts to keep it there.

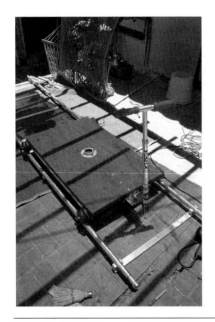 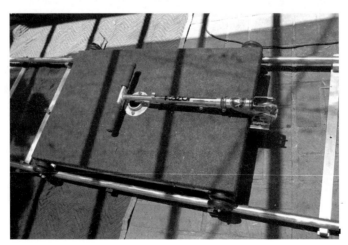

9 Admire your handiwork!

Killer Camera Rigs That You Can Build

Adding a Way to Hold a Tripod without Using a Spreader

In this project, we'll be drilling some holes in your dolly deck and adding some straps to hold the tripod down.

Important: This project is for either the surveyor's tripod or a cinema tripod. Both of these types of tripods have pointy little daggers as feet. A video tripod will more than likely *not* have these pointy little feet.

If your tripod feet look like this, you're good to go.

Materials List

☐ (3) 14" (0.35 meters) long rubber straps. These can be a little shorter or longer, depending on your tripod.

☐ (3) anchors. There are tons of different types out there. You can find them at most home centers or automotive supply stores.

☐ (6) wood screws 1½" long. My anchors take two screws each, so that's six in all. If your anchors take four, make sure you get enough screws.

☐ (3) nylon spacers with at least a ⁵⁄₁₆" (8 mm) hole or bigger.

☐ (6) 1" (25 mm) long flat-head wood screws.

Tools List

☐ A drill.

☐ A ⁵⁄₁₆" (8 mm) drill bit.

☐ A drill bit the same size as the 1" (25 mm) long flat-head wood screws.

☐ A screwdriver bit for your drill or just a plain ol' screwdriver. Make sure you have the right type of screwdriver bit as your screw. Mine has a Phillips head.

☐ Some masking tape.

☐ A marker.

☐ A combination square.

Let's Build It

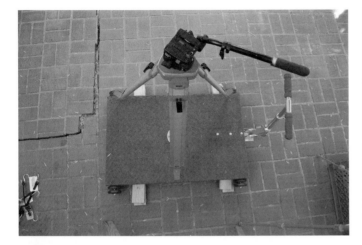

① First we need to determine where to put our holes for the legs. Two legs of the tripod should be at each edge of the long side. The third leg should be dead center of the opposite side. You'll be operating the camera from the one leg side.

Let's do the single leg side first. My dolly is 40" long, so the leg needs to be at 20", halfway up the deck, right?

Take your combination square and set it to 1½" (38 mm). Set the leg so it is 1½" (38 mm) in. Then mark that point. If you don't want to put a mark on your carpet, use a bit of masking tape under the leg point and make your mark on that.

Now we need to mark the placement of the two-leg side. From the end of the dolly, I'm going to go in 3½" (89 mm).

And 1½" (38 mm) from the long edge (the same measurement as the single leg side).

Do the same for the third leg.

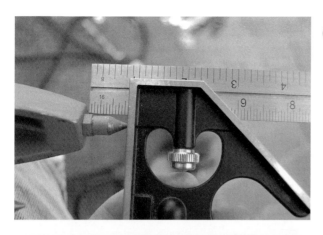

2 You can now remove your tripod. Get your combo square and determine how long the spiked feet are. Lock the combo square at that point.

Put a ⁵⁄₁₆″ (8mm) bit in your drill. Take your combo square that you used for the spike length and set it against your drill bit. Put a piece of masking tape on your drill bit at that point. This is how far you can drill into the dolly deck.

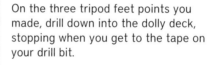

On the three tripod feet points you made, drill down into the dolly deck, stopping when you get to the tape on your drill bit.

3 Now we need to figure out where to put our anchors.

Loop the rubber cord around a tripod leg and through the anchor. Stretch it tight, then put your anchor just a little farther than that. You don't want the thing to be too loose.

Make sure you are coming straight back from the leg.

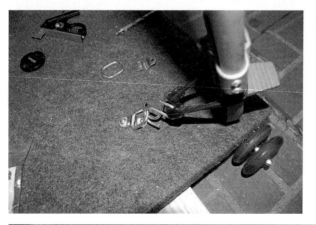

Screw the anchor in place.

Do the other two legs and you're done.

4 You don't have to do this next bit, but it makes it look nice. We're going to add a little plastic ring around the holes.

Know those 1" (25 mm) screws you bought with the drill bit to match? Take that drill bit and drill little holes in each side of the spacer as shown here.

5 Set the spacer over your tripod foot hole...

...and drill it to the dolly deck using those flat-head wood screws.

Repeat on the other two holes.

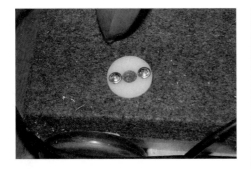

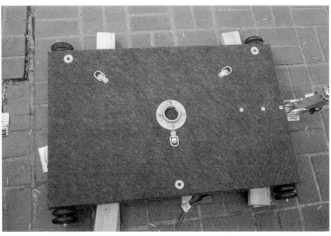

Holy cow! Look what you did! Hey, are you wondering what that floor flange bolted to the center of the dolly is for? You'll find that out in the next chapter.

The *Gun Crazy* Camera Pedestal

Hey, Dan. Why do I need a camera pedestal?

Well, maybe you don't. Do you have "baby sticks" (a very short cinema tripod)? Or a Hi-Hat (a very, very, low-to-the-ground camera mount)? If not, you might want to consider the simple-to-build rig in this chapter: the *Gun Crazy* camera pedestal, made especially for the dolly I hope you just finished. What a pedestal does is raise your camera to different heights; anywhere from just about dolly level to 3' or 4' above (or more if you want, but at that point you might consider building one of the jibs in the book).

Materials List for the *Gun Crazy* Camera Pedestal

☐ (2) 6" (15 cm) × 6" (15 cm) squares of ¾" thick plywood.

☐ (2) 2" (50 mm) floor flange. You'll find this in the plumbing section.

☐ (1) 2" (50 mm) × 3' (90 cm) plumbing pipe threaded on both ends. Most hardware stores can cut and thread 2" pipe for you.

DOI: 10.1016/B978-0-240-81337-0.00003-3

☐ (1) 2" (50 mm) × 12" (30 cm) plumbing pipe. Frankly, the length is up to you. If you want your camera 6" above the dolly, get that instead. I keep a whole range on hand. You might also want a 2" (50 mm) connector, also seen in the photo. This is so you can turn your 3′ pedestal into a 4′ pedestal. But this is up to you.

☐ (4) big fat wood screws 1½" (38 mm) long. "Big fat" is a technical term meaning just small enough to fit through the hole on the flange. Get flat or round head ones.

☐ (4) 2¼" (57 mm) long × ⁵⁄₁₆" (8 mm) bolts. They don't have to be carriage bolts like in the photo. Any bolt will do. If you can't find the right length, get longer ones. You will also need (4) ⁵⁄₁₆" (8 mm) nuts for these bolts.

☐ (1) ³⁄₈" (9 mm) bolt with a washer... maybe. OK, work with me here. This bolt is used to mount your fluid head on the pedestal. Most fluid heads that take cameras under 20 pounds use a ³⁄₈" (9 mm) bolt. And just how long does it need to be? How far does the bolt go into your head? Screw a bolt in there, and wrap the base with tape like in the photo. Unscrew the bolt and measure from the end of the bolt to where the tape begins.

☐ For my fluid head, that's ½" (14 mm). So now I can add a ½" (14 mm) (or slightly less) to the thickness of any camera platform in the book that takes a fluid head. The camera platform for the pedestal is 1½" (38 mm) thick (two ¾" (19 mm) pieces of plywood). 1½" (38 mm) plus ½" (14 mm) is 2" (50 mm). So I need a 2" long bolt. Once I add a washer to mount it to the platform, I'll be able to really get a tight fit.

Tools List for the *Gun Crazy* Camera Pedestal

☐ If you need to cut your plywood, you'll need a wood saw of some kind.

☐ Wood glue.

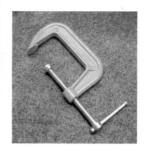

☐ (4) C-clamps.

☐ A drill.

☐ A drill bit about half the thickness of your big fat screws.

☐ A ³⁄₈″ (9 mm) drill bit (you can go slightly larger if you want. No big deal.).

☐ A ⁵⁄₁₆″ (8 mm) drill bit.

☐ A big honkin' screwdriver to fit the head of those big fat screws.

☐ A combo square.

☐ A sander and some sandpaper. This is optional; you don't have to sand it if you don't wanna.

☐ Also optional is a grinding bit. This one is cone-shaped. It's for enlarging the bolt hole a bit at the top, which makes it easy for getting the bolt through the plywood.

☐ Pliers or a socket wrench.

☐ A big set of channel lock pliers.

Let's Build It

1 Glue the two pieces of plywood together. I won't go over this since you should be an old hand at this by now after building the dolly.

2 Determine the center of the plywood by drawing an X to each corner.

3 Use the ⅜″ (9 mm) drill bit to drill a hole in the middle of the X.

Use the cone-shaped grinding bit to make the hole look like...

...this.

4 Sand it so it looks nice.

5 Center a flange over the middle and mark the holes in the flange.

You should have four little marks.

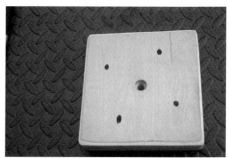

6 Drill holes with the smaller bit for the fat screws. Be careful *not* to drill all the way through to the other side of the plywood.

7 Screw that flange on tight!

8 Go get your dolly and tip it over. We are going to do the exact same thing to the dolly deck.

Find the center of the dolly deck.

Use a 5/16″ (8 mm) drill bit to drill four holes through the dolly deck.

Lay your other flange on there and mark the holes.

Push your bolts up through the bottom.

Add the flange, add the nuts to the bolts, and tighten the daylights out of it.

If the bolts are too long, just cut them off with a hacksaw or bolt cutters.

ATTACHING YOUR FLUID HEAD

 9 Take your ³⁄₈" (9mm) bolt and put a washer on it.

Run it up through the hole in the pedestal mount (on the flange side, please).

Position the fluid head bolt hole over the bolt.

Tighten it down tight!

It should look like this when you're done.

Note: I don't really have a problem with the fluid head moving around on this plywood platform. But if you do, you can easily solve the problem by gluing a little mat to the top of the plywood. Throughout the book, you'll find tons of different things I've used as mats on camera mounts; yoga mats, tool tray mats, floor mats, etc.

Here's a grip mat I found at the 99 Cents Only store. Things you can use for nonskid mats are everywhere! Just glue this stuff on with a little spray adhesive.

HOW TO SET UP YOUR CAMERA PEDESTAL

This is really easy.

You'll need your 2" (50 mm) pipe, a big pair of channel lock pliers, and your fluid head mounted to the pedestal mount.

Screw whatever length of pipe you need into the dolly floor flange.

Tighten it down with the channel locks.

Screw the fluid head on top. There. Done. In this case I now have a 3' (90 cm) pedestal.

Want a 4' (120 cm) pedestal? Add another 12" (30 cm) with a connector.

Any higher than 4' or so, and your tripod can take over.

Need something more like a Hi-Hat? Use a shorter pipe.

You get the idea. Just get whatever length of 2" pipe you need and you have a whole range of camera heights without spending a fortune on a bunch of different equipment.

Killer Camera Rigs That You Can Build

The *Naked Kiss* Upside-Down Dolly Camera Mount

Why in the world would you need this dolly setup?! Suppose you were in a location where laying dolly track on the ground is impractical like in the uneven mountains, or my apartment (if you saw my apartment, you'd understand—there's not one bit of floor in this tiny place that doesn't have something on it)? In most cases, directors just give up trying to get a dolly shot in these instances. Now you don't have to. Hang the dolly overhead! I should point out that the overhead rail that I built for this book isn't something I'd want to do day-in and day-out. If I were going to spend days in the mountains, for example, I'd come up with something that is easy to haul around and easy to set up. How about a rig that has two cables coming from a bar on each end that you could run between two trees? Run the cable through the PVC, ratchet it down between a couple of trees, and there you go. Use your imagination; there are tons of ways you can suspend track. I'll show you a few to get you started at the end of the chapter.

DOI: 10.1016/B978-0-240-81337-0.00004-5

Materials List for the *Naked Kiss* Upside-Down Dolly Camera Mount

☐ ¾″ (19mm) plywood. How much, you ask? It depends on your camera. You'll have to take some measurements shown later in this chapter. If you just want to buy some now and not worry about it, a 2′ × 4′ piece should be enough for just about any camera out there.

☐ (2) 2″ (50mm) floor flange.

☐ (1) 2″ × 12″ (50mm × 30cm) long plumbers pipe. When you hang the dolly upside down, you need to have some clearance for the rig to rotate without hitting the track. This lowers it with plenty of room no matter what you are going to use as track. If you don't need to rotate the camera, there's no need for the floor flanges or this pipe. At some point on some shoot, you'll probably have a need to rotate the camera, so I'd advise going ahead and building this aspect of the rig.

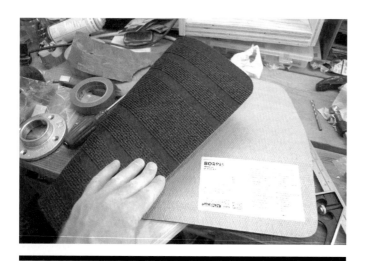

☐ Some kind of mat for the camera/fluid head mounting section. On this rig, I'm using a door mat. You can use a yoga mat, tool tray liner, hobby foam, a mouse pad... I've used tons of different materials in this book for padding. Thumb through the book for other ideas.

☐ (2) inserts that take ¼″ (7mm) bolts or larger. I'm using ⁵⁄₁₆″ (8mm) inserts. Inserts are little barrels that have machine threads on the inside and big wood threads on the outside. If you've ever built furniture from IKEA®, you've probably run across some version of an insert.

36

Killer Camera Rigs That You Can Build

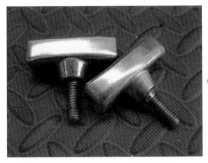 

☐ (2) knobs with ¼" (7 mm) bolts (or larger) on them. I'm using ⁵⁄₁₆" (8 mm) bolts on my knobs. These screw into the inserts. So if you can't find ⁵⁄₁₆" (8 mm) bolts, get knobs and inserts that have the same thread size. I'm using metal knobs used on C-stands. Unless you're in a major filmmaking city, these will be hard to find, but plastic knobs work great too. You'll want the bolt part to be to be 1½" (38 mm) long.

☐ Here it is with the insert screwed on just so you're clear on what you're buying.

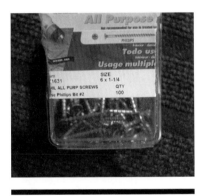  

☐ (10) wood screws 1½" (38 mm) long or longer.

☐ Did you build the camera pedestal? Well, you're going to need those same 1½" (38 mm) long big fat wood screws—eight in all.

☐ Some kind of wood treatment like polyurethane. Not necessary if you don't care how the rig looks.

Tools List for the *Naked Kiss* Upside-Down Dolly Camera Mount

☐ A wood saw for cutting the plywood. The one pictured is a hand saw, and not the best way to go. I think most of you probably have a power circular saw for this task! A table saw is even better (wish I had one!).

☐ A drill.

☐ A Phillips head attachment for your drill.

☐ A ½" (50 mm) drill bit. Attention: This is the size drill bit my inserts take. It will tell you on the package they come in what size drill bit the insert takes, so check it out before leaving the hardware store.

☐ A ⁵⁄₁₆" (8 mm) drill bit (or a bit that matches the knob bolt size). It can be a little bigger, but not smaller.

☐ A ³⁄₈" (9.5 mm) drill bit. It can be a little bigger. This is to drill the holes to mount your fluid head onto the rig.

☐ A ¾" (19 mm) drill bit. This may not be necessary for your rig. Please read step 10 to see if you might need one too!

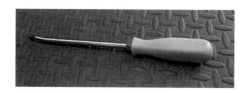

☐ A big flat-head screwdriver.

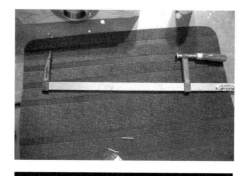

☐ A bar clamp at least 2 4" (0.60 meters) long.

☐ (6) C-clamps. A 3" (76 mm) mouth is plenty big enough.

☐ A combination square.

☐ A tape measure.

☐ Some wood glue.

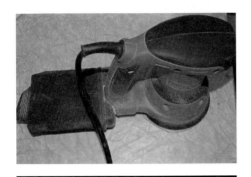
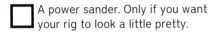

☐ A power sander. Only if you want your rig to look a little pretty.

☐ A utility knife.

☐ Spray adhesive.

☐ Some masking tape.

Let's Build It

1 Take a look at the next photo. Side A and Side B are a single thickness of ¾" (19 mm) plywood. The top, bottom, and dolly mount are two thicknesses of ¾" (19 mm) plywood glued together.

The dolly mount is 12" (30 cm) square because that's the size dolly I'm going to use. All the sides of the rig box are 6" wide. The length depends on your camera. So let's do some measuring.

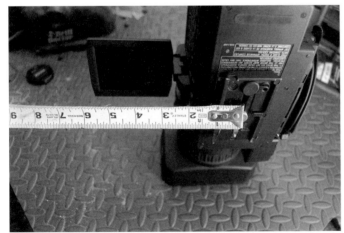

2 Open the screen on your camera. Now measure from the camera's mounting hole to the edge of the open LCD screen. Take that measurement and *double* it. So if the measurement to the edge of the LCD is 6", the total measurement is 12" (30 cm).

Cut four pieces of plywood 6" (0.15 meters) wide by whatever your measurement is. Glue them together in groups of two with some wood glue and clamp them together. If you built the *Killers* dolly, you should be an old hand at this by now.

You should end up with your top and bottom of the rig exactly the same size.

3 Mount your camera on your fluid head and tilt your camera at the angle shown in this photo. Measure from the base of the fluid head to the top point of your camera, then add 4" (100 mm). The measurement for me is 13" (33 cm) from base to top. Add 4" (100 mm) and the final measurement is 17" (43 cm). You don't have to use a fluid head on this rig, but it's a good idea to allow for that anyway.

Cut two pieces of plywood 6" wide × 17" long for Side A and Side B. You do *not* need to make these double thickness as with the top and bottom.

4 Did you make yourself a small dolly? It's a very handy dolly to have, so I'd get started on one if you didn't. Mine is 12" (30 cm) × 12" (30 cm). So I'm going to make the dolly mount part of my *Naked Kiss* Upside-Down Dolly Camera Mount the same size. Cut two pieces of ¾" (19 mm) thick plywood the size of your dolly.

Glue them together and clamp them until they dry.

Killer Camera Rigs That You Can Build

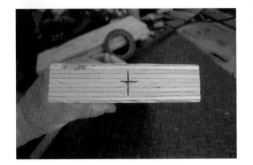

5 Once the glue is dry on your bottom portion, remove the clamps.

Measure halfway across one edge. Since mine is 6" wide, that would be 3", right? Make a mark at that halfway point.

Measure halfway up from the bottom and make another mark. So a 1½" (38 mm) thick block is going to be ¾" (19 mm) at the halfway point.

6 Clamp it to your bench...

...place your drill bit point right on the middle of the cross and drill the hole for your insert. My insert takes a ½" (50 mm) hole, so I'm using a ½" (50 mm) drill bit. Make sure you drill the hole straight and level!

7 Set your insert into the hole. Make sure you get your insert started straight!

Use a big flat-head screwdriver to screw the insert into the hole.

Make sure you screw the insert in so it is slightly below the surface of the plywood.

Make sure your knob fits!

Now turn the base around and do the same thing on the opposite side.

8 Take the plywood for the top of the rig. Determine the center, and use those big wood screws to screw one of the floor flanges to one side.

9 Take the Side A bit of plywood and measure halfway across and mark it.

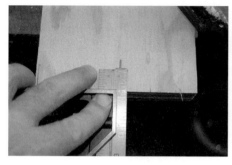

Then measure up ¾" (19 mm) from the bottom edge and make another mark across your first mark.

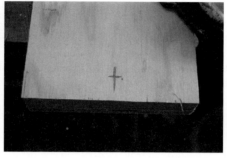

You should have something that looks like this.

Drill a 5/16" (8 mm) hole through the center of that mark. (If your knob bolt is ¼" (7 mm), for example, drill a ¼" (7 mm) hole through that mark.)

See if your knob bolt is long enough. Because I'm using this damned fancy knob, mine isn't! If yours is, you can skip step 10.

Repeat the steps for Side B.

10 Use a ¾" (19 mm) bit to drill a hole about ¼" (7 mm) deep. Do not go all the way through your plywood!

Like this, see?

Now my knob rests low enough to get some extra length out of it.

Killer Camera Rigs That You Can Build

11 Grab your glue, your drill with a Phillips head bit in it, the wood screws, your combo square, your long bar clamp, Side A, Side B, and the Top.

Spread some wood glue on each edge of the Top plywood section.

Set Side A against one edge and Side B against the other. Make sure everything is square with your combo square and clamp the sides to the top with the bar clamp. The only way this will *not* be square is if your Top section was cut wonky.

 12 With the clamp still on, screw in some wood screws with your drill. Do the same on the opposite side.

You can now take the clamp off and add a few more screws. Not pretty, but strong like moose.

13 Put the bottom in and screw in the knobs. See how you can tilt it, tighten down the knobs, and freeze it in place?

 14 Remove the knobs and take the bottom out. We're going to add some holes so you can mount your camera or your fluid head to the base.

Determine the center and make a mark there. Then, for good measure, add a mark on each side of the center one.

Take a ⅜" (9.5 mm) drill bit (or a little larger is OK) and drill holes through the base on each mark.

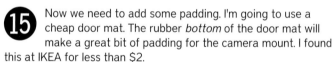

Take a utility knife and cut the mat around your camera platform.

15 Now we need to add some padding. I'm going to use a cheap door mat. The rubber *bottom* of the door mat will make a great bit of padding for the camera mount. I found this at IKEA for less than $2.

16 This is the top of the door mat, but I'm using it as the bottom.

Since I'm using a spray adhesive, I don't want it getting on the sides of the platform. I'm using masking tape to, well, mask the edges.

Follow the directions on your adhesive. Usually they want you to spray both pieces and wait a few minutes until it's tacky.

Careful when you press it down on the platform. It's hard to move if you're off a bit.

17 While we're waiting for that to dry, add your second floor flange to the dolly mount part of the rig. Just use wood screws and attach it just like you did to the Top in step 8.

18 Once your mat is dry, you need to add some holes in it. This material is tough! Here's how I did it: take a ³⁄₈″ (9.5mm) drill bit and drill up through the holes until you punch through the mat. This looks pretty bad still, so I took a ³⁄₈″ (9.5mm) bolt and grabbed it with some vice grips. I then heated the bolt up on a stove flame. Once it was really hot, I melted through the rubber part of the mat. It doesn't look perfect, but it will work just fine.

19 This step is optional, but makes it look nice. Sand it all down nice and smooth, and add some kind of wood treatment like polyurethane.

Make sure you mask off the floor flanges before you finish the wood.

How to Use Your New Rig

Screw in the 2″ (50mm) pipe into the flange on top of the rig.

Screw the dolly mount part on top of the pipe.

Use two C-clamps to mount the dolly on top as shown.

If you're going to use a fluid head, you can go ahead and mount that on too.

Now You're Ready to Hang It on Some Rails

There are lots of ways to do this. Really. Especially if you need it for only a short run like 10' or under. I'll get you started with a couple of ideas. If you have any specific needs for long dolly runs overhead, just shoot me an e-mail at dan@DVcameraRigs.com and I'm sure we can come up with some ideas.

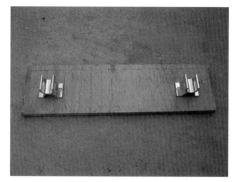

A very simple thing you can do is get some pipe clamps and attach them to a piece of lumber the correct distance for your dolly wheels. You'll need two sets: one for each end of the rail run.

Mount the board to a tripod, a ladder, or for something adjustable and portable, a speaker stand (you can find this at any big musician supply). I'm using ¾" (19mm) electrical conduit for track. You can't really join electrical conduit together, but for short runs, it works great. You can use almost any diameter of the stuff, so you can use much longer pieces than 10' if you get larger diameter conduit.

Add your dolly and attach the mount and you're good to go!

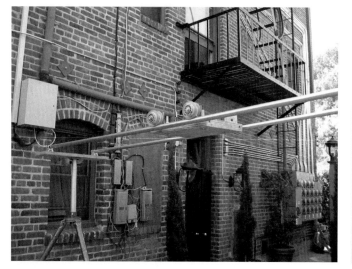

Now this track setup is a big pain. I just wanted to show you what was possible with some 2×4 lumber and clamps! I certainly wouldn't want to use this setup day-in and day-out, but if you're stuck for a way to get your dolly working for a shot, this will do.

Take a look in the section on Dolly Track about attaching PVC to a strip of lumber.

This dolly run is almost 20' (6 meters), so to support the track I used C-clamps to connect three lengths of 2×4s together. Of course, you'll need three lengths (or however many you need) for each side.

Put your PVC track together, and use drywall screws to attach it to the 2×4.

Use your dolly as a spacer to determine the distance between rails. Use some big C-clamps to attach a short 2×4 across each end of the track run to keep the spacing correct.

One end of this run is sitting on top of a fence. For the opposite end, you can see I've hobbled together a bunch of 2×4s to support it. Like I said, I wouldn't want to do this every day!

The Way This Rig Works

Mostly, it's pretty clear. But let's say you want to pan farther than your fluid head allows. When you put the rig together, tighten down on one of the flanges, then back off one turn. Now you can rotate the camera on the threads of the flange. It's as smooth as glass.

If you want the lens to look straight down, loosen the knobs a bit and tilt the platform, then tighten up the knobs again. I've even used this without a fluid head because it's so versatile in panning and tilting without one.

Now you can dolly across or over most anything: a mountain stream, a wall, uneven terrain... I've even used this rig to go across an alley, running the rails from one rooftop to another. Use your imagination and blow your audience away!

Killer Camera Rigs That You Can Build

The *Dark Corner* PVC Dolly Track

You're going to need dolly track for your dolly to ride on. PVC is the easiest and cheapest way to accomplish that.

In this section we'll be going over various ways to use PVC, from super easy "just throw it on the ground and get started" to slightly more time consuming, but sometimes needed, ways to use PVC as track.

The reason I like PVC so much is that can hold a ton of weight and is easy to connect lengths together without getting a bump from your dolly every time is goes over a joined section; truly the most tricky part about dolly track, whether professional or not!

Materials List for the *Dark Corner* PVC Dolly Track

This is for a 20' (6 meter) run. If you need longer, just buy more of what you need.

☐ (4) 10' (3 meter) lengths of ¾" (19 mm) PVC. When you look around at the hardware store you'll see two different types: one with a very thin core and one with a thicker core. Get the thicker-core stuff. You can also use 1" (25 mm) diameter PVC. Either is fine.

☐ (2) ½" (14 mm) closed plumbing nipples. If you are making more track, you need one nipple for each two sections you'll be connecting. If you're using 1" (25 mm) PVC, you'll need to get ¾" (19 mm) nipples instead.

DOI: 10.1016/B978-0-240-81337-0.00005-7

I'm going to make a little track spacer. This makes laying out the track at the correct distance for your dolly wheels really easy.

A 3" to 6" (76 mm to 152 mm) wide, ¾" (19 mm) thick piece of plywood or pine. The length should be at least 2" (50 mm) longer than the middle distance between your dolly wheels.

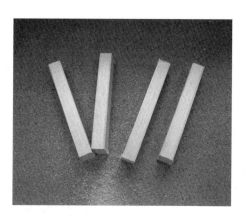

(4) little strips of wood about an 1" (25 mm) wide. Make them as long as your plywood is wide.

(8) wood screws long enough to go through your plywood and into the little strips of wood above.

Tools List for *The Dark Corner* PVC Dolly Track

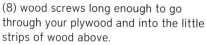

☐ Vice grips or other pliers.

A Phillips head attachment for your drill.

A drill.

Let's Build It

This just doesn't get any easier! Here's what you do:

① Take your ¾" (19 mm) PVC and screw the nipple in halfway. You'll basically be making your own threads as you screw the thing halfway in. Then screw the other PVC onto the other half of the nipple. You just turned 10' (3 meters) of track into 20' (6 meters). After a while the PVC will become worn and not hold the nipple any more. Just cut an inch off the PVC and start over. Simple!

Hey Dan! I'm not as butch as you! I can't screw the darn nipple in!

No Worries. Not everybody has the strength of 10 men.

② Grab those vice grips and lock them down on the middle of the nipple.

Careful! You must screw this in straight and true. Once it's in, screw the other length of PVC on.

Are you crazy?! It's still too difficult!

Yeah. Sometimes it's real hit or miss on a true diameter that stays the same in the manufacturing process. Sometimes these are very easy to screw in, sometimes near impossible.

③ Grab the nipple in the middle with the vice grips.

④ Heat up the nipple on your stove. *Now be careful! It's hot, right?!*

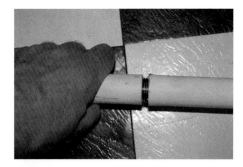

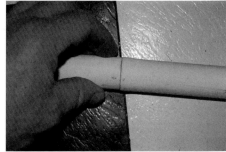

5 Carefully screw the nipple halfway in. The hot nipple will melt the PVC just enough to very easily make threads inside the PVC. Let it cool a bit, then unscrew it. Take another length of PVC and do the same thing, *but leave the nipple halfway in*. Yep. Just leave it there. It's done.

6 Now it should be easy to screw the other length of PVC in by hand because you made threads with the hot nipple.

Warning: If your nipple is too hot it won't make threads, but will just melt the inside smooth. It might take some experimenting to get it right. If you do mess it up, don't worry. Just cut an inch off the PVC and try again.

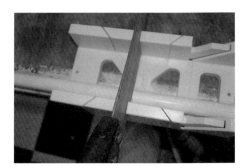

You can use vice grips or pliers to twist the PVC together if you need to. Be careful not to chomp down too tightly, though or you'll crack the PVC.

7 Cutting PVC: Use a mitre box and saw. That's the easiest. The reason is that you need a perfectly square edge, otherwise the track won't screw together right and you'll get a bump in your dolly move. Often, I cut 10' (3 meter) PVC down to 4' or 5' (1.2 meter or 1.5 meter) lengths so it's easier to haul around. Just remember, for every cut, you'll need a nipple.

The Dolly Track Spacer

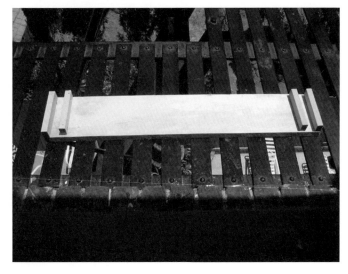

OK, let's make a little jig to keep the track spaced correctly for your dolly wheels. It's not completely necessary, but it does make things easier.

First, get a piece of wood that will span the tracks by at least a couple of inches with your dolly sitting on it.

Then cut four strips about the width of the board.

Set the strips on each side of the track and screw them into the board. Do this on the other side and you're done.

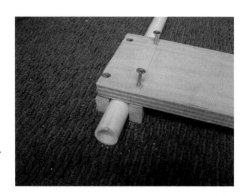

You can make another one for the other end of the track run if you want. I generally just set one end of the track, throw sand bags on it, then set the other end. (Check out the pant leg sandbags later in the book. They are super easy to make.) Your track spacer doesn't have to be pretty, it just needs to set the track at the same width as your wheels.

Here's the spacer in use on a long dolly track run, being helpful while leveling track.

If you're shooting inside or a level place outside, this track setup will work great. Sometimes on concrete you can get some vibration. Putting a quilted moving blanket down first will help that. FYI, a moving blanket in the film world is called a *sound blanket*. They're the same thing, except sound blankets cost twice as much. For a really cool and effective way to solve putting your PVC on weird surfaces, check out Chapter 6, "The *Cry Vengeance* Dolly Rail Padding."

Attaching Dolly Track to Lumber for Dolly Shots over Rough Terrain

If you are going to be using your dolly on uneven surfaces, like just about anywhere outside, you'll need to make this PVC so you can level it. Attaching it to long lengths of lumber is a really easy solution.

Materials List

☐ You'll need one 10' (3 meter) length of ¾" (19 mm) PVC and one 8' (2.45 meters) × 3" to 6" (80 mm–150 mm) wide bit of lumber. I'm using a 3" (76 mm) wide piece of pine, but if you've got a lot of track to make, cutting down a sheet of ¾" (19 mm) thick of plywood into 4" (100 mm) strips would be a cheaper and better way to go.

☐ (4) 1" long wood screws.

Tools List

☐ A drill.

☐ A drill bit smaller in diameter than your 1" long screws.

☐ A drill bit larger than the *head* of the 1" long screws.

☐ A screwdriver. Keep in mind if your screw head is a Phillips, you'll need that kind of screwdriver.

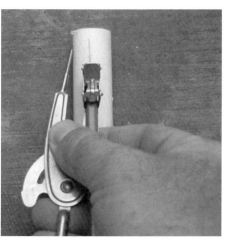

☐ A compass. The cheap, sharp dangerous ones you used in elementary school are fine.

Optional

A drill guide. Now think this through. A drill guide will be necessary for other projects in the book like the cranes. They run about $35. A drill press runs about $100 and can easily make your life $70 easier. If you decide to build the pro track later in this section, you *have* to have a drill press. So your decision is to get this or get a drill press. Something to think about.

Let's Build It

1 Take a compass and adjust it so the pointy end rests against the side of the PVC and the pencil rests on top. Don't move it from this position and carefully run a line down the entire length of the PVC. This marks the "top" of the pipe.

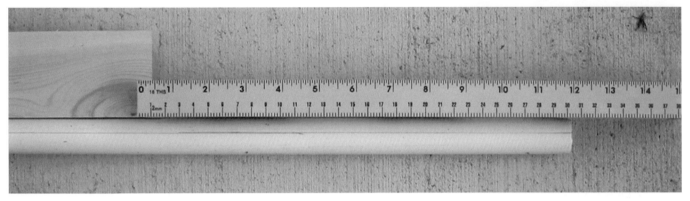

2 Lay the PVC next to the lumber and adjust it so the PVC extends one foot (30 cm) beyond each end of the lumber.

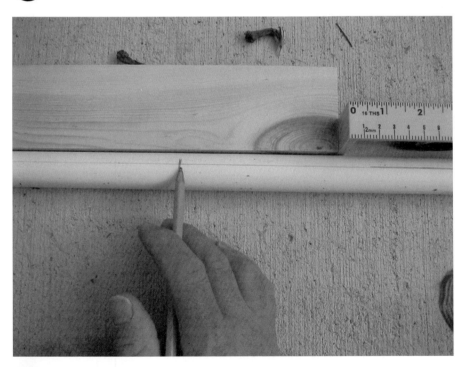

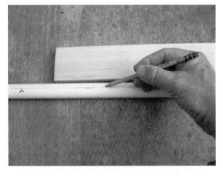

Do this on the opposite end...

3 Draw a line across the line that runs down the PVC (from step 1) around 5" (130 mm) from the end of the board.

...and at two or three points in-between along the length of the PVC.

4 Drill a small pilot hole straight through both sides of the PVC on each of the cross marks. I'm using a $^{3}/_{32}$" (2.38 mm) bit. Just make sure the bit size is smaller than the screw you're going to be putting in here. I'm using the drill guide to do this. It really helps making your holes straight. A drill press can do the same thing.

5 Now load up a bigger bit. The diameter of the bit must be bigger than the head of the screw you're using. Mine is $^{5}/_{16}$" (8 mm).

Drill a hole through the top of the PVC on each of your pilot holes. Do not go all the way through as you did on the smaller holes!

As you can see, the large hole is just an access hole for putting a screw through the bottom hole.

6 Center the PVC pipe on the lumber and put a screw in each of your holes. Make sure the PVC is straight before you screw it down.

And there it is.

If you have more than one length of a run, put a bit of wood (the same thickness as your track wood, please) under the connecting points of the track. Also, you may think that screwing together section of track attached to lumber would be difficult. It's really not.

Hey! Wait a minute, Dan. How come the track coming off the end of the lumber is so much shorter in the photo than the stuff I just made?

Because I actually do *use* this stuff on shoots. After a lot of use, the nipples no longer grab, so you have to cut an inch or so off the end of the track to have a fresh bit of PVC to make new threads. It does take quite a lot of use to get to this point though.

If the track is up off the ground, and you'll be riding on the dolly, we'll get into making this a lot stronger with only a few lengths of 2×4 lumber. But more on all this in Chapter 9.

The *Cry Vengeance* Dolly Rail Padding

Yet Another *Dark Corner* PVC Dolly Track Option!

This is my dog Silvie's favorite. Sometimes you have a level surface, but it's something like brick, or a slick hardwood floor you can't just throw PVC down on. Here's a way of holding PVC track nice and straight, so that it protects the floor, and gives it a very smooth ride on less than ideal surfaces like brick, tile, or concrete.

Materials List for the *Cry Vengeance* Dolly Rail Padding

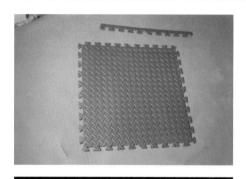

☐ "Anti-Fatigue" floor mat. You can find this in most hardware or automotive supply shops. It is 2' × 2' (0.60 × 0.60 meter) square interlocking rubber mat. It usually comes in packages of six mats.

58

DOI: 10.1016/B978-0-240-81337-0.00006-9

Tools List for the *Cry Vengeance* Dolly Rail Padding

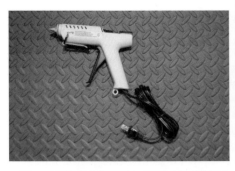  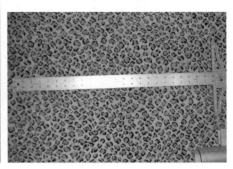

☐ A hot glue gun with a big package of hot glue sticks. I like the long sticks because you don't have to keep reloading your gun that way.

☐ A utility knife with a new sharp blade.

☐ Some kind of straight edge.

Let's Build It

 1 Link the mat together in one long stretch.

Take your blade and straight edge and cut off the puzzle-looking pieces on each side.

2 Measure across the mat, putting a mark every 4" (100 mm).

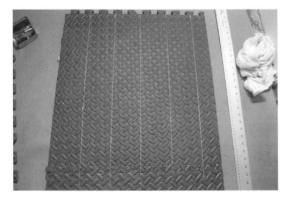

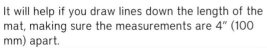

3 Use your utility knife to cut the mat along the lines, working your way down the entire length. You'll have a little left that is narrower than 4" (100 mm). Put that aside, and we'll be able to use it later.

It will help if you draw lines down the length of the mat, making sure the measurements are 4" (100 mm) apart.

 These mats have edging included to give them a finished look on the outer edges. We're going to use these for making a gutter for the PVC track to lay in.

On the bottom of these edges, coat them with some hot glue...

...line up the puzzle side with the edge of your 4" (100 mm) pieces...

...and glue them in place. Work fast! This hot glue dries quickly! Do this on each side. You may need to cut off the ends of your edging so these pieces are easier to connect together for your dolly track run.

If you run out of the edging, use what's left when you cut the mat into 4" (100 mm) wide lengths.

5 All that's left now is to connect your strips together and lay your PVC track in the gutter.

Don't worry if you get two pieces that don't fit together. It's perfectly fine just to lay them end-to-end without connecting them.

There you have it. You'll be amazed what a smooth ride you get out of these cheap little pads over really rough surfaces.

Killer Camera Rigs That You Can Build

The *Thieves' Highway* Angle Dolly Track

Because you're using my dolly wheel design (you *are* using mine, right?), this opens up a lot of possibilities for track you can use.

The *Thieves' Highway* dolly track uses aluminum angle connected together to give you as much dolly track as you need for a shot. It's a little more difficult and a little more expensive to make than PVC track, but a lot easier and a lot less expensive than the "pro" dolly track in Chapter 8, *The* Glass Key *Pro Dolly Track*.

Make sure you read the appendix, *Working with Metal, before* starting this project—it's important! Please read it (or you might just go blind or put a hunk of metal through your kidney). And dog-ear that corner while you're back there. You'll need to refer to it throughout this book!

Let's take a look at *Thieves' Highway*:

It is simply aluminum angle set on the open end with the dolly riding on the top of the triangle.

The track is joined by a piece of aluminum that the angle is bolted to.

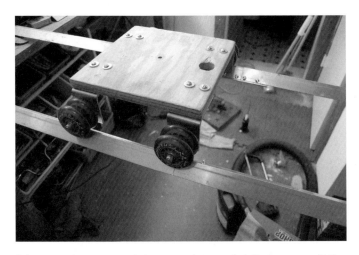

It is even strong enough to support a small dolly for runs off the ground.

I typically just lay the track out on blocks of wood at the correct distance apart for my dolly wheels, but if you know how to weld, you could very easily weld aluminum bar cross sections for every 4' or 5' (1.2 or 1.5 meters) of track. If this interest you, take a look at the way the *Glass Key* track is made with cross-sections for support.

DOI: 10.1016/B978-0-240-81337-0.00007-0

61

Dollies

Materials List for the *Thieves' Highway* Angle Dolly Track

☐ You'll need aluminum angle that is at least 1½" (38mm) on each side of the angle and at least ¼" (3mm) thick. These are *minimums*! You can certainly have angle that is 2" (50mm) or more, and thicker than ⅛" (3mm). I prefer ¼" (7mm) thick stuff, which is really bomb proof, but it is more expensive. You can use however long angle you want. I cut my sections at about 4' (1.2 meters) long so it's easy to haul around, or set up short dolly runs in tight places. The more sections you have, the more work it is because you have to connect each section.

☐ To connect the angle, you'll need aluminum bar: 6" (15 cm) long, ½" (14mm) thick, and as wide as your angle is on one side. My angle is 1½" (38mm) wide on each side, so I need bar that is 1½" (38mm) wide. You can go just a little wider or a little narrower. The *minimum* length is 6" (15 cm). The longer this bar is, the sturdier the track will be. So if you plan on doing long runs off the ground with no support underneath, the longer bar you use, the longer your unsupported track run can be.

☐ ¼" (7mm) round head machine screws ½" (14mm) long and a Nikon lens cap. *Just kidding about the lens cap!* (There have been some pretty late nights making this book, so things make it into some of these shots that I hadn't planned on.)

Optional

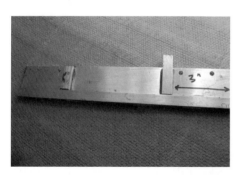

This crummy looking thing is a jig I made. It keeps the holes you'll be drilling in the angle and bar in the same place on every piece you make. This way you don't have to worry about matching which bit of angle track connects to another specific bit of angle track.

Now, having said that, let's think about this for a second. Unless your aluminum angle is cut perfectly straight on each end, making the jig in the photo will be a waste of time. If I were the least bit unsure about my cuts, I would *always* join the finished track to its mate. To be clear: If I cut a 10' long piece of angle down to two 5' long pieces, I would make sure that when setting up my track on a shoot, these two pieces always went together. It is very easy to *color code* two pieces that go together. Just spray paint a little across each mated section a different color for each section. You also then don't have to worry about your machine screw holes being in the perfect place either!

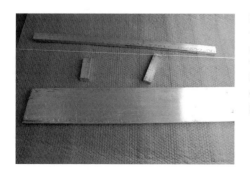

But if you want to make this jig, you'll need a flat piece of aluminum 7" to 12" (17 cm to 30 cm) long and ½" (14mm) wider than one side of your angle. You'll also need aluminum bar ¼" (7mm) thick and as long as your aluminum flat piece (7"–12"), and two shorter pieces of the same stuff that are long enough to span the width of your bar. One of mine is longer than the other. The only reason is because I didn't feel like cutting a ½" off of it. It doesn't matter if the bit is longer than the width of the flat piece; it just can't be shorter than the flat piece.

Killer Camera Rigs That You Can Build

☐ A vice.

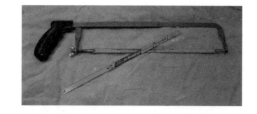

☐ A hacksaw or some other metal cutting device.

☐ A screwdriver.

☐ ¼" (7 mm) tap with matching drill bit. A tap is something that you twist into a hole you've drilled into metal that makes threads so that you can screw a screw into that hole. You can buy tap sets all by themselves, but they are a little pricey. It's much easier to go to an automotive supply and purchase a single tap for the size you need with a drill bit specifically for that tap. If you've never used a tap before, it's easy and kind of cool.

☐ A tap wrench. You'll need this to screw the tap into your aluminum.

☐ A ¼" (7 mm) drill bit.

☐ Thread cutting oil.

☐ A drill.

☐ A metal file.

☐ (4) C-clamps. See, didn't I tell ya in the dolly chapter you'd need a bunch of these?

☐ J-B Weld (only if you're making the jig). This stuff is great for gluing metal together.

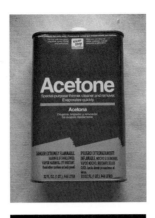

☐ Acetone. You'll need this if you're using the J-B Weld. It's to clean your metal before applying the J-B Weld.

☐ A prick punch or center punch. If you made the bomb-proof dolly, you know what this is for. If you didn't, pick one up now and we'll get into using it later.

☐ A hammer.

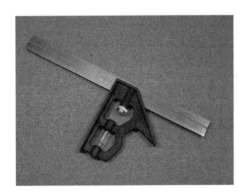

☐ A combination square.

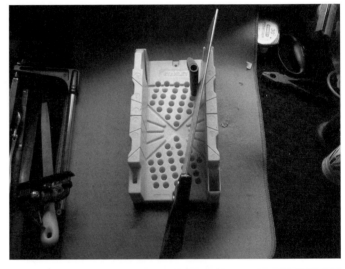

☐ A mitre box. You really only need to use this if you really want to try your hand at cutting the aluminum angle very straight. Don't use the mitre saw, but use the hacksaw. If you're going to color code your track, or you have precut pieces of angle, don't worry about getting a mitre box.

Let's Build It

1 Cut your aluminum angle to any length you want. Mine are usually 4' or 5' (1.2 or 1.5 meters) long. If you have a good way to haul them around to different locations, you can even get away with 8' long pieces. Any longer than 8' (2.45 meters), you're asking for trouble. What if the room you need to do the dolly shot in is only 8' 3" long and your dolly track is 10'? You can also mix lengths together if you want. It really doesn't matter as far as the operation of the dolly goes.

2 Cut your aluminum bar. Mine is 6" (15 cm) long. 6" is minimum! This is used for joining track together, so I'll need one bar for each section of track that needs to be joined to another section of track. So if you have four pieces of track, that's two bars, right?

A JIG FOR KEEPING EVERYTHING THE SAME

3 If you want to make the jig for keeping all the track the same, let's do that now. If you'd like to save yourself a big headache and just color code your sections, skip this part.

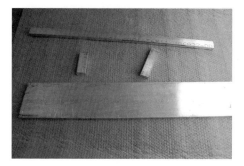
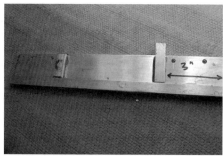

Gather up your flat aluminum and the small aluminum bar. The small bar has three bits: one long piece that is as long as your flat aluminum, and two short pieces that are nearly as long or longer than the flat piece is wide.

4 Clean all the pieces with acetone. You need to do this, or the J-B Weld won't stick well.

Now, how long is your aluminum bar for connecting the track together? If it's 6″ (15 cm) long like mine, divide that in half: 3″. If your bar is 12″ long, half of that is 6″. Easy. Set your combination square to whatever that half measurement is.

Set the combination square at the end of the flat aluminum piece and measure in 3″ (in my case), and use your prick punch or center punch to scratch a line across the flat piece at that point. Do the same at the opposite end.

5 Mix up some J-B Weld according to the instructions on the package. You don't need much. Just enough to cover the three aluminum bar pieces on one side.

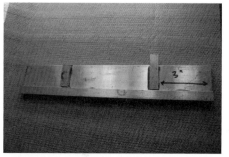

Glue them up as shown in the photo. The long piece goes along the top edge. The short pieces go 3″ (76 mm) in (or whatever your measurement was) from against the long bar at the top, across the width of the flat piece. Use your combination square to make sure these pieces are square!

Clamp the pieces against the flat aluminum and allow the J-B Weld to dry. Make sure to clean up any J-B Weld that has squeezed out.

6 Set your dolly up on the track as shown in the photo.

Mark the aluminum angle at the bottom of the dolly wheel.

The machine screws for joining the track must go below that mark so that your wheels don't bump over the screw heads.

Use your combination square to take a measurement of where that mark on your track is from the bottom of the aluminum angle. Make a note of that measurement, then split that measurement in half again. This is how far up from the bottom you can safely drill the holes for the machine screws that will join your track together.

7 After the J-B Weld has dried on your jig, take the measurement from step 6, and from the bottom of the jig, make a few marks with your prick punch from the edge to the vertical bar. Do this on both ends of the jig.

Now set the combination square to 1" (25 mm). Set it against the end of the jig, and mark a line across the line on the bottom you just made. Do this on the opposite side as well.

Set the combination square to 2½" (63 mm) and mark another vertical line across the bottom line. Repeat on the opposite end.

8 Take your prick punch or center punch and set the tip directly on the intersection of the lines you just made and give it a good thwack with a hammer. This photo *is not* the project we are working on now, but it's a good clear photo of the whacking in progress: make sure the point of the punch is right on the mark, the punch is straight up and down, and you give it a good solid thump or two with the hammer.

Back to our jig: you should have some little dimples in the metal that look something like this.

 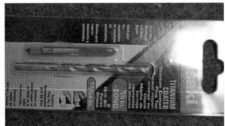 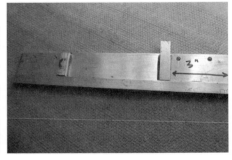

You *did* do both ends, right?

9 Take the drill bit that is the match for your tap and load it into your drill. Clamp your jig to the table or vice. Set the point of the drill bit into the first dimple you made with your punch, and drill away. Since you read the appendix, I know that you know you need some drill oil and a slow drill speed.

You should now have four holes in your jig. It is now ready to use!

10 If you're using the jig, take one of the angle pieces and set it in the jig as shown: the top edge of the angle against the long bar at the top of the jig, and the end against the 3" stop.

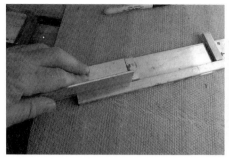

If you're not using the jig, simply measure in from the end of your angle half the length of your aluminum bar. In my case, 3" (76mm). Scratch a line at 3" with your punch. You can now move to step 11.

Being careful to keep the jig and the angle in place, use a C-clamp to clamp it together.

11 Load the drill bit that came with your tap into your drill.

If you're using the jig:
Drill two holes in the angle where you already drilled two holes in your jig.

If you are not using the jig: Pick two spots *under* where your wheel mark is and at about 1" (25mm) in from the end of the angle, and about 2½" (63mm) in from the end of the angle. Use your prick punch to make the dimples (see step 8) and drill two holes.

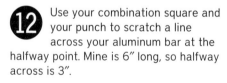
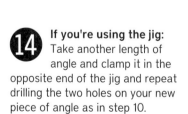

12 Use your combination square and your punch to scratch a line across your aluminum bar at the halfway point. Mine is 6" long, so halfway across is 3".

13 Line up your halfway mark on the bar to the end of the angle, and clamp your bar there. Drill two holes in the bar where the holes in the angle are. You don't need to use your prick punch, as the holes in the angle will hold your drill bit in the proper place.

This is the underside of the bar clamped to the angle. Make sure it is snug against the top of your angle aluminum.

Once you've drilled the holes, leave it clamped together!

14 **If you're using the jig:**
Take another length of angle and clamp it in the opposite end of the jig and repeat drilling the two holes on your new piece of angle as in step 10.

If you are not using the jig:
Repeat the steps for drilling two holes *under* the wheel line on your new piece of angle as in step 11.

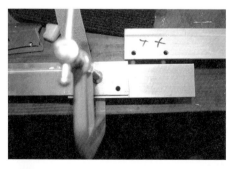

15 Take your newly drilled angle (shown in photo with a double X on it)...

...and clamp it to the bar, making sure that the edges of the angle are pushed hard together so that there is no gap at all!

16 You may now remove the first angle. Drill two holes in the other side of the bar where you drilled the holes in the angle.

You should now have a bar with four holes in it.

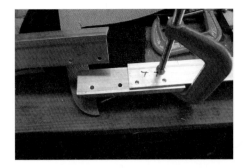 

If you are not using the jig, make sure that you mark the bar and both angle pieces so that you will know which bar and angle goes together.

If you are not using the jig, repeat the steps for each section of track:

1. Drill the holes in the angle.
2. Use the angle holes as a guide to drill holes in the bar.
3. Repeat the process for the joining track.
4. Mark each track's "mate" so you'll know how to color code them later.

17 **If you are using the jig:**

There is no need to go through all the steps again for the bar.

Use the first bar as a drill guide and stack two or three bars under the guide bar. Clamp them all down in a vice, and drill away. You'll need as many bars as you have pairs of track to string together.

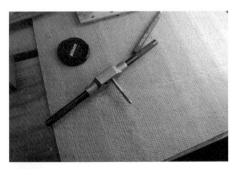 

Load one of the bars into your vice. Use thread cutting oil on your tap, and carefully twist it down through all four holes of the bar. For every turn or two of the tap into the hole, back off about a half turn, then proceed until you are all the way through the hole. Make sure you are going straight!

Repeat this step on all of your bar holes.

18 Take your tap and load it into the tap wrench.

19 Load a ¼" (7 mm) drill bit into your drill.

Clamp the angle into your vice, and drill out the holes in the angle so that they are now ¼" (7 mm).

20 Screw the ¼" screws through the angle and into your bar. There ya go. Track!

HEY! Dan! I think I screwed up. My holes don't match! Do I have to start over?

Don't panic yet. Chances are they are really close.

Take a ⁵⁄₁₆" (8 mm) drill bit, and drill out the holes on the angle so they are a little bigger.

See? Problem solved. The screws will still hold your track tightly in place.

Even with only 6" (15 cm) long bars holding the track together, this track is really very sturdy. It's holding this small dolly off the ground with no sagging at all.

When I use this track on the ground, I usually put blocks under it so that leveling the track is easier.

In the end, this track is pretty easy to build, and is light and strong. If you know how to weld, you can even weld cross pieces if you want. Take a look at the *Glass Key* Pro dolly track in the next chapter for ideas.

The *Glass Key* Pro Dolly Track

In this chapter I'll be showing you how to build "professional grade" dolly track. It's not too difficult, but it is very time intensive. The materials listed are for two 5 (1.5 meters) lengths of track for a total of 10 (3 meters). Of course, you can keep adding 5 (1.5 meters) long extensions until you run out of money or room.

There are a couple of power tools you'll need at a minimum: a drill press and a chop saw. I say at a minimum, because even these are not the best way to drill out large cores of aluminum or even cut thick pieces of aluminum. But they are relatively inexpensive tools, and can do the job... although slowly. In fact, a machine shop could pop out the pieces you need very quickly, and a welder could put them together for you. But in the end, would it be cheaper to go buy the commercial track and be done with it? If you don't already own a drill press and a chop saw (great tools for other projects in this book, by the way!), would it be cheaper to have a machine shop make these pieces for you rather than buying this equipment? That's something that you'll have to check out in your corner of the world. I know if you live in Thailand or China, you can get this done for you for very little cash indeed.

Since there is no welding anywhere in this book, there are steps that you'll have to do that would be unnecessary if you knew how to weld aluminum. So this might be another place to ask yourself, "I've made these pieces. I wonder if it would be dirt cheap to have them welded together?" Again, if you're reading this book in Bangkok, let somebody else do it!

I should let you know right now that I cheated. Take a look at the photo. These are aluminum blocks that hold the track. In these plans, you *have* to have these on each end of your track. But there are two cross-sections in the middle of the track that are there for support, and don't need the strength that each end of the track needs. So...

...see the black block supporting the track on the two middle sections? These are made of wood. Only because it is easier to make them out of wood and I don't need the strength of aluminum that I need at each end of the track. If you are going to have a machine shop make your blocks or if you are going to be welding them, you should make these out of aluminum as well. Once you read through the plans, it will be much more clear.

This is great track. It's easy to set up, very strong, and the dolly goes over the joints as smooth as glass. So if you still want to tackle this, let's get started.

Important: First, make sure you read the appendix, *Working with Metal*.

DOI: 10.1016/B978-0-240-81337-0.00008-2

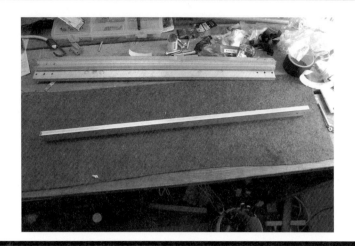

☐ (8) 1″ (25mm) thick × 2½″ (63mm) × 2½″ (63mm) aluminum bar. The metal supplier where I get all my stuff sells this aluminum bar in 12″ (30cm) lengths. I cut it down to the proper length myself.

☐ (8) 1½″ (38mm) wide by ½″ (14mm) thick by 30″ aluminum bar. My metal supplier has this in 36″ (91cm) lengths that I cut down. Depending on your dolly, this may be shorter or longer than 30″ (76cm). It depends on how far apart your dolly wheels are. I like to keep everything under 32″ (81cm) in case I want to dolly though a doorway (the standard door opening in the United States is 32″).

☐ (4) 1¼″ (31mm) diameter aluminum tube × 5′ (1.5 meters) long. This is what your dolly will ride on. I really wouldn't go smaller than 1¼″ (31mm) in diameter, but you can go larger. It would also be best if it were ⅛″ (3mm) thick. A 1/16″ (1.5mm) thick is absolute minimum.

☐ (4) 1″ (25mm) diameter round bar. This needs to fit into the aluminum tube. See the next photo.

☐ I get mine in 12″ (30cm) lengths. If you are *not* going to be welding the track together, you'll be cutting a bit off the end of this round bar.

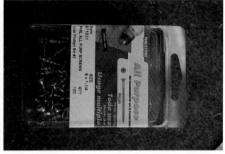

☐ Metal mend tape. You can find this in most automotive stores. You'll be using this on the round bar to give it a snug fit inside the aluminum tube. You don't need much at all. This package is 3" (76 mm) wide × 60" (1.5 meters) long, and is plenty.

☐ (16) #6 × 1¼" (31mm) long wood screws.

☐ ¼" (7 mm) flat-head machine screws. Take a close look at the photo. Since we won't be welding anything, we need to attach everything together with machine screws. The short two are 1½" (38 mm) long × ¼" (7 mm). The long one going into the tube is 2" (50 mm) long × ¼" (7 mm). You can go a little shorter if you want (by ¼" [7 mm] to ½" [14 mm]) and you'll still be OK. For this project of 10' of track, you'll need eight of the long screws and 16 of the shorter ones. If you're welding, you don't need any at all.

☐ (8) ¼" (7 mm) nuts.

☐ (4) ⁵⁄₁₆" (8 mm) wing nuts.

☐ (8) ⁵⁄₁₆" (8 mm) washers.

☐ (4) ⁵⁄₁₆" (8 mm) nuts.

☐ (2) ⁵⁄₁₆" (8 mm) × 2" (50 mm) long flat-head machine screws.

☐ (1) ⁵⁄₁₆" (8 mm) turn-buckle. This needs to be around 8" (20 cm) long when both eye-bolts are unscrewed as shown in the photo.

Killer Camera Rigs That You Can Build

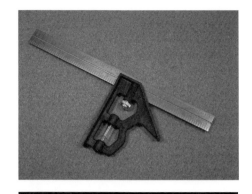

☐ A combo square.

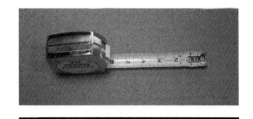

☐ A tape measure.

☐ A 24″ (60 cm) or longer level.

☐ A drill press.

☐ A hand drill.

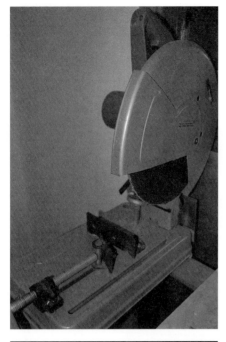

A chop saw.

C-clamps, 3" (76mm) and 4" (100mm).

A screwdriver, probably a Philips head, and probably a big one for the flat-head screws.

A vice. It would be a good idea to have a drill press vice too.

A 1³⁄₈" (34mm) hole saw. This is because I'm using 1¼" diameter aluminum tube for track. You want this hole saw to be slightly bigger than the diameter of your tube.

A prick punch or center punch.

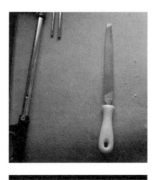
A metal file.

A hammer.

☐ A wire buffer wheel. This fits into your drill for buffing metal. A 2" (50 mm) wheel is a good size.

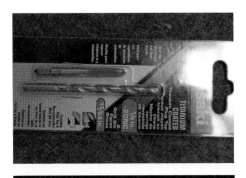

☐ ¼" (7 mm) tap with matching drill bit. A tap is something that you twist into a hole you've drilled into metal that makes threads so that you can screw a screw into that hole. You can buy tap sets all by themselves, but they are a little pricey. It's much easier to go to an automotive supply and purchase a single tap for the size you need with a drill bit specifically for that tap. If you've never used a tap before, it's easy and kind of cool.

☐ A tap wrench. You'll need this to screw the previously mentioned tap into your aluminum.

☐ A ¼" (7 mm) bit.

☐ A ⁵⁄₁₆" (8 mm) bit.

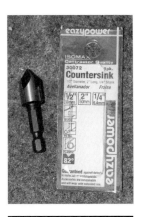

☐ A countersink bit. This allows the flat-head screw to fit flush against the metal.

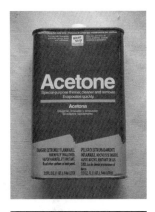

☐ Acetone. Really necessary for cleaning metal for J-B Weld prep.

☐ J-B Weld. This is great for gluing metal together.

☐ 60 grit sheet of sandpaper.

☐ Sharpie® marker.

☐ Framing square.

☐ Thread cutting oil.

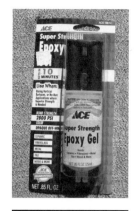

☐ Metal/wood epoxy.

☐ Masking tape.

☐ Spray or other kind of paint. This is to paint the wood portions of the track. Use any color you'd like.

☐ Heavy duty paper towels or rags.

Let's Build It

1 Make sure you are wearing eye protection, as I pointed out in the appendix, *Working with Metal*, which you must have read several times by now. If you're not wearing eye protection, please make sure your health insurance covers being blind. *Am I getting through to you?*

If you need to cut the 2½" (63 mm) square aluminum blocks, take your 2½" (63 mm) wide aluminum bar and use your prick punch and combo square set to 2½" (63 mm) to mark a line across the bar. Cut the bar so you get a 2½" (63 mm) square block.

Killer Camera Rigs That You Can Build

If you are using a chop saw to cut the block, go slow. Make sure you are allowing for the thickness of the blade when cutting. You want this block to be perfectly square. Also, the friction when cutting block this way is substantial; the metal will get really hot. It might be a good idea to have a bucket of cold water on hand to drop the block into to cool it down. Seriously, it gets really hot!

Draw an X from corner to corner to find the exact center of the block. I'm using a Sharpie so you can see it, but a prick punch or center punch is a better way to go.

Set a prick punch or center punch at the intersection of the X and give it a good thwack with a hammer. This will put a dimple in the metal where you'll need to drill. *Be very careful here*: The hole must be drilled in the exact center. We'll be cutting this piece into two pieces in step 3, and the measurement from the bottom edge of the bar to the bottom edge of the hole must be the same in every piece you make. (See step 3 if you're confused about where we're going with this).

2 Drill a large hole through the center of the aluminum block. I'll tell you right now that this is not the best way to do this. It's slow and painful. A metal shop might use an *annular cutter,* which makes quick work of cutting a plug out of steel or aluminum. Don't bother looking up annular equipment on the Internet—a single bit can cost over $1000. So we'll be doing it the best we can for the cheapest we can!

Before you start drilling this hole, set your drill press to the slowest speed it will go. Yep, I said the slowest speed. If the bit goes too fast, it will cause a lot of friction and heat and will actually weld the bits of aluminum you're drilling to the teeth of the bit. You don't want that.

It's very important to have some drill lubricant standing by, and lots of it. For this book, we'll be using thread cutting oil. It does a pretty good job and is reasonable on the wallet. Something like Ultra Lube for cutting and drilling metal is even better, but it is very expensive. But lubricants used for everyday stuff, like WD-40, 3-in-1 Oil, etc., are out; they simply won't hold up under the heat of the bit. Of course, since you read the appendix, *Working with Metal*, you know this already... right? If you haven't read that section, go read it now. And if you have read that section and are not wearing eye protection, you are taking a big risk with your eyesight. How many times do I have to tell you? Buy and wear the protective glasses!

Load the hole saw (1⅜" [34mm] drill bit) into your drill press. If your drill press is new, I assume you've read all the instructions and safety section on the information that came with your new drill press.

Take a quick look at this photo. I'm using a bench top vice and not a drill press vice. The reason for this is that we need some room underneath the aluminum block for this big plug we are about to drill out. A drill press vice will also work, but you'll need to set the block a little higher in the vice so there is room at the bottom, so that you don't start drilling a hole in your vice!

I'm using the level on my combo square to make sure the block is level in the vice. Make sure it is level both front-to-back and side-to-side.

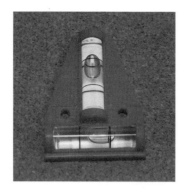

A bubble level or a level like that in this photo will work even better. You'll need one of these for filmmaking anyway, so don't be shy about buying one or the other.

If everything is not level with your drill bit, it will be a whacky hole, and you don't want that.

In the middle of your hole saw, there is a bit to guide things. Set this bit so that it is dead center on the dimple you made in the center of your block. Once it is set, use C-clamps to clamp your vice to the deck of the drill press.

Start drilling. Go just a touch into the aluminum. Add drill oil and start drilling again. Bring the bit out and add more oil. Just keep doing this until you are all the way through. The idea is to keep the bit wet with the oil. Think how well your car would run without oil. Same thing here.

A lot of metal waste will start to pile up. It will help a lot if you take a shop rag and clean the metal scrap off the teeth of the hole saw every once in a while. Fill the drilled aluminum with more cutting oil and keep going.

Sometime around Christmas, you'll make it all of the way through. Don't rush, keep adding oil and cleaning the bit and I promise you'll make it.

Clean all the oil and scrap metal off of it and you're done. The really good news is that this block makes *two* cradles for the dolly track. The bad news is that you'll need to drill a total of four blocks if you're not going to be welding. If you *are* going to be welding, you have to keep going until you have eight blocks for 10 of track.

3 Grab your prick punch and combination square and mark your drilled bar directly in half.

Cut your bar into two pieces. If you are a little bit off, and one is slightly taller than the other, that's OK. What's important is the distance between the bottom of the bar and the bottom of the now half hole. That distance *must* be the same. The track rests in this semicircle, and if the measurement from the bottom of the hole to the bottom of the bar is different between the bits you've made, the finished track will be wobbly.

Hey, Dan! I screwed up! The measurement from the bottom of the hole to the base of the bar is not the same on all my pieces. Do I have to start over?

If your measurement from the bottom of the bar to the bottom of the hole is off, you are allowed to cheat. If you need to add a bit more, try gluing a bit of aluminum to the bottom of the bar with some J-B Weld to make the distance the same. If the measurement is too great, you can simply trim a bit off the base of the aluminum block.

Everybody makes a mistake now and again, and most everything is fixable without starting over completely.

If you have any stray bits of aluminum hanging off your piece, you'll need to clean those up.

A metal file will make quick work of the stray bits.

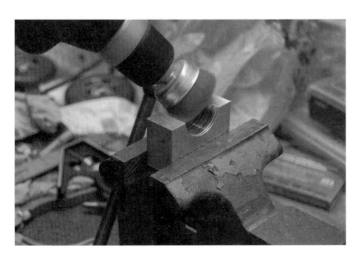

A wire brush in your drill is really handy. Just clamp the piece in your vice and have at it.

You should now have two pieces that look like this. If you're making the track exactly as instructed in this chapter, you will need four pieces for each 5' section of track. We'll call these pieces "track supports."

4 For this step, you'll need your four finished track supports, the aluminum bar that measures ½" (14mm) thick and 1½" (38mm) wide, the aluminum tube that is your track, and your dolly.

Set up your track as seen in the photo. The aluminum bar goes down first, then the track supports go on top of the bar, then the aluminum tube goes into the gutter on the supports.

One of the track supports should be aligned exactly at the end of the bar. Set this up on each end of the round tube.

Set your dolly on the track, and adjust the track support that is *not* aligned with the end of the aluminum bar.

My metal supplier sells this bar in 36" (91cm) lengths, which is very handy. If you are going to have the metal supply house cut your bar, it would be a very good idea to build your track supports first, set up your dolly, *then* take the measurement for the length of the crossbar. *Or* build the track first and make a dolly to match the track. It's much easier to have a dolly first.

Make a mark in the crossbar against the outside edge of the track support.

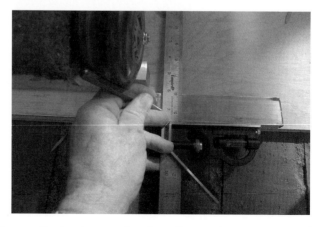

Once you have everything lined up to the wheels and to one end of the crossbar, take a combination square and set it up against the track support and the edge of the crossbar. Make sure that the track support is square with the crossbar.

Remove the track support and use the combo square to scratch a line all the way across the bar where you made your mark against the track support.

I used a chop saw to cut this bar to length. *Make sure* that you cut this bar on the outside of the line you made. If you cut *on* the line, the thickness of the saw blade will make this bar a little short.

You will need four crossbars for each section of track. Since I'm making a total of 10', or two sections, I'll need eight bars in all.

You should have something that looks like this. All of your cross pieces are now going to be this length. In this case, my bar is 30" (76 cm) long.

I'm using one of the bars as a guide for all the rest I'll be making. To make things easy on me, I'm not going to cut this bar yet. I did mark the length, then used some gaffer's tape to mark the end of the bar at the correct length. We'll be drilling holes in this bar later, then using those holes as a guide for the rest of the crossbar sections. That way every bar we make will be the same. Why not cut this bar now and still use it as a guide? Well, I could. But having the extra little bit of length helps me quickly know that this bar is the guide bar, and sometimes a little bit extra at the end helps in handling the bar for clamping and whatnot.

 If you're welding the pieces, you can skip this step, and all the steps that require bolting the track support to the crossbar.

We're going to be bolting the track support pieces to the crossbar, so we need to determine where to drill the holes for the machine screws.

The flat-head ¼" (7 mm) bolts will be screwed into the track support and the track itself as seen in this photo. As you can see, the middle bolt will go well into the track. Later, we'll be adding round aluminum bar so that the middle bolt will have something to screw into.

Take one of your track support pieces and determine the exact center on the bottom. Usually, I'd draw an X from corner to corner to give me the center, but we'll be putting a few more marks on here, so it's best just to measure across halfway and up and down halfway to find the center.

Now we need to make marks for the shorter machine screws. Set your combo square to ½" (14 mm) and measure in ½" (14 mm) from the left edge and make a mark, then do the same for the right edge. Then set your combo square for half the distance across the track support piece, and mark a line across the lines you made ½" (14 mm) in from the edges.

Take the marked up track support and line it up with the edge of the crossbar.

 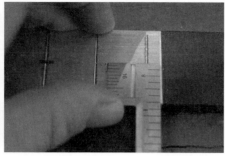 

If you're using an uncut bar as a jig like me, use this bar instead. For either bar, you want to use your prick punch and your combo square to draw lines across the crossbar from the three measurements you have on your track support bar. I'm using a Sharpie marker because it's a little easier to see in a photo, but using a prick punch or center punch to scratch a line in the aluminum is a better way to go.

Once you have those lines, measure the width of your bar. Mine is 1½" (38 mm) wide. Set your combo square to half that width. So mine is going to be ¾". Set your combo square against the edge of the bar and measure it in half, and mark a line across each of the three vertical lines.

Take your prick punch or center punch and put the point of it directly on the cross where the vertical line and horizontal lines meet and give it a good thwack with a hammer. You should now have three dimples in your crossbar.

Repeat these steps for the other end of your crossbar.

 Important: Read about drilling into metal in the appendix!

Remember the tap set you bought with the matching bit? Time to take that bit out. We'll be using the tap later to make threads for the ¼" (7 mm) machine screws. To be clear, this bit is *not* a ¼" (7 mm) bit. It has to be smaller than the ¼" (7 mm) tap, so don't think you can get away with a ¼" (7 mm) drill bit here!

Load this bit into your drill press. Be very careful to line up the dimple in the crossbar to the tip of the drill bit, then clamp the crossbar down. Use this bit to drill the holes on *each side* of the center mark. Repeat the steps on the opposite end of the bar.

Now load a ¼" (7 mm) bit into your drill press. Line it up with the center dimple and drill the center hole at ¼" (7 mm). Do the same on the opposite end.

Now you should have a crossbar with six holes in it: three on each end. The center hole is ¼" (7 mm) and the two holes on either side are from the drill bit that came with the tap. Set this bar aside for the moment.

Killer Camera Rigs That You Can Build

8 Now let's drill out the holes in all of our track support pieces. You can leave the ¼" (7 mm) bit in the drill press.

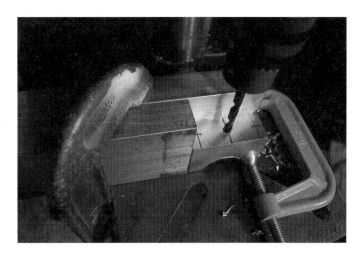

Take a close look at the photo. I'm using some extra aluminum bar that I used to make the track supports as a make-shift guide. I've lined up the ¼" (7 mm) drill bit to the center hole on the support bar. Then, I've taken an extra hunk of aluminum and placed it behind the support bar. I've taken a second piece of aluminum and placed it firmly against the edge of the support bar. I've clamped the extra hunks of aluminum bar down, then clamped the track support bar to the rear hunk of aluminum. Why? Now I never have to measure the rest of my track support pieces. Once I've finished drilling the center hole in this piece, I can remove it, and slide another track support piece in and drill the center hole on that one, and so on.

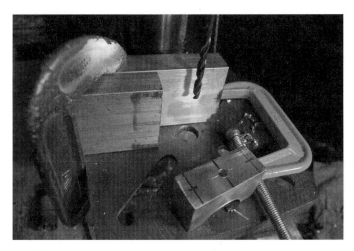

To be clear: I'm *not* touching the big hunks of aluminum once they are clamped down: these hunks are now a guide for the center hole on all of my track support pieces.

This way, I only have to mark up one track support piece, set the aluminum bars as a guide, and simply insert the new track support piece against the extra aluminum bars, clamp it, drill the hole, remove it, and go to the next support piece. Get it?

Now, drill the center hole at ¼" (7 mm) on all of your pieces.

9 Now let's finish all of our crossbars.

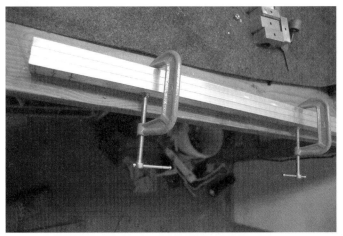

Take your guide crossbar (the one with the holes in it) and clamp it on top of two crossbars that are cut to the correct length.

Make sure the ends of all three line up exactly when you clamp them together.

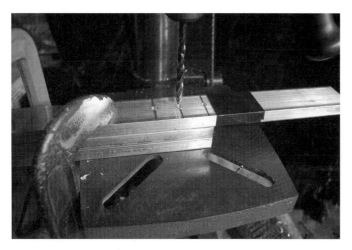

Line up the center hole on the stack with a ¼" (7 mm) bit in your drill press. Clamp the stack down! Use tons of drill oil or lubricant and drill through the bottom two pieces. Once that's done, turn the stack around and drill a ¼" (7 mm) hole through the center hole on opposite end.

Keep the stack clamped together, but change the drill bit to the one that came with your tap. Now use the same method to drill the smaller holes on each side of the center hole.

Now you may remove the clamp. You should now have two exact copies as your guide bar.

Use your original guide bar to keep making these crossbar sections until you have all of them drilled and ready to go.

If there are any metal bits hanging out of the holes on any of these bars, use a metal file to file them off.

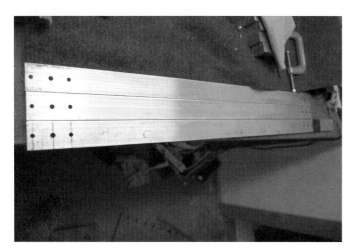

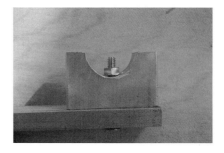

10 First, this next step may seem like extra work to some of you, and it is. In step 8, you set up extra hunks of aluminum on your drill press to act as a guide to drill a ¼" (7 mm) hole through the center of your track support. In this step, we'll be drilling the two holes for the tap in your track support pieces. So why didn't we use the same method to drill the tap holes? Well, originally, I did. But I also have a little experience in working with metal. When people that had no experience did it this way, for some reason a hole or two was a little off, and they were not able to screw a machine screw in there when the time came. To solve that, I came up with this fool-proof method. It's a little more work, but who said perfection was easy? If you're comfortable in your metal shop, go ahead and make the pieces mass factory style. Fine by me.

But if you are the least bit worried that your holes in any of your crossbars are off, here's a way to make sure they all fit together.

Take one of your crossbars and your track support bars and use a ¼" (7 mm) bolt and a nut to bolt them together through that ¼" (7 mm) center hole on both pieces.

Use your combo square to make sure that the track support piece is square to the crossbar.

Tighten the nut down, making sure the support piece doesn't move out of square.

If you have enough ¼" (7mm) screws, go ahead and screw all the track support pieces to each end of all of your crossbar pieces.

Line up the crossbar hole under the tap kit's drill bit, add some thread oil, and start drilling.

These outside holes do *not* go all the way through! If you are using machine screws that are 1¼" (31mm) long, the outside holes should be about 1½" (38mm) deep! All drill presses have a stop on them so you can set the depth of the hole you are drilling. Keep in mind that when setting the drill stop, you have an additional ½" (14mm) thickness of the crossbar.

Once you are done with one hole and have your stop all set up, it's pretty easy to drill the rest of the holes in your support pieces. Just don't get lazy and forget to clamp each piece! Always clamp your metal work!

You should now have something that looks like this photo (above) for each end of each piece of crossbar. It might be a really good idea to put a mark of some kind on the crossbar end and the corresponding track support bar so you know that *this* support bar goes with *this* particular end of crossbar. Theoretically, they should all be the same, but the few times it doesn't work out that way is a real drag.

⓫ Now load the ¼" (7mm) drill bit into the drill press and drill out all the outside holes on the crossbar to ¼" (7mm). The reason we didn't do this to begin with is that you needed to have the smaller holes to use as a guide for drilling the tap holes.

⓬ Next we are going to countersink the holes on the crossbar. This allows the head of the machine screw to sit flush with the bottom of the crossbar.

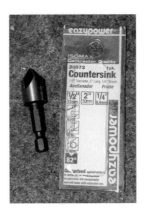

A countersink looks like this. It must be slightly bigger than the diameter of the head of your machine screw. Mine takes a ½" (14mm) countersink. I've also used big ½" (14mm) drill bits as a countersink. Either will get the job done.

Load the countersink into your drill press and line up one of the holes in your crossbar dead center with the point of the bit. Clamp the bar down.

Drill down a bit until you get a countersink going.

Drop one of your flat-head ¼" (7 mm) machine screws through the hole. If it is flush with the aluminum bar, you can set your drill stop at that point. If the head of the screw is sticking up above the surface of the bar, you'll have to drill out a little more. Just drill the countersink a bit, check it, then drill a bit more, check it, and so on. If you go too deep, it will weaken the bar so be careful. Once you have the drill stop set, you won't have to worry about drilling too far or too little on the rest of the countersink holes.

13 Tapping the holes in the track supports.

What is a "tap" anyway? A tap is like a drill bit with threads on it. As you twist a tap into a previously drilled hole, you will create threads in that hole. You can then screw a bolt, or in our case, a machine screw into it. Don't worry, it's very easy to do.

First, I like to keep the tap and the drill bit matched to that tap in the same place, so whenever I'm done drilling with that specific bit, I put it in a little box with its tap. There is nothing worse than digging through all of your drill bits to find the matching bit to a tap. If you keep them together, you will never have that problem.

The other thing you'll need is a tap wrench. This is a specialized tool that the tap fits into.

Load your track support piece into your vice with the bottom facing up so you have access to the holes on the bottom. Load your tap into your tap wrench.

Fill the hole you'll be tapping with thread cutting oil or drill lubricant. Set the tap into the hole and make sure you are going straight and true.

Twist the tap into the hole by grabbing the ends of the tap wrench and turning just like you would a bolt: clockwise. (Ever heard the term righty-tighty, lefty-loosey?)

With every full turn or two turns, reverse for a half-turn. You need to get the cut metal bits out of there by reversing a half-turn or each turn will become more difficult because you'll be cramming more and more metal bits into the hole with each turn. So don't skimp on this. Make sure you go all the way to the bottom of the hole you drilled (and remember that the hole is deeper than the machine screw is long, right?)

Killer Camera Rigs That You Can Build

When you hit bottom, unscrew the tap. There will be metal dust on the tap; clean it off before doing the next hole. Now do the second hole on your track support piece.

Once you have both holes tapped, take the piece out of the vice, and rap it hard on a surface to get all the metal and oil out of it.

ATTACHING THE TRACK SUPPORT PIECES TO THE TRACK CROSSBAR PIECES

14 Mix up a good bit of J-B Weld. Please follow the instructions on the J-B Weld package. If you don't, it won't work. If you do, it will work great.

Clean the piece with some acetone. Make sure your screws screw in. Good. Done. Now move onto the next one. Tap the outer two holes on all of your track support pieces.

Apply a thin layer of J-B Weld around the two outer holes of a track support piece. Avoid getting J-B Weld on the center of the piece.

Use your shorter ¼″ (7 mm) machine screws, and screw the track support to the crossbar. Use acetone and a rag to clean up any J-B Weld that has squeezed out.

Make sure your screw heads are flush with the crossbar base. If they don't screw in all the way, you'll have to cut these screws with a hacksaw or buy shorter screws. You can't fix it by drilling deeper holes. Too late for that!

It should look like this when you're done. Attach the rest of the track supports to the crossbars: one on each end of the crossbar. Work quickly! You don't want your J-B Weld to dry up!

If you're following my directions for 10′ (3 meters) of track, you should have four crossbars with aluminum track supports on each end. Set them aside and let the J-B Weld dry for 24 hours.

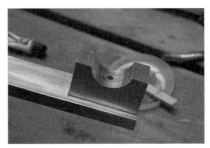

15 Now we are going to add round bar inside our round aluminum tube. This will allow one section of track to slide into another section, giving us a seamless joint between sections so that we don't get a bump when the dolly glides over it.

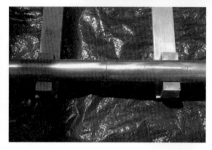

When you are all finished, it will go together as shown in these three photos.

My metal supplier sells this bar in 12" (30 cm) lengths, which is incredibly handy.

First we need to determine how far apart our crossbars will be from the end of the track aluminum tube. A turnbuckle will tighten these two pieces of track together. If we space the track crossbars too far apart, the turnbuckle won't be long enough to reach. If they are too close, the turnbuckle will not be able to tighten down. For my turnbuckle, the edge of the crossbar to the end of the round aluminum tube is 3" (76 mm). So that's where I'll be attaching my crossbar to the round tube. If your turnbuckle is different from mine, unscrew the eye bolts an inch or more. Lay the eyes of the bolts on the center of the crossbars as you can see in the photo. Half the distance between the two crossbars is the measurement of aluminum tube that needs to come off the edge of the crossbar. *Do not* make the total distance between the two crossbars more than 8" (20 cm). If it is longer than that, your turnbuckle is too long and you'll need to get a shorter one.

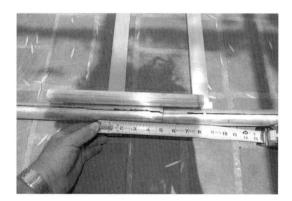

Once you've determined the distance between crossbars, we need to figure out how long our round aluminum bar that goes inside the round aluminum tube needs to be. The round bar on one side will go into the tube permanently. Then when assembling the finished track, slides into the tube on the adjoining track. The round bar must go over the track support piece completely on the permanent side. In the receiving side, we will be cutting a section off of the bar to go over that side's track support. The permanent side will extend outside the tube up to the point of the receiving side's track support. Take a close look at the photo: in my configuration, it is 8" from the outside edge of the track support to the inside edge of the receiving tube's track support. Therefore, the round bar length is 8" (20 cm).

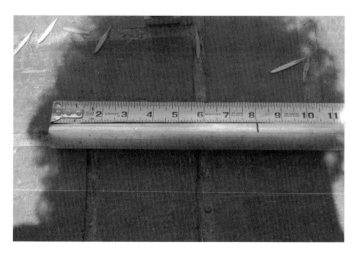

If you are copying my design exactly, measure and mark your round bar at 8" (20 cm) long. Your measurement might be different, depending on the length of your turnbuckle. Cut four bars at your determined length. Don't throw the leftover bar away! You'll be needing it later.

GLUING THE ROUND BAR INSIDE THE ROUND TUBE

16 Take another look at this photo: From where the receiving bar starts to the edge of the track support is 3" (76mm) (starting at the 5" [12cm] mark and going to the 8" [20cm] mark). We could let this round bar go right to the edge of the track support, but to be on the safe side, subtract ¼" (7mm). So the part of the bar that extends out of the permanent side will be 2¾" (69mm) instead of the true total of 3" (76mm).

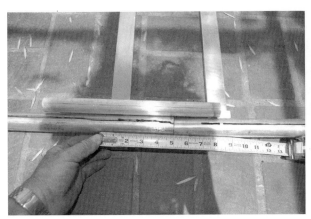

Measure from the end of each of your four 8" (20cm) bars, and make a mark at 2¾" (69mm). Take some 60 grit sand paper, and roughen up the aluminum bars up to that mark. Once that is done, take a rag or shop towel with acetone on it, and clean the sanded part of your round bar.

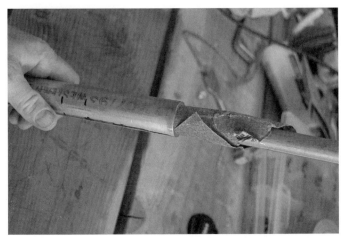

Collect your four 5' long pieces of round tube. Wrap some 60 grit sandpaper around a wood or metal dowel, and sand the inside of one end of each of your tubes, at least 5" (12cm) in.

Once you've sanded it really well, wrap a shop towel around the dowel and soak it with acetone. Stick it inside the tube and clean it.

Make sure it's spotless! No grease, dirt, or metal filings please.

Slide your bar inside the tube. In mine, there is a tiny bit of wiggle room. We don't want that. It needs to fit snugly into the tube. So let's fix it.

Get your metal mend tape (the stuff used for fixing mufflers and such on cars). Cut a strip about an inch wide or so.

Determine the length of the tape by wrapping it around the round bar. Once you've got the length, go ahead and cut a dozen or so more.

Peel the backing off the tape, and carefully wrap it around the end of the sanded part of the bar.

Slide the taped end of the bar into the round tube. Is it snug, or still a little loose? If it's loose, add another layer of tape on top of the first and test it in the tube again. Keep adding layers until it fits into the tube just a little snug. I had to add three layers of tape before mine was perfect.

Now add the same amount of metal mend tape to the end of each bar and a touch below the mark on the bar you made earlier. Don't add any tape to the middle of the bar.

Collect your four bars and your four sanded and cleaned tubes. Mix up a batch of J-B Weld and completely slather the sanded part of the bar with it.

Insert the bar into the tube up to the mark you made on the bar. J-B Weld is going to ooze out. That's ok. Use acetone and a rag to completely clean off the J-B Weld that has oozed out before it starts to dry!

Make sure the J-B Weld is completely cleaned off. If there is any left, it will cause the track to not fit together properly!

When you're done, you should have four round tubes with round bar sticking out of one end. Set these aside in a safe, out of the way place to dry for 24 hours.

 While the tube dries, let's finish up our crossbar pieces.

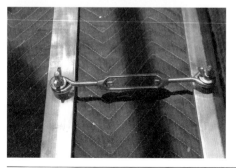

As you know, the ends of the track are joined tightly together with a turnbuckle. Let's put these turnbuckle pieces on our end crossbar sections. Since I am only making two 5' sections, I'll only need one turnbuckle. But as I add more track, I'll need to add a turnbuckle to each end section of track. At this point, you should have four crossbar sections with the track support pieces attached with J-B Weld and machine screws.

Measure the length of the crossbar on the bottom, and make a mark at the halfway point. Then measure the width of the track and make a mark halfway across. You should now have a point dead center of the crossbar piece. Drill a ⁵⁄₁₆″ (8 mm) hole at that point.

Do this on all four crossbar pieces.

You may be wondering about the other crossbar pieces you cut and drilled. Don't worry, we'll be getting to those. Right now, we need to get the end sections done.

As you know from drilling the end holes for the track support pieces, the flat-head machine screw can't stick out like this. So let's drill the countersink hole so that the ⁵⁄₁₆″ (8 mm) screw fits nicely flush with the bottom.

Like we did on the ends, load your countersink bit into the drill press, line it up with the hole, and drill out a countersink hole. Remember, this screw is ⁵⁄₁₆″ (8 mm), so the countersink bit has to be big enough to accommodate the head of that machine screw. As you did on the ends for the ¼″ (7 mm) screw, drill a bit at a time until you determine the correct depth this bit needs to go, then set the stop on the drill press for drilling out the countersink hole on the other three bars.

When done, you should have something that looks like this. Clean them up well with acetone, making sure to get all the drilling oil off!

At this point, we'll put off adding the machine screw permanently to this hole, as we still have some work to do, and we'd have to wait for the J-B Weld to dry before moving on.

ADDING ROUND BAR TO THE RECEIVING TRACK ALUMINUM TUBE

18 Remember this photo from earlier in the chapter? We've connected the track support to the crossbar with the two shorter machine screws. The longer middle one didn't have much to screw into until we added the round bar into one end of our round tube. Now that tube is good to go. But what about the receiving end of the track? We need to add a bit of bar inside the receiving end so that we can bolt the round tube securely to our track support.

Make sure that the J-B Weld has had 24 hours to dry the round bar we put in earlier before moving on with this step!

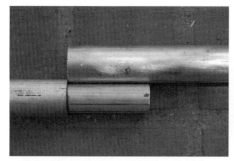

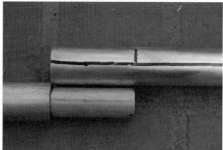

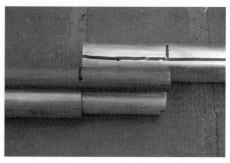

Collect your four pieces of round tube. One end should have a bar sticking out of it, and the opposite end should have nothing sticking out of it. This end of the bar is now the receiving end. Take two of the aluminum tubes: Set the receiving end against the edge of the aluminum tube that has a bar sticking out of it as seen in the photo.

Put a mark on the receiving tube where the round bar from the other tube ends. (Pay no attention to the mark running down the middle of the tube in these photos! That's from a failed experiment of mine.)

Remember the wood or metal dowel you used to sand out the interior of the round tube? Take that and line the end of the dowel up with the mark you just made on the receiving tube. Make a mark on the dowel where the receiving tube ends.

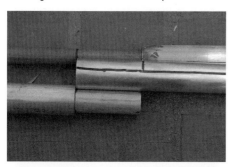

Since my round bar was 12" (30 cm) long, and I cut it to 8" (20 cm), I have 4" (100 mm) of scrap left. We'll be gluing this inside of the receiving tube. Your scrap *does not* have to be 4" (100 mm)! All you need of this round bar is 2" (50 mm) or more. The reason we made a mark on the dowel is that when you push this bar into the tube, you'll know exactly how far it needs to go.

Mix up some J-B Weld. Take your dowel and spin it around in the J-B Weld until you get a good-sized glob on the end of it.

Just like you did when adding the bar to the tube before, sand out the inside of the tube, and clean it well with acetone. Then sand the round bar a bit and clean it with acetone. Add some metal mend tape to the middle of this bar (you don't need to add it to two places as you did with the other bar on the opposite end of the tube).

Here comes the tricky part: Slide the glob end of the dowel into the round tube, being very careful *not* to touch the sides of the tube until you reach the mark on your dowel! If you ever played the game "Operation" as a kid, it's kind of like that. To be clear: The tube must be clean up to the mark. After the mark, smear it around against the wall of the tube. Remove the dowel carefully, then clean the J-B Weld off the dowel immediately.

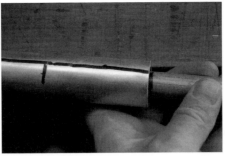

Use your dowel to push the bar in up to the mark on the dowel. It's ok to go a tiny bit further in, but not too much.

Carefully set this bar aside out of the way of clomping feet and curious dogs.

Finish up the other three bars.

If you got any J-B Weld on the wall of the tube before the mark, use acetone-soaked shop towel to clean it out, being careful not to push the round bar any

Insert the round bar into the tube, and push it in.

further in! This is a real pain, so it's best to just have a steady hand when applying the glue in the first place.

Let the interior bar dry for 24 hours!

19 Attaching the end crossbar sections to the track. When we are done, we'll have two 5' long sections of track that look something like the photo.

Remember measuring the distance between crossbars for the turnbuckle? This is why we did that. Our rough measurement was 3" (76 mm) from the end of the round tube. We can now attach the crossbars to the tube between 3" (76 mm) and 4" (100 mm), because our round bar now glued to the inside of the track is plenty long enough that an inch here or there won't make much difference. But once we determine where to attach our crossbars, *all* the crossbars on each end of the track must be that distance.

It's also a good idea to slide the male end of the track into the female end to see if your bar hits any snags, or goes all the way in so that the two pieces of track meet.

To determine where to drill our holes to bolt the crossbars to the track, we'll be using a lot of clamps to clamp the round tube track to the crossbars. The best approach is to work upside-down so that the bottom of the crossbars are facing up. To do that, arrange some milk crates or apple boxes to set the track on.

Since the crates are narrower than the track is wide, I've added some scrap bits of lumber to hold the round tube track.

Lay the track on the lumber, then lay the crossbars on the track, one on each end, of course. Don't worry about perfection at this point; everything will be adjusted and readjusted as we go. Make sure that the male ends (with the bars sticking out of the tube) are on one end and the female ends are on the other.

Clamp the round tube track to the scrap lumber. Try to clamp it so that the ends of the track are somewhat equal.

The round bar in my track begins at 3" (76mm) in. That, combined with the turnbuckle measurement, means I can attach this crossbar piece anywhere from 3" (76mm) to 4" (100mm). So I'm going to split that, and make it 3½" (88mm). I set my combo square to 3½" (88mm) and measure from the end of the round tube (*not* the round bar sticking out of one end!). Move the crossbar so that the side of the track support rests against the end of the combo square.

Don't let any of this freak you out. It is simply this: (1) the turnbuckle needs to be able to tighten when your track is finished, and (2) the crossbar has to be over a piece of the round bar that is inside the round tube so that the machine screw has something solid to screw into.

Once the track support is in the proper place, use a marker to mark the round tube track on each side of the support.

Now move to the other side and make the same measurements and marks.

Move to the male end and do the same thing. Make sure you are measuring from the edge of the round tube and not from the round bar.

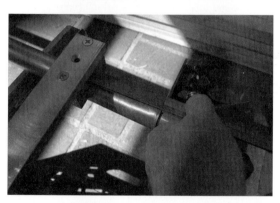

Once the marks are made for attaching the crossbars to the track, we can't have them moving around. Take a look at the photo. The round tube is clamped to the support pieces using lumber and a big clamp.

Here's a closer look.

If your clamps aren't big enough, you can use thinner material like a scrap bit of aluminum or steel.

Make sure you do all four corners.

With the support pieces clamped between the marks on the aluminum tube, we now have to make sure the track is square. *This is the most important measurement you will make!* If your track is out of square, it won't fit together properly, and your dolly won't run on it! So take your time on this part. Maybe you should go have lunch now. This is not something to measure while you're hungry.

Killer Camera Rigs That You Can Build

It's hard to get a big framing square up against a round tube and be accurate with it. To solve this, get a scrap bit of plywood and clamp it to the inside of the round tube near the crossbar.

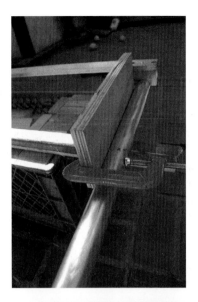

Unless you have a friend around to lend an extra pair of hands, you might need to stack something under the framing square to hold it in place. One side of the framing square should be up against the plywood clamped to the tube. The other side should be up against the crossbar. Now take a close look near the middle of the crossbar in the photo. Do you see the gap between the framing square and the crossbar?

Carefully grab the tubes and shift the whole thing so that it's square against the framing square. Picture a rectangle that is more of a parallelogram than a perfect rectangle. You need to shove one corner of the parallelogram to make it a perfect rectangle.

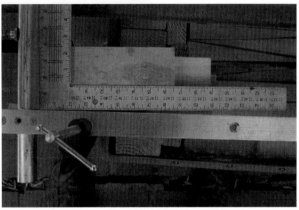

Here's a closer look. That gap is bad. Both sides along the entire length of the framing square should be touching the crossbar and the plywood.

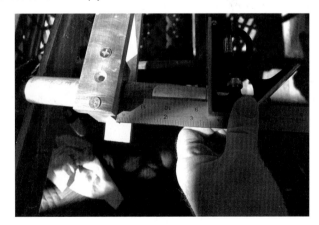

Take your combo square and remeasure the distance from the end of the tube to the track support on all four corners. If it is the same as it always was, you're good. If not, you'll need to readjust the track support to the proper measurement (in this case, 3½" (88mm)). If you needed to adjust the support, make sure you go back to the framing square to see if the entire track needs to be squared again. Redo these steps until the track is square and the track support is in the proper place.

Once everything is perfect, clamp everything down tight to keep it that way.

Take a hand drill and load a ¼" (7 mm) bit into it. We are going to use a drill to make a mark on the tube. We are *not* drilling a hole! You simply want to use the drill to "start" a hole. And by "start" I mean, make a mark in the tube just big enough to find later. Carefully guide the bit into the center hole on the track support and drill away. You don't need to use a lubricant, as we are not going into the tube, but just marking the tube. Do this on all four corners.

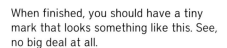

When finished, you should have a tiny mark that looks something like this. See, no big deal at all.

Before you take the track apart, label the round tube and the track support with the same mark. Something that says: this track support goes with this end of the tube. Of course you want to use a different label for each corner. This way when you put the whole thing together, the holes you'll be drilling in the tube and the track supports will match up perfectly.

Now you can take the track apart. If the mark you drilled into the tube is barely visible, it would be a good idea to circle it with a marker so it's easier to find later.

Given you probably have at least one more section of 5' of track, you'll need to repeat all of these steps for each section you have.

TAPPING THE SCREW HOLES IN THE TUBE

 Load the bit that matches the tap into your drill press. Clamp the aluminum tube under the bit so that the bit will go perfectly straight down the mark you drilled with the hand drill. Make sure you set the stop on the drill press so that the bit does not go all the way though the tube! You need to drill this hole nearly to the opposite side of the tube, just short of going all the way through.

For each section of track, you'll have four holes to drill.

You should be an old hand at tapping by now. Clamp the tube down and tap each of the four holes. Now do you see why we put a section of round bar inside? We've got a nice threaded hole to take the machine screw.

ATTACHING THE CROSSBARS TO THE ROUND TUBE

21 Lay the track out on the floor, making sure that the track support marks match the marks on the tube. We are still working upside-down; the crossbars are on top of the round tube.

Once everything is matched up, load a wire brush into your hand drill. Move the crossbar aside a bit and roughen up the bar around each tapped hole with the wire brush.

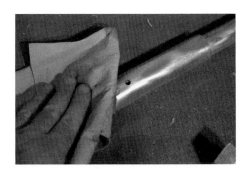

Use acetone and a shop towel to clean the tube.

Do the same cleaning on the gutter of the track support.

Have your long ¼" (7 mm) machine screws ready. Mix up a batch of J-B Weld and apply it in the gutter on each end of one crossbar.

Flip it over, and screw the crossbar onto the tube on both sides.

Repeat these steps for the opposite end.

While the J-B Weld is still wet, double-check to make sure the track is still square. It should be, but if it isn't, loosen up the screws a bit and adjust the track to square, then tighten the screw down.

Repeat for each section of track.

Let the J-B Weld dry for 24 hours.

MAKING THE CENTER TRACK CROSSBARS

22 Now that we have the ends done, the track needs some support between the ends. We need to add two crossbars in the middle of the track. For the ends we used aluminum block to make the track support because lots of strength is needed. For the middle, we can get away with using wood. No more nasty drilling into big blocks of aluminum! You're welcome. (Of course, if you are welding the whole thing, you'll have to keep using aluminum for the track supports. Sorry.)

These are just like the aluminum supports, but are made of 2×4 lumber.

Remember the width of our aluminum bar: 2½" (63mm)? Then we cut that into a 2½" (63mm) square? We'll be doing the same with 2×4 lumber. The lumber will be thicker than the aluminum, but that's perfectly fine. In fact, it's a good thing.

Cut the lumber into 2½" (63mm) squares. You'll need one square for each crossbar. I'm using a power miter saw for this. A hand saw and mitre box works just as well, it just takes longer.

Once you have them cut, draw an X from corner to corner to find the exact center.

Use the same hole saw (big drill bit) that you used to cut the aluminum version of these to cut a hole through the middle of the block.

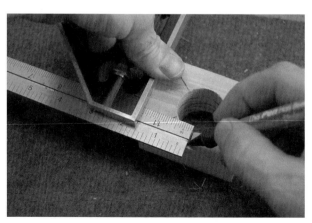

Use your combo square to make a mark halfway across the block.

98

Chop it into two pieces as you did with the aluminum supports. As with the aluminum track supports, make sure that the measurement from the bottom of the gutter to the bottom of the block is the exact same measurement as that on your aluminum version of these.

Since I am making two 5' (1.5 meters) sections of track, I'll need four crossbars with the wood supports: two for each section of track. It might be a good idea to sand these blocks to make them look nice, but it's not necessary for them to do their job. Don't bother sanding the bottom; it will glue better if it's a little rough.

Draw an X on the bottom of each block to find the center. Then drill a ¼" (7 mm) inch hole through the middle of the X.

You'll need to protect the wood some way. I'm painting mine black. You can also use a polyurethane on the wood if you don't want to paint it. Either way, there are a couple of places on the block that you want to keep untreated wood. Use masking tape to cover the bottom of the block, and the base of the gutter.

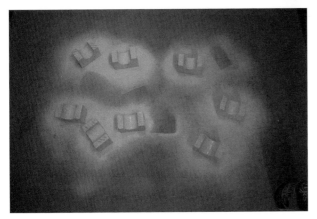

If you are going to paint the blocks, it's a good idea to use a primer first. Frankly, it's better to use a brush to paint these, but I'm lazy so I'm going to use spray primer and spray paint.

Put at least two coats of paint on these. I kind of wish I'd painted them red, only because I think that would look really cool.

Once the paint is dry, remove the masking tape from the gutter and the bottom.

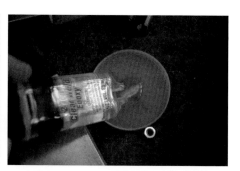

Mix up some epoxy. Make sure that the epoxy is for wood and metal (most are). Have a ¼" (7 mm) bolt and nut handy.

Spread some epoxy on the bottom of a wood track support.

As with the aluminum version, use a ¼" (7 mm) bolt and nut to temporarily attach the wood support to the crossbar. Again, use your combo square to make sure the wood support is square.

Use wood screws to attach the block while the ¼" (7 mm) bolt is holding it in place. If you are using large wood screws, you'll need to predrill some holes in the block so that the screws don't crack the wood.

Once you have the screws in, remove the ¼" (7 mm) bolt! You don't want the epoxy drying with that in there.

Repeat these steps for the opposite end of the crossbar.

You should have two crossbars for each 5' (1.5 meters) section of track when you're done. It's not shown in the photo, but you should have one block on each end of the crossbar.

ATTACHING THE MIDDLE CROSSBARS

 Lay out a section of track upside-down. Clamp a piece of plywood to one of the crossbars you just made. Clamp another piece of plywood to the round tube rail.

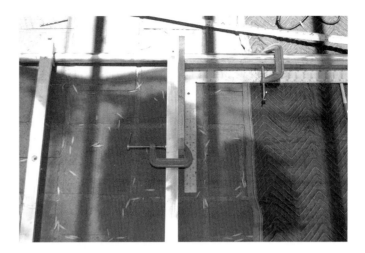

The two middle crossbars should be somewhat equally spaced. Measuring from one of the end crossbars down the round tube rail, find a good place to place your first middle crossbar. My measurement is about 17" (43 cm). For the second middle crossbar, I'll measure down 17" (43 cm) from the opposite end crossbar. This will place each crossbar somewhat equally spaced down the track.

Take a look at the photo. When you're all done, you should have four crossbars equally spaced like this.

Use your framing square to make sure the new crossbar is square, just as you did with the end crossbars. (You don't need to have the track up off the ground for the middle crossbars. The two end crossbars are now holding everything together quite well for you.)

Mark each side of the wood track support with a marker.

Use a hand drill and a ¼" (7 mm) bit to mark the round tube by using the center hole on the crossbar as a guide. This is the same method you used before on the aluminum track supports. Repeat on the other end of the crossbar to mark the opposite round tube.

You can now move the crossbar aside. It's a good idea to draw a circle around the bit mark so you can find it easily.

Label each end of the crossbar and track with a unique mark so that you'll know which support goes to each hole.

Repeat for the second crossbar and any other sections of track you're making.

Load the bit that matches your tap into the drill and drill a hole through each mark on the round tube. Do *not* go all the way through the tube; just get through the wall on one side.

As you've done many times before, tap each hole with the ¼" (7 mm) tap.

Note: Originally, I did all the holes on the round tube, including the aluminum end pieces. This made drilling all the holes in the tube easy to work with. Once the end pieces are J-B Welded and screwed, it's awkward to do the center holes for the middle crossbars. Unfortunately, the "beta builder" (I have people actually follow the instructions to build these things to make sure my plans are clear; I call them "beta builders") had a problem at some point, and the holes at a couple of points were off just a tiny bit. That's enough to cause big problems. By adding the end pieces first and keeping everything square, making the holes in the middle of the round tube as you just did keeps everything perfect. If you feel comfortable doing all the tapped holes first, go ahead. It is easier, but one mistake means redoing a lot of work.

Clean the aluminum round tube over each tapped hole with your wire brush and acetone. Mix up some epoxy as you did for the bottom of the wood block. Smear it into the gutter on the wood blocks on each end of a crossbar.

Use a ¼" (7 mm) machine screw to screw the crossbar onto the round tube. Make sure that each track support matches the hole for that support. Repeat for the opposite end of the crossbar.

Repeat for each crossbar.

ATTACHING THE MACHINE SCREW FOR THE TURNBUCKLE

 24 This is what the ⁵⁄₁₆″ (8mm) hole is for in the center of each end crossbar. Use your wire brush on the drill to clean up that hole, then wipe it down with some acetone.

Mix up a little bit of J-B Weld. Add some to the bottom of the hole in the middle of your end crossbar.

Add some J-B Weld to the head end of a ⁵⁄₁₆″ (8mm) flat-head machine screw.

Run the ⁵⁄₁₆″ (8mm) machine screw up through the hole and add a nut. Tighten it down really tight.

Use some acetone and shop cloth to clean up the J-B Weld.

Make sure you clean the J-B Weld completely off the threads of the machine screw!

Repeat these steps for each of the end crossbars.

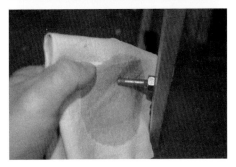

ATTACHING THE TURNBUCKLE

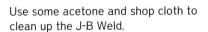

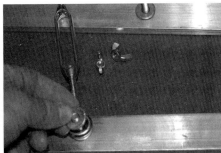

25 Once the J-B Weld is dry, add a washer to the ⁵⁄₁₆″ (8mm) machine screw.

Slip the eyebolt of the turnbuckle on the machine screw, then add a another washer on top of that, then screw the whole thing down with a wing nut.

On the matching crossbar on your other section of track, add two washers and a wing nut.

26 We are almost done!

Flip the track so it's right-side up.

Check each support that is now attached to the track. You might find some J-B Weld or some epoxy that has dripped down onto the round tube rail; use a big flat-head screwdriver to chip that stuff off the rail.

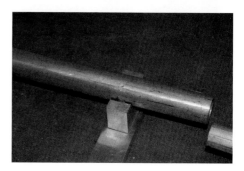

The reason I didn't have you clean all the rail in the beginning is because a dirty rail makes it easier to chip off the glue. If you want, now that all the glue is off, you can load the wire brush into your hand drill and shine up all of the rail, then clean it with some acetone.

PUTTING SECTIONS OF YOUR TRACK TOGETHER

 27 Line up a female end of your track with a male end.

Slide the male end (the part with the round bar coming out) into the female side of the second section of track.

Push the two sections of track together.

Remove the wing nut and one washer from the end crossbar that doesn't hold the turnbuckle.

Slip the eyebolt of the turnbuckle onto that screw.

Add the washer and wing nut. You can now tighten both wing nuts down.

Turn the middle of the turnbuckle to tighten it down. This will tighten each section of track together.

And there it is. You can just keep making 5′ (1.5 meters) sections of track until you run out of money.

Try out your dolly on it. Put a clamp on the track support on one end of the track to keep your dolly from rolling off.

Read the chapter on how to level track before using it for real!

How to Lay Out and Level Dolly Track

Since you'll be seeing this track design every now and again in these pages, I wanted to give you a closer look at it. It's basically a wood version of the PVC padding in Chapter 6. The PVC lays in a gutter on a 2×4 length of lumber.

Hey, Dan! Why didn't you include this in the book?

In this chapter, we'll be learning how to lay out dolly track, level it, and put down markers for dolly moves. This is all basically the same whether using PVC track or the professional grade dolly track in the last chapter. We'll also be getting into stuff you'll need to do this. Sometimes a few wedges will do the trick. Other times a combination of wedges, apple boxes, and wood blocks are needed. It all depends on the situation.

Mainly because 12′ of track and a dolly looks like this. It's a lot to haul around if you don't need to. Now there will be times when you need the support of a big 2×4, and there will be times, mostly in fact, that PVC attached to a 3″ wide bit of lumber is plenty. Wouldn't you rather haul less to the shoot when you need it than haul more when you don't need it? Although this track system works great, it's also a big pain. But if you'd like to know how to build it, just email me at dan@DVcameraRigs.com and I'll fill you in.

DOI: 10.1016/B978-0-240-81337-0.00009-4

What You'll Need to Lay Out Dolly Track

2" × 4" × 10" long wood blocks. Lots of them.

Why 10" long? Because 10" fits perfectly into a legal milk crate:

Just grab a length of 2×4 lumber and starting cutting it in 10" lengths until you fill a legal milk crate. And that's only a good start. You need tons of these. (What's the difference between a legal milk crate and an illegal one? A legal milk crate is one you *pay* for.)

Wedges. A wedge is a big shim. It's a 2" × 4" × 12" block cut at an angle. It is nearly impossible to make this simple little thing without a band saw. They sell for about $2 each at grip supply stores like Studio Depot in Hollywood or Film Tools in Burbank (both these have Web sites where you can have them shipped to you), and are much easier to buy than make. Get at least 20 for a short track run; 40 would be even better. There never seem to be enough blocks or wedges around when you need them.

Of course you have to have a long level, 36" minimum! And 48" is ideal. Depending on the type of track you'll be using and the layout, you might need C-clamps, ¾" (19 mm) thick plywood, and grip clips (in the ordinary world, grip clips are called spring clamps, but if you call them "grip clips" you can charge more for them). You'll see whether you'll need this other stuff later in the chapter when we cover laying out the different types of track.

What you don't see here, and something that is often used to raise and/or level track, are apple boxes. As hard as I try to get people to make sandbags and apple boxes, most of the time these tools are seen as afterthoughts. An apple box just isn't as sexy as a crane. But in reality, sandbags and apple boxes are the most used and important tools on a film set. In the meantime, I'll forego the use of apple boxes in this section. Just know you can use them for leveling track, and they can be a total lifesaver for a variety of uses on a film set.

The First Step for Any Type of Track

First things first. You need to determine *where* the track will be laid, and *how much* track you'll need for your shot. The easiest way to do this is to block your actors. Blocking is simply deciding where and when your actors move, if at all. It may be a simple *push in* from 6" away. Or your actors may be all over a room, needing to hit a half dozen *marks,* with the camera moving from close-ups to two shots, to singles. What seems simple can turn very complicated very quickly!

Once you decided where the actors will be, take your camera or director's finder and determine your start point. Let's say you are starting on a Close Up of actor A, then pulling the camera back to an over-the-shoulder of actor B. Hand-hold your camera to get the first starting point on that close up. That's where the lens of the camera needs to be. Now, keep in mind that your dolly may be 40" long or longer, and if the lens of the camera is on a tripod in the middle of the dolly, you need to have at least enough track so that the dolly doesn't fall off the end! The next step is to move the camera to the over-the-shoulder shot. That's where your dolly shot ends. Your track, like the opening shot, needs to extend beyond that point to accommodate the length of the dolly.

Take these steps a bit seriously. Once you have leveled out dolly track, it is a big pain to move it another 8"!

Laying Out and Leveling Dolly Track

PVC Track

We've covered PVC on its own, and with the track padding. This is just fine on level ground. (True level is found mostly indoors. The only level outdoor locations I have ever come across are a tennis court and a patio.)

PVC TRACK PERMANENTLY ATTACHED TO WOOD PLANKS

There are two methods for laying out this track you may have built. One is to support the track on the 10" long wood blocks. The second is to attach the track to 2" × 4" lumber lengthwise. You'll need to use either of these methods if the surface is not level, or you are shooting in rain or snow. (See Chapter 5.)

Supporting the Track with Blocks

Of course the first step is to attach lengths of track together until you have the proper length for your shot.

If you made this handy little dolly track spacer, use it now!

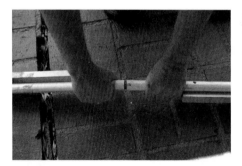

Run it down the length of track to make sure all of the track is spaced apart correctly. If you don't have one of these, you can use the dolly itself.

Place wood blocks under the track about 2' apart.

On each end of this type of track, you will have PVC that is not supported by the lumber the track is screwed into. You'll need to support each end of the wood plank, and underneath the point where the track is joined together. Since the plank holding the PVC is ³⁄₄" thick, use a piece of lumber that thickness. I'm using a scrap piece of plywood.

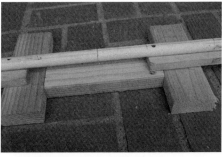

Start at the high end on one side of the track. Place a level on top of the PVC to determine how out of level you are. I'm laying out this track on a nasty bit of patio. At first glance, it *seems* level, but in reality, it's a mess going every which way. To my surprise, the upper part of this side of the track is level. *But* there's a small space under one of the blocks that will have to be supported.

So I'm going to put some wedges under this block to lift it high enough to support the track.

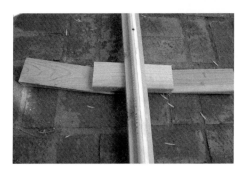

Move to the "low end" of the track and determine how much higher that end needs to be. In this case, it's huge! To make this track level, I've had to stack two blocks supported by wedges.

Once each block is supporting the track, put your level back on top of the PVC and press the level down—put some weight behind it! Make sure it is still level along the length of the track.

Go to each block and add wedges or extra blocks to eliminate the "air" between the block and the track, so that the track is supported at each block.

Go back to the high end and set the level *across* the two sides of track.

Add blocks and/or wedges until the opposite side of track is level with your balanced side of track. In this photo, the right side of track is obviously lower than the left side.

Keep moving down the track, stopping at each block to see if you need to add wedges until you reach the end.

Don't forget that the joined section of track will need some extra attention. It's especially important that this section be supported.

Add a C-clamp or throw a sandbag on top of the track at the end of the run to make sure that you don't dolly off the end!

There you have it. All leveled and ready to go.

Supporting PVC track with 2×4 lumber

There may be some cases where you can't use the single 10" block method. Perhaps your dolly shot requires you to go off a curb or over a small ditch of some sort. You'll need to support the entire length of lumber your PVC is attached to.

Lay out your track at the start and end points of your dolly shot as before.

Next lay 8' lengths of 2×4 lumber alongside the track. Where two sections of track are joined together, be careful that one length of 2×4 goes completely under the joined sections.

Slide the lengths of lumber under the track.

You'll still need to put 10" blocks under this track as you did without the 2×4 lumber support, *but only two or three 10" blocks per 8' of 2×4,* not every 2' or closer as before.

Attach the track to the 2×4 lumber.

There are a few ways to do this.

On each end of the track run, it's easy: simply clamp them in place.

In the middle, you can still clamp them, but you have to adjust the clamp so that it is at an angle. You don't want the dolly wheel hitting the clamp!

My personal favorite is to use grip clips (spring clamps) to do the job. They are quick and easy.

And lastly, attaching them with dry wall screws. Dry wall screws are just as easy to get out as they are to get in!

Don't forget to support the joined sections of track!

Level the track as you did in the previous section.

Make sure that the wheels don't hit any of the clamps!

Leveling the Pro Dolly Track

This is exactly the same, but will go faster.

Once one side is level, put the level across the track and work your way back up, adding wedges/wood blocks to level the left side with the right side.

Determine the high end, and place a wedge under one end of the crossbar.

Work your way down to the low end and add blocks and/or wedges under each crossbar. Then go back, adjusting the wedges to remove the "air" between the crossbar and the wedge.

Remember, a wedge needs to go under each side of the crossbar.

112

How to Use Your New Dolly

Actors have to "hit their marks." Well, so do dolly grips.

While blocking the camera to the actor's blocking, it's important to know where the dolly stops and starts. This may be in just two places. Or it may be in half a dozen places along the track run. Basically any time the camera operator says "Stop" is a dolly mark when working out the careful choreography between the camera and the actors. As camera rehearsals go, you may be changing these points by inches throughout the rehearsal.

What I like to do is to make a bunch of slips of gaffer tape with consecutive numbers written on them with a Sharpie.

The number one position is where the dolly push begins. Ever hear an AD yell *"Back to one!"*? That's what he or she is talking about; the camera and actors are going to start the take over from the first position. Place the gaffer tape with the number 1 on it at the back wheel of the dolly at this position.

As you go through the camera rehearsal, the operator will say "Stop." That's his position 2. Place a piece of number 2 tape at the back wheel. Now at a certain line of dialogue or the actors moving, you'll know that you'll need to move the dolly from position one to position two.

This will go on until all the positions are marked for the camera.

There might be a time where position 3 is exactly the same as position 5. That's OK, just go ahead and put a piece of tape for position 5 as well.

You might have five positions or more within 8' of track. Choreography between the camera and the actors can get very complicated, and often it can mean moving only inches!

Speaking of moving the dolly; you want to *feather* your moves. This means gently but quickly moving the dolly up to the correct speed. You don't want to start a dolly move by shoving the thing up to speed. Keep your shots smooth! The same with stopping. You don't want to jerk the thing to a stop.

Working with a dolly takes practice! It's not as easy as it seems. A good dolly grip is worth his or her weight in gold. Actors are allowed to screw up. Dolly grips and camera operators... well, not so much.

Know that laying out dolly track and getting the moves down takes time! I don't care if it's PVC or the sweetest pro track on the planet. Both small indie pictures and the biggest budget blockbuster shoots have this in common. Both have to haul a ton of equipment to get that shot (ever see the back of grip or rigging truck? Nothing but plywood, 2×4s, and speed rail, and lots of it). So take the time to make or buy all the wedges, 10" blocks, sandbags, and apple boxes. You really do need this stuff.

Again, if you have any questions about anything in this book, e-mail me at Dan@DVcameraRigs.com. I'm happy to help.

Troubleshooting Dolly Problems

First, let's tackle what every dolly on the planet has at one time or the other: squeaking.

Squeaking

In the "old days" (around 1979!) I used to use WD-40 spray lubricant on the big Fisher dolly wheels when it was used on track. You can still use it, but that makes a big mess that is time consuming to clean up after the shoot. There are better, cleaner ways.

There are two things that are good for taking the squeak out of PVC. The first is baby powder. Just sprinkle it on the squeaky part of the track and run the dolly over it a few times.

For PVC and aluminum track; a spray-on furniture polish works great!

Just spray it on the track and wheels as you are moving the dolly back and forth. It might take a lot to get to the point of no squeak.

Dolly Bumps

I personally have never had this problem, and have heard of it only once, when I got an email from a filmmaker that had bought an earlier edition of this book. (And I came up with this in-line skate wheel design in 1987, so that's a lot of wheels over the years!) There was a consistent bump when he pushed the dolly down the track. I could only think of two reasons: that one of the bolts acting as one of the axles was bent, or one of the wheels was defective. It was the latter. I had to go through dozens of wheels at my supplier until I found a defective one to try this out.

To determine if this is your problem too, turn the dolly upside-down. Grab a length of PVC and lay it into the wheel grove.

Killer Camera Rigs That You Can Build

DOI: 10.1016/B978-0-240-81337-0.00010-0

Put some weight on the PVC as you roll it back and forth. If you feel it give somewhere along the wheel, you've got a defective wheel.

Examine it closely and put an X on the part that feels like an indentation. These are almost impossible to see, so you have to go by feel. Check out the other wheels to make sure you didn't get a bad batch!

The Dolly Rolls Off the Track Before It Reaches the End

There are a few places to check:
1. Your track is not spaced the same distance apart.
2. The brackets on your dolly are not square.
3. The dolly platform is not square.

The Dolly Creaks or Groans

This is incredibly rare. Somewhere the bolts aren't tight enough or the plywood is funky. Adding a third set of wheels to the midway point on each side of the dolly will get rid of this.

The Dolly Vibrates

This is almost always putting electrical conduit or PVC on a hard surface like concrete. Usually this type of track resting on concrete is no problem at all, but sometimes you get a slight vibration. Throw down a sound blanket, carpet, or anti-fatigue mat, and put your track on top of that. The vibration will vanish.

SECTION 2: HANDHELD RIGS

A handheld rig is pretty much what it sounds like; any rig that is held or attached to the camera operator's body. Probably the most famous is the Steadicam™. Many manufacturers over the years have done their version of this great rig, both in a vest-style full Steadicam rig and a version for smaller cameras that is literally hand-held. The *Shock Corridor Stabilizer* falls into this category. It certainly has been the favorite of filmmakers buying this particular book over the years!

You will also find a rig that holds your camera inches off the ground for cool traveling shots called The *Sweet Smell of Success* Pooper-Scooper Cam. The City Streets Circle Rig was designed by filmmaker Mike Figgis for his film *Timecode* and is available commercially under the name *FigRig*™. My version is much the same, and is really easy to build yourself. And finally, you'll find a shoulder mount that is custom designed for *your* shoulder.

The *Shock Corridor* Camera Stabilizer

When the first edition of *Killer Camera Rigs* was released, cameras where much smaller and lighter. Now it seems everyone has an HD camera, some of which are over 5 lbs. The *Shock Corridor* can easily hold a camera over 5 lbs, but the question you need to ask yourself is can *you* hold a heavier camera on this rig before your arm and wrist start to fall off? I've used this rig with my Panasonic HD camera for short periods without any problems, but I wouldn't want to use it all day for every shot!

Ever since Garret Brown invented the Steadicam™, every filmmaker has been drooling over getting one. Now, because of the lighter cameras, there have been a horde of copycats for the DV market. Most of these commercial ones cost upward of $1,000, putting them way out of range for most of us.

Well, here's one you can make for around $50. Does it work as well as the commercial versions? In my experience, yes. In fact, I made a little improvement (a rotating handle) that isolates wrist movement, something the lower cost stabilizers don't have. Take your time when building this, because everything has to be perfect.

A word to the wise: A camera stabilizer is not the be-all, end-all. It's great for some things and lousy for others. (For example, if you're doing a tracking shot, a dolly is easier and better. If that tracking shot is over the bombed out rubble of a building, go with the stabilizer.)

Whether you're using a homemade rig or a commercial one, these babies take a ton of practice. Garret Brown used to teach (maybe he still does) workshops to professional operators. These are guys who use this stuff day in and day out, and they still take workshops. This is a great tool, but you'll need to practice, practice, practice.

At the end of this chapter you'll find instructions on how to balance your new rig and some helpful lessons to get you started.

Be sure to read the section, "Make It Groovy" before heading off to the hardware store!

Materials List for the *Shock Corridor* Camera Stabilizer

☐ (1) in-line skate wheel with bearings. Some wheels come with bearings, some don't. If they don't, just buy a package separately. You can use the rest of them on the dolly and crane handle projects.

☐ Also, if your wheel has an axle in the bearings you'll need to remove it. (The bearings pop right out with the help of a screw driver, then just remove the axle and push the bearings back in.)

DOI: 10.1016/B978-0-240-81337-0.00011-2

☐ (2) in-line skate wheel bearings. These are in addition to the ones in your wheel (one advantage of buying your bearings separately from the wheel). Otherwise, you'll have to pop these out of an extra wheel.

☐ (1) foam handle bar pad, either bicycle or razor scooter type. If you're making the crane handle, you might get two. You'll also need a tube of water-based personal lubricant to oil up the handle pad to be able to slip it onto the handle.

☐ (2) 5/16" (8mm) jam nuts for the threaded rod. (Jam nuts are narrower–thinner–than regular nuts. If you can't find them, you can use normal ones.)

☐ (2) 5/16" (8mm) lock nuts for the threaded rod. Lock nuts have a nylon ring that holds it tight to the bolt. (You might also see these called stop nuts.)

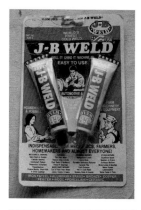

☐ J-B Weld. This is like a super glue for metal. It comes in two tubes that you mix together.

☐ Pro Lok or Loctite. This keeps nuts in place. If you can't find a lock nut, you'll need to use this stuff on the nuts.

☐ (1) 1/8" (3mm) thick × 3/4" (19mm) wide aluminum bar. They usually come in 3' (1 meter) lengths, but you'll only need 9" (22 cm) or so.

☐ 1¼" OD (outside diameter) and 1" OD aluminum tubing. There are a couple different types of tubing you can get: regular aluminum tube or anodized aluminum. The anodized stuff comes in an assortment of colors and is pretty hip.

You'll need (1) 1¼" OD and (1) 1" OD. The color ones usually come in 5' lengths, so you won't use the entire lengths of these, but you can use what's left over for other projects.

Before You Go Searching for Aluminum Tube

In Los Angeles, where I live, aluminum tube is easy to find. (If you live here too, go to Industrial Metal Supply). But I've gotten e-mails over the years from filmmakers who have one of two problems: They can't find a local supplier, or metal shops on the Internet are price gougers pure and simple. Truly, I can't believe the prices some of the online suppliers charge for this stuff.

If you can't find aluminum tube in your area, the easiest thing you might try is taking the bearings that go into the handle and head for the hardware store (to make things easy, you might slip them on a bolt and tighten them down with a nut). There are tons of things made out of tube aluminum. You just need to find something the bearing fits into exactly. I've had builders use an aluminum flag pole, a squeegee handle, a paint roller extension, an expandable shower curtain rod... you get the idea. Start pulling the handles off things and slipping the bearings in to see if they fit (if an employee bugs you for doing this, tell them I said it was OK). Don't worry so much about the 1¼" OD tube for the top of the rig. Size isn't that important for that part. If you find, say, a paint roller extension and the inside tube is perfect for the bearing size, you can use the outer tube (even if it is fiberglass) for the top tube that the camera plate attaches to. (If you do use fiberglass, the best thing to cut it with is a hacksaw).

(4) ⅞" (22mm) plastic sockets. These come in packs of four and are used to shove into metal chair legs to hold wheels. Note: Different brands may be designed differently. My measurement is for *Shepards* brand sockets.

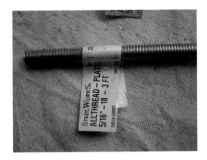

(1) ⁵⁄₁₆" (8mm) threaded rod by 36" (1 meter). Threaded rod is just a big bolt with the head cut off. I've never seen a hardware store that didn't have these. The actual length you'll need is 30", but they are sold in 36" lengths.

You'll need a piece of hardwood for the camera platform. Try to get one ¼" (6mm) thick and 3" to 4" (76–100mm) wide. You'll be cutting it down later to 10" (25cm) long. Usually you'll find this special lumber in its own section of the store. It might read "Hobby Lumber" or something like that. Or if you want a metal camera plate instead of wood, see what's coming next.

Make It Groovy

Instead of wood, use a ⅛" (3mm) thick piece of aluminum by 3" to 4" (76–100mm) wide by 10" (25cm) long. Pay attention in the section, "Tools You'll Need" for working with aluminum for the camera base.

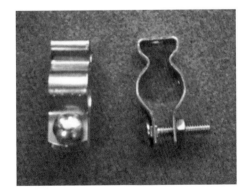

(2) #2 conduit hangers. You'll find these in the electrical department. They're used for hanging electrical conduit. The #2 size is for 1" pipe. See those bolts at the bottom of the hanger? Go get yourself two wing nuts that fit that bolt before you leave the store. If you live outside North America, check out the *Stabilizer Alternate Mount* at the end of this chapter. It's very possible you won't be able to find this item in your country.

These would be the wing nuts for the earlier *conduit hangers*. Mine are ¼" (6mm). Yours may or may not be, so it's always best to screw the wing nut onto the bolt in the store, just to be sure.

This holds the camera to the platform. Usually the camera base has ¼" (6 mm) thread, but yours might be metric. Just take the camera to the hardware store and get the right size. Get one ½" (14 mm) long unless you're going to use a mouse pad to pad your camera base, then get one a bit longer: ¾" (19 mm). This is an Allen head. A flat head or hex works fine too.

This is for the counterweight base. Get one 12" (30 cm) long, ¹⁄₁₆" to ⅛" (1.5–3 mm) thick, and about 4" (100 mm) wide. Or you can "make it groovy" by getting channel aluminum instead (see next).

Or Make It More Groovy

The channel allows you to set the rig upright on a flat surface. This is for the counterweight base. Get one 12" (30 cm) long, ¹⁄₁₆" to ⅛" (1.5–3 mm) thick, and about 3" to 4" (76–100 mm) wide. The sides should be more than ½" (14 mm) deep.

Since there will be a nut and bolt sticking out the bottom of this plate on your rig, the idea of the channel aluminum base is to allow you to set it on the floor without it falling over. That is the only advantage to channel aluminum. If you'd like to use the flat aluminum, you can stick little rubber feet on the bottom of the rig and get the same result.

Pick up about 10 to 12 heavy duty washers between 1" and 2" (25–50 mm) in diameter. These are for the counterweights. If you have a heavier camera like a Panasonic HVX200, you'll need more. Go ahead and pick up 20 or so.

(2) #10 to 24 size by ½" (14 mm) long screws and nuts. These will hold the conduit hangers onto the camera plate. They don't have to be exactly this size, just no longer than ½", and they need to be able to fit through the hanger hole. A flat-head screw is even better. You won't need these outside North America because they attach the conduit hangers that you couldn't find, right?

This is an Allen bolt, a wing nut, and a large washer with a small hole (called a fender washer). These will hold the counterweight washers to the base. Length of the bolt is relative to the thickness of the base and 6 to 10 counterweight washers stacked like poker chips. The additional washer has a smaller hole than the larger ones. You need this, otherwise the wing nut would just drop down the big washer holes. You'll need two sets. Also, there is no reason I'm using an Allen bolt here—they just look really nice. You could just as easily use any bolt. I'm using a ¼" (6 mm) bolt.

(1) This is called a cap nut. You can use any ⁵⁄₁₆" (8 mm) nut, but this one looks nice, and makes your rig look a little more professional.

(2) Around ³⁄₁₆" (5 mm) or larger by 1¼" (32 mm) to 1½" (38 mm) long bolt. These hold the handle bracket to the wheel. The length of these depend on wheel diameter. Take a look at steps 5 thru 16 for more information. Allen bolts look good here too.

Some cork or tool drawer liner or best of all: a mouse pad. Get the cheap cloth covered one, and rip the cloth off. This is for covering the camera plate. Use the mouse pad if you're using the "make it groovy" materials. You only need a piece big enough of whatever you're using to cover the size of aluminum plate you bought for the camera plate.

A little square of 60 grit sandpaper. You'll use this to roughen up the bearings and aluminum tube before gluing.

Super-strength epoxy. This is for the wheel bracket bolts.

Tools List for the *Shock Corridor* Camera Stabilizer

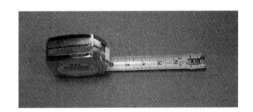

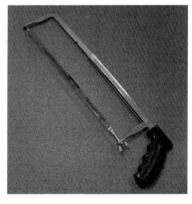

☐ Pipe cutter. Make sure you get one that will go around the 1¼" (32 mm) OD tubing.

☐ A hammer for thwacking the prick punch.

☐ A tape measure.

☐ A hacksaw. Get extra blades. We'll be cutting aluminum, so get blades that have no more than 16 teeth.

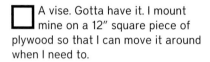

A vise. Gotta have it. I mount mine on a 12" square piece of plywood so that I can move it around when I need to.

A metal file and some grinding stones for your drill. If you're making the wood camera platform, you can get by with just the grinding stones. Make sure they're cone shaped. Get a few, they wear out fast. If you're making the "groovy" camera plate, get a file and some grinding stones.

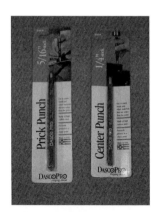

Center punch and/or prick punch. Officially, a center punch is used to put a small dimple in metal where you're going to drill a hole. You have to have this or your drill bit will "walk" across the metal, and that's not good at all. The prick punch scratches into the metal for marking (a pencil comes off too easily). In reality, you can use one for both marking and dimpling.

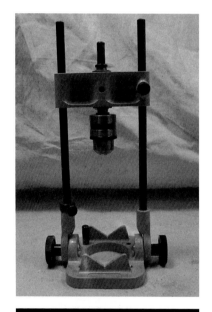

If you don't have a drill press, I really encourage you to get one of these. It's a handy drill guide, and will keep your holes straight and true—very important in this type of work. It also has a V in its base to hold a round piece of pipe for perfect center drilling (something we do a lot around here). It runs about $35—a good investment if you build more than one project in this book.

A combination square. One of the most useful tools on the planet. You'll especially need it on this project.

Vise grips. One is good, two pairs will make life much easier.

A flat-head screwdriver.

A plug-in variable speed drill or drill press.

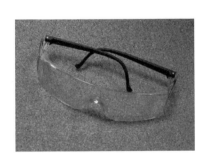

A ½" (14 mm) socket. This isn't absolutely necessary, but it's very handy when building the handle.

Safety glasses. We're drilling into metal–these are important and not to be left out! In fact, every project in this book that requires drilling into metal requires safety glasses. You need to read the appendix, *Working with Metal*!

Cutting oil. You use this when drilling into metal. You might want to pick up a little oil can to put it in or find a brand that has its own little spout. To be clear: this is not 3-in-1 Oil or WD-40.

Drill bits. You need the following sizes: 5/16" (8 mm), 7/32" (5.5 mm), 9/64" (3.5 mm), ¼" (6 mm).

Note: The 5/16" (8 mm) bit is the only size you must use. The other sizes depend on the size bolt you use on these parts of the rig or whether you're "making it groovy." Please read through the plans carefully. It might be easier to simply buy a kit with all different sizes in it.

☐ A utility knife for cutting the cork or tool drawer liner (although scissors work better if you're cutting a mouse pad).

☐ A back saw or mitre saw. If you're getting the home center to cut your wood, you can leave this one out, and you do not need a back saw if you're making your camera bracket out of aluminum! Otherwise, you might want to pick up a mitre box too. They often come as sets, and you don't need a high priced one.

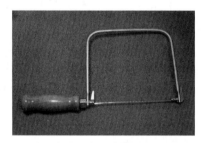

☐ Coping saw. If you've got a router or jig saw, you don't need this. Otherwise, you do. But if you're making an aluminum camera bracket, then you will not need a coping saw. As an alternative, check out the "drill and saw power bit" next.

☐ This handy little drill bit/saw combo. The shaft of the bit acts as a saw. Very handy and cheaper than the coping saw (but harder to control too!) You will need one of these if you are making your camera bracket from aluminum, and of course you can use it on wood too. This one is ¼" (6 mm). It's fine to go a bit larger. If you have a router, you can use that instead to cut the slots in the aluminum. I'll assume if you have a router, you know how to use it.

Let's Build It

Please read the appendix before starting this project!

Since I think you'll probably be building this project over a few days, I've gone a bit crazy labeling the steps. I think this will really help you out, so don't freak out on how many steps this project takes!

 Cut a 3" (76 mm) length of the smaller (1") aluminum tube with the tube cutter.

Well done!

3 Take the plastic sockets and shove them in as far as you can by hand, then take a hammer and give them a few good thwaks to drive them the rest of the way in. Do this on both ends of both sections.
Take a utility knife and trim off any plastic that may be sticking out from the thwaking.

2 Cut another 16" (40 cm) length of the smaller tube. Speeding right along, aren't we?

4 Cut a 9" (23 cm) long piece off the larger 1¼" tube.

Make a little mark on the 9" tube at the halfway point: 4½" right? If you are using the drill guide, load a 5/16" (8 mm) bit into it and place the marked tube in the V of the jig. If you're using a drill press, load the tube into a vice under the bit.

Drill a hole with the 5/16" (8 mm) bit down through both sides of the tube (you don't need drilling oil for this thin tube).

Beautiful, Baby!

5 Next we'll make the wheel gimbal unit. This is probably the hardest part to make, and it's not really hard at all. Just take your time and make sure you make everything just right.

Measure the diameter of your wheel. This one is 2¾" (70 mm). Add ¼" (6 mm) to whatever your measurement is. In this case that would put our measurement at a total of 3" (76 mm). (The angle of this photo makes it seem that the wheel is 2½". Trust me, it's not.)

This is what we'll be using that measurement for. We want the left and right side of this bracket to be 3" (76 mm), regardless of wheel size. Then take the wheel measurement of 3" (76 mm) and add all that together: 3" side + 3" side + 3" wheel = 9", right?

6 Take that ¾" (19 mm) wide by 3' (1 meter) piece of aluminum bar, put it in your vise and cut it down to 9" (or whatever your measurement ended up being).

7 Set your combo square to 3" (76 mm). Measure 3" (76 mm) in from each end and use your prick punch to scratch a mark square across the bar. Measuring in 3" (76 mm) from each side will give you the correct width for the center section.

3 inches	3 inches	3 inches
	✕	

8 In the center section, between your two marks, make an X going from corner to corner of the rectangle made by the marks. Where the two points cross will be dead center of the middle section.

9 Use your punch and a hammer to make a small indentation on the center of the X.

10 Measure in ½" (14 mm) from the end of your bar and hammer a dimple halfway across the width of the bar. Do this on both ends.

You should now have three little dimples halfway across the bar: ½" in from each end and one smack dab in the middle. Now we're going to drill some holes on those dimples.

Killer Camera Rigs That You Can Build

 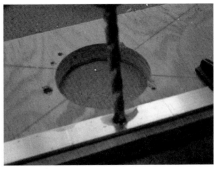 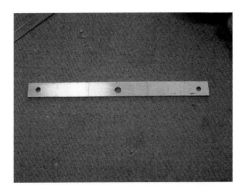

 Clamp the bar (dimple side up, please) down tight against your bench on a piece of scrap wood. Put a ⁵⁄₁₆" (8 mm) drill bit in your drill, add a little lubricant to the center dimple, and drill away. Start slow, about half speed. Metal likes a lower drill speed.

Change to a smaller bit for the size bolts or machine screws (mine are #10–24) you got to attach the bracket to the wheel. The hole should be slightly larger than the diameter of that bolt, so the bracket moves freely. Drill the holes in the dimples on each end. The size bit I used is ⁷⁄₃₂" (4 mm).

You should now have something that looks kinda like this (above). I have a confession: take a close look at the center hole. See how is it not quite dead center from top to bottom? That is because I didn't make my dimple deep enough, and the bit walked. I should have thwacked the prick punch one more time with my hammer! Learn from my mistakes!

12 Let's do some bendin'!

Clamp the bar in your vise with the 3" (76 mm) line you made earlier an ⅛" (3 mm) above the teeth of the vice. *Hint*: Since this aluminum is an ⅛" thick, you can lay a scrap piece on top of the vice, and line the mark on your bendy piece up with the top of the aluminum laying on the vice. Use your combination square to make sure it's, you know, square. Like this:

Hey, lose that gap, Sister!

That's more like it. Nice and square. Now you can bend it.

 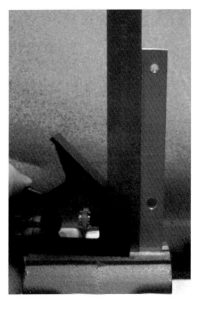

Just muscle that thing over, Junior. To get a clean 90°, use a hammer to tap it down the last few centimeters. If you can't seem to get the bar bent, slide some of that spare tubing over it (at least a foot or so) and use that as leverage. It'll bend like butter.

Some of the aluminum I've used for the handle has broken when bent as far as this, and it was always scrap stuff that sold in 12" lengths at the metal supply shop. On the other hand, the 3' lengths sold at home centers like Lowe's® or Ace® have never failed me. So if you find yourself at a metal supply getting cheap stuff, buy a few of them!

Next, flip it around and do the same on the other 3" (76 mm) mark. Don't forget to square it up!

And there she is. Nice job.

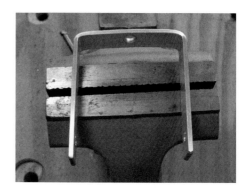

13 Now we need to drill a couple of holes in the wheel for bolts that hold the handle bracket. Use a felt tip pen to mark the center of the edge of the wheel. There is usually a manufacturing seam along the outside edge that makes this easy.

A Few Ways to Find the Direct Opposite Side of the Wheel

We need to find the direct opposite side of the mark you just made. Basically, we're just cutting the wheel in half.

The lazy way is to just use a ruler and eyeball it. Not the best way to go about it.

Or...

130

Grab a piece card stock, something along the lines of an index card will work fine (or if you have a piece of graph paper around, that's good too). Set the wheel on the corner of the card so the edge of the wheel lines up with the sides of the card. Locate the edge of the wheel opposite the outside edge of the paper. Make a small mark on the remaining two sides.

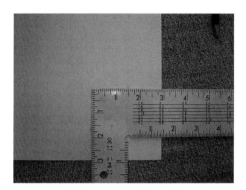

Measure your marks to make sure they are the same distance from each side.

Trim your card on the marks so that you get a perfect square.

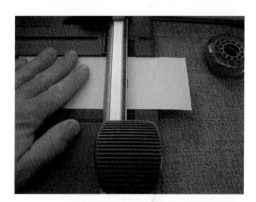

Draw an X on the card from corner to corner.

Then draw a line through the center of the X, cutting the card into two equal halves.

Set the wheel dead even on the card and line up the mark you made on the wheel to the center line across the card.

Now it's a pretty simple matter to follow that line to the opposite side of the wheel and make your second mark.

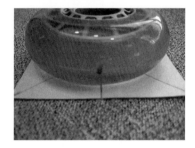

14 Clamp the wheel to the bench—and I mean this—clamp the wheel to the bench! Carefully and slowly drill straight and level through to the center of the wheel using a bit a little smaller or the same size as the Allen bolt or machine screw you're using to attach the handle bracket to the wheel. In my case, I'm using a $^{9}\!/_{64}$" (3.5 mm) bit. Do this on each side. A level on your drill is very helpful here. Go ahead and drill all the way to the center of the wheel from each side.

This is one time where a drill press would be great. If you have one, just clamp the wheel between two pieces of scrap lumber (2×4s work nicely) to hold the wheel vertically under the bit and drill away. Also, if you screw up, don't worry. There's no need to get a new wheel—it's a circle, just move to a new point and start over. If you'll look closely at the photo you'll see the mess I made on the left side of the wheel. Hey, no editing the mistakes in this book! It's all a part of being human. Let me also take this opportunity to say, do all of this work on a full night's sleep and a stuffed belly.

15 OK, gather up all the parts for this little section: the handle bracket, the two machine screws for the holes you just made, and the wheel of course. You'll also need a toothpick and something to mix the epoxy together.

Follow the directions on the epoxy and mix the two parts together. And *please* use epoxy. Super-glue types of glues just won't last on this kind of work.

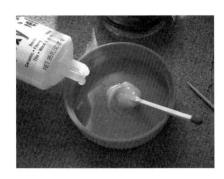

If you used the paper X method to locate where to drill your holes, leave it under your wheel when drilling. The line in the middle makes a handy guide.

When you're done, blow out the excess rubber in the holes. (As Ms. Bacall sez: "Just put your lips together and blow.")

Next, get a nice coating of glue on the toothpick...

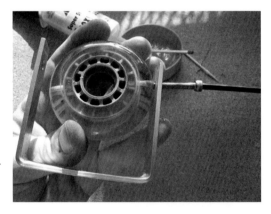

...and coat the holes in each side of the wheel with a good glob of the stuff.

Before the epoxy starts to harden, grab your bracket and screw and quickly attach the bracket through the side hole.

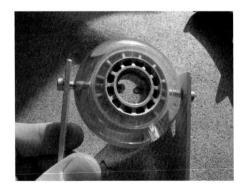

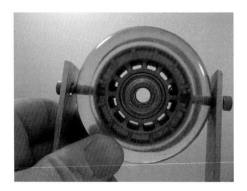

When you're done it should look something like this. You'll notice I've used long Allen bolts that go all through the hub. This isn't absolutely necessary, especially if you're using a lighter camera, but you should at least get into that first layer of the plastic part of the hub.

Look closely at the photo. Notice how the bolts don't go as far as to block the bearing hole. If you can see your bolts in the bearing hole, back them out quickly before the epoxy sets! The idea is to have bolts long enough to get into the plastic, but not so long that you've got a lot of wiggle room between the bracket and wheel.

Clean off any excess epoxy and don't tighten the bolts down too much. You want the wheel to spin freely in the bracket.

16 Take the threaded rod, measure off 24" (61cm) and clamp the thing in the vise.

Take your hacksaw and start hacking. See how I'm holding it, using my left hand to steady the blade? Load the hacksaw blade so the teeth are pointed away from you. Don't go too fast or you'll wear the teeth down. About 40 strokes a minute is good. Now, 24" is still going to be too long. We'll be trimming it down again later. I'm doing it this way, because mistakes can be made, and it's just safer to cut it to final length once the tubes are on. Your other option is to not cut it at all right now, but you'll be sorry you left it long when you get to step 21.

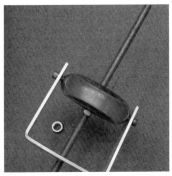

17 Take a jam nut and screw it down onto the rod about 7" (178mm) or 8" (203mm). I like putting the wheel label toward the bottom of the rig so that you can't see it, but there is no "top" or "bottom."

Then slip your gimbal unit on the rod down to the nut.

Add the second jam nut on top of that.

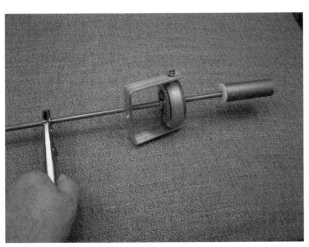

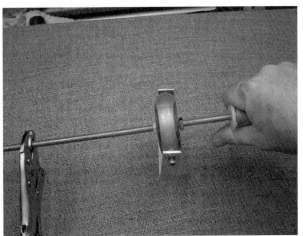

18 Grab a section of the bottom part of the threaded rod with a pair of vice grips or pliers. Then take the 3" (76mm) section of tube and screw it down to the top nut.

Don't worry too much about how much bolt you've got showing at the top. We'll adjust everything as we go.

19 Take the top 9" (23 cm) tube and slide it onto the bolt on top of the smaller tube. The larger tube goes horizontally, passing the rod through the hole you drilled into the middle of it. Make sure there is enough room for a stop nut at the top of the threaded rod.

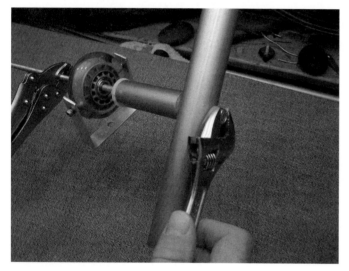

Take a ⁵⁄₁₆" (8mm) stop nut and tighten it so that the threaded rod is flush with the top of the nut. (You'll still need to hold the bottom of the rod with vice grips to tighten the stop nut on.)

20 Tighten the top jam nut (the one above your wheel) tight against the bottom of the 3" (76 mm) tubing. Even better: Use a dab of J-B Weld on the jam nut and let it dry over night. Basically, we want the big tubing on top and the 3" (76 mm) tubing below to feel like one piece by tightening the top and bottom nuts toward one another.

Move the wheel against the top jam nut, and screw the bottom jam nut up against the bottom of the wheel. (You can use J-B Weld here too, if you want). Not too loose and not too tight! The wheel should spin freely without moving up and down on the rod.

21 Next, screw the long part of the tubing onto the rod. This isn't easy. It will seem like forever before you get that thing twisted all the way up to the wheel.

Killer Camera Rigs That You Can Build

LET'S MAKE THE HANDLE UNIT

22 Cut a 5" (127 mm) piece off the smaller tubing. Don't get any bright ideas about making this piece longer; it really will affect the balance of the unit.

Roughen up the inside of the 5" tube on each end with sandpaper.

Do the same on the outside of two bearings. Wipe the tube and bearings clean with acetone.

 23 Squeeze an equal amount of J-B Weld onto a lid and mix it fully. A popsicle stick works great (although I prefer an Eskimo Pie stick).

Glob a thick layer of the J-B Weld all the way around the outside of the bearing. Be careful that it's only on the outside.

Now, these in-line skate bearings fit perfectly into this ⅞" (22 mm) ID (inner diameter) tubing. Coincidence? I think not!

Slide the bearings into the tube—one on each end—and wipe away the mess that oozes out. Make sure these are sitting straight inside the tube!

As you can see, on one end of the tube I've set the bearing flush with the top. On the other end I've inset the bearing about a ½" into the tube. This is to hide the nut that will be on the bottom end of the handle. This isn't necessary, it just looks nice. Carefully set the handle aside in a safe place away from cats and clomping people for 24 hours until the J-B Weld sets.

SOMETHING TO THINK ABOUT

I've never had these bearings come loose—ever—though I've gotten just a few e-mails over the years where people had problems with them popping out. Why? Because they didn't sand and clean the tube and bearings before gluing them in there with the J-B Weld. J-B Weld works amazingly well, but only if you follow the instructions! I also heard from a filmmaker who used a "tube crimper" to crimp the tube around the bearings. That's perfectly fine to do, but I could *never* find one of these mythical tools! (Just kidding. I'm sure they exist somewhere on the planet, but I simply couldn't find one.)

MAKING THE BASE

 Before starting, you might want to look at the section, "Make It Groovy."

In some of the photos, I'm using a 4" × 12" × ⅛" (100 mm × 30 cm × 3 mm) hunk of aluminum. The commercial versions base is only about an 1½" wide. The wider base works much better for placing counterweight when balancing the rig, but it need not be

as wide as 4". With a little practice, a 2" wide base works just fine. With that in mind, anything between 2" and 4" you find in the metal scrap pile will work. Also, a ¹⁄₁₆" (1.5 mm) thick piece of aluminum is plenty thick if you're using aluminum channel for this part. A ¼" thick piece is out—much too heavy!

If you can't find aluminum, you can use a ¼" thick piece of oak or other hard wood.

Remember the X we made from corner to corner to find the dead center of our handle bracket? We're going to do the same thing here.

Take your center punch and place the tip right on the X. Give it a good thwack or two with a hammer.

You should end up with a dimple in the middle of your aluminum base.

Now we need to make a minimum of six more marks (see the section, "Make It Groovy" at the end of the chapter for more details on more holes). Measure in about 1" (25 mm) from one end and put a mark dead center. Move 2" (50 mm) from the end and do the same. Move in 3" (76 mm) and make one more. Do the same on the opposite end and use your center punch on the marks.

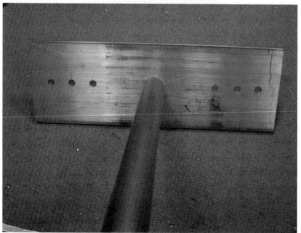

If you want to get really fancy, you can add a bunch of holes for your counterweights; 99% of the time, those six holes down the middle are all you need. But there have been rare cases with cameras that want counterweights on an outside hole. It's very weird, because it shouldn't be that way, but sometimes weird comes visiting.

Here's the idea on hole placement for seven holes.

Killer Camera Rigs That You Can Build

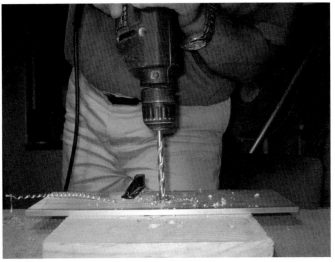

 26 Just a reminder: you *did* read the appendix, right? It's really important. You could get seriously injured!

Clamp the aluminum to the bench on top of a piece of scrap lumber. Put a bit of cutting oil into the dimple and load up your drill with a 5/16" (8mm) bit.

Here's what you'll have when you're done.

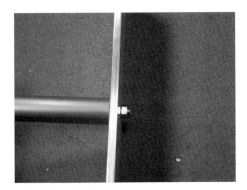

27 Put on your safety glasses and drill away on the center hole. If you want, you can use the 5/16" (8mm) for all the holes. I prefer the outer holes to be 1/4" (6mm), but your center hole *must* be 5/16" (8mm).

Warning: As you learned in the appendix (if you've been putting off reading that section, now is the time!), sometimes the bit will jam and try to rip your arm off in the process. As soon as it jams, let go of the trigger. If you didn't clamp your work down and this happens, have your first aid kit handy. Clamp your work!

To work through the jam, reverse your drill rotation and back the bit out. Starting slightly above the hole, get your bit moving forward at a good clip, *and then* lower the bit into the hole. If you start with the bit in the hole, it *will* jam again.

28 Slide the base on through the threaded rod. Allow enough room on the rod for the lock nut and trim off the rest of the rod. You can check out the section, "Make It Groovy" if you need pictures for this bit.

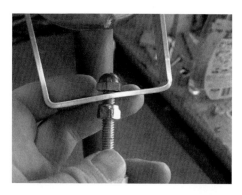

 Next we'll attach the handle. Your bearings should be well adhered to the tube before this step!

Grab what's left of the threaded rod after you cut it. Screw on a lock nut down about an inch. Slide the rod through the hole on the bracket and put on another nut. I used a cap nut in this case.

Tighten the lock nut hard against the bracket. We don't want any movement here.

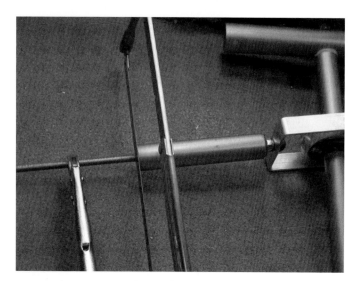

Slide the handle on, and cut the threaded rod at the base of the handle. Hold the rod below the handle with some vice grips or put it in your vice to cut it. It might be easier for you to mark the threaded rod with a marker and remove the handle before you cut the rod. If there is a little piece still sticking to the rod after you cut it, file down that piece or the nut will be difficult to screw on. If you got a bright idea of cutting the rod with bolt cutters, you'll never get the nut on! Use a hacksaw.

Take some water-based lubricant and oil the inside of the foam handle. Do *not* use a petroleum-based lubricant. This will eat away at the foam. It must be water-based.

Muscle the foam onto the handle and wipe away any lubricant that oozes out.

Slip the handle on the bolt and add another stop nut at the bottom of the handle. A socket is a big help in tightening this down. Don't tighten too much; you want the handle to turn without moving up and down. And if you really muscle that nut down, you *will* force the bearing loose from the tube. Just tighten a little at a time, making sure the handle spins on the bearings, but doesn't slip up and down on the threaded rod. It's a thin line!

Killer Camera Rigs That You Can Build

30 The camera base. See the section, "Make It Groovy" if you're making it out of metal!

Get a piece of ¼" (6 mm) thick oak × 3" to 4" (76 mm–100 mm) wide and cut it down to 10" (25 cm) long. I'm using a cheap mitre box to make sure the cut is perfectly square. If you don't want to purchase a mitre box, most home centers can cut this for you.

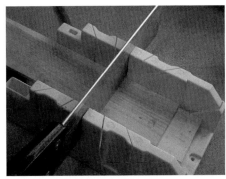

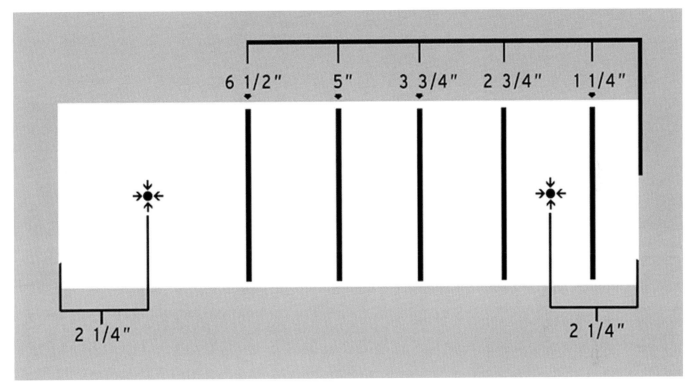

6 1/2"   5"   3 3/4"   2 3/4"   1 1/4"

2 1/4"   2 1/4"

31 **Metric Conversion:** 1¼" (32 mm), 2¼" (57 mm), 2¾" (70 mm), 5" (127 mm), 6½" (165 mm).

OK, mark up the camera base matching these measurements. (The white rectangle represents your camera base, whether wood or aluminum.) The X at 2¼" from each end is where you will drill holes to attach the conduit hangers. Make sure the Xs are placed halfway across the width of your plate. It would be a good idea to use your prick punch to scratch the lines into a *metal* camera plate. The other measurements start at the right edge. You can start on the left edge if you want. It doesn't matter. Use your combination square to draw these lines across the plate to make sure they are square!

32 Let's drill some holes.

Use a ¼" (6 mm) bit for all the holes except the ones at 2¼" (57 mm). These are for the pipe clamps, and we'll be doing something different here. This is why I had you make your marks on these holes different from the others.

First we'll drill the holes that hold the pipe clamps. The idea here is make a hole big enough to go around the head of the bolt that holds our clamp, and only deep enough so the bolt head doesn't stick out above the surface of our camera plate.

To do this I'm going to use a large bit that has a guide point on the tip and is slightly bigger than the diameter of the bolt head. I like these bits with the guide point for wood because they're easy to place and they don't tend to "walk."

Next we need to determine how deep we can drill without going all the way through the wood. (If you happen to do this, you'll have to start the camera plate *completely* over, so take your time and get it right.)

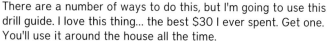

There are a number of ways to do this, but I'm going to use this drill guide. I love this thing... the best $30 I ever spent. Get one. You'll use it around the house all the time.

OK, see that little thumb screw? That is a *stop*, and it will keep my bit from going deeper than that point. So the first thing we need to do it to set that *stop* to its proper place.

I'm simply going to align the top of the bolt head flush with the top of the camera plate. Then I align the bottom of the drill bit (not including the guide point) with the bottom of the bolt head. That's where I'll tighten the stop on my little jig.

If you don't have this drill guide or a drill press, then make stops that go onto the bit itself. Just make sure you get the right size for your bit—in this case ½" (14 mm). Another trick you can do is to wrap some masking tape around the bit at the stopping point. That works great a lot of the time, but I wouldn't recommend it for this particular operation. We're only working with a ¼" (6 mm) thick board, and it would be too easy to go too deep.

Drill down to your stop and you'll end up with something like this. *Beee-u-ti-ful!* Now drill another one on the other mark.

Now finish this up with a smaller hole for the bolt. I'm using a ⁷/₃₂" (5.5 mm) bit. This is just a tad larger than my bolt shaft diameter.

140

Killer Camera Rigs That You Can Build

You should now have two countersunk holes that fit the bolt or machine screw just right.

The rest of the holes are for camera placement. Most, if not all DV cameras take a ¼" (6mm) bolt, so that's what we'll make our holes.

Using a ¼" (6mm) drill bit on each line of the plate will allow you to thread a coping saw blade through the hole to cut your slots. So on each line you drew across the camera plate, measure in about ¼" (6mm) to ½" and make a mark across the original line. Do this at the top of the line and at the bottom.

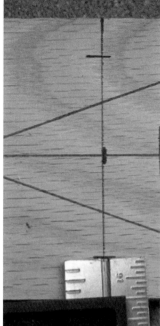

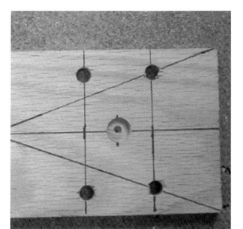

Drill a ¼" hole at the top and bottom of that line.

An Important Note: I use a lot of different cameras, so I'm putting in a lot of slots. If you are using your own camera, start with the two lines from the right of the center. Most cameras work here. Finish making the plate minus the cork and try it out. If it balances, you don't need to make any more slots, or you might find you need a slot across the center of the plate. That's the beauty of building this stuff yourself, custom design! Keep in mind that different battery sizes will shift the weight, so you might want to try it with both long- and short-run batteries.

Now we have to cut some slots between some of the holes we drilled so we can slide the camera back and forth.

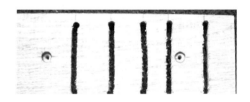

As you can see, they don't have to be pretty. The best way to do this is with a router. If you've got one, use it. Or you can use the sawing drill bit (see "Make It Groovy"). We're going to use the cheapest method: a coping saw. It'll set you back about $5.

Clamp your plate in the vise in between two pieces of scrap to protect your wood.

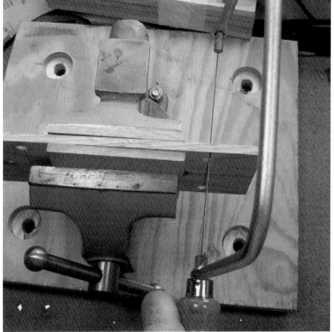

A coping saw's blade is removable by unscrewing the handle, so loosen the blade on one end, slip it through the hole on the board, and clip the blade back in place.

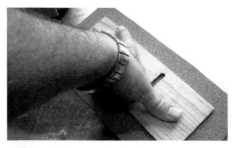

Cut down the edge of one hole to the other, back the blade back up to the top through the cut you just made, and go down the other side of the hole. A coping saw blade will cut through this oak like butter. Do this on the other pairs of holes and sand the edges of the slots a bit.

Don't worry if it's not pretty. It'll still work just fine. Just make sure your camera bolt slides from one side to the other without getting stuck or falling through.

33 Let's put some cork on the top to help hold and cushion the camera. You have the option of using a mouse pad here, but for the wood camera platforms, I really like the cork. Cut a piece of cork off your roll a little bigger than your camera plate. (You can buy a big roll for around $10. It's very handy for covering all sorts of camera platforms.)

Put some type of adhesive on the top of the plate. I'm using a hot glue gun, but there are a ton of glues that will work. Yellow carpenter's glue is an excellent choice if you're using cork.

Once the glue is dry, trim the excess cork from the edges.

Then trim the cork from the camera screw slots and hanger holes.

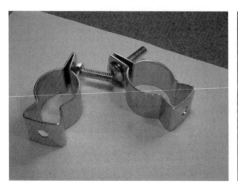

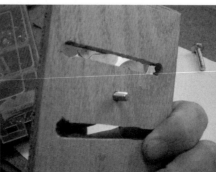

34 Now let's add the electrical conduit pipe clamps.

Put a bolt through the hole.

Thread on the nut, add some Loctite to the threads, and tighten the nut down.

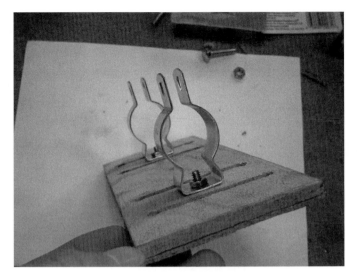

Do this on the other hole and you're done.

Add the camera plate to the top tube.

Replace the nuts that came with the conduit hanger with wing nuts.

Grab about four big washers and one with a small hole (a fender washer) for each end of the counterweight base.

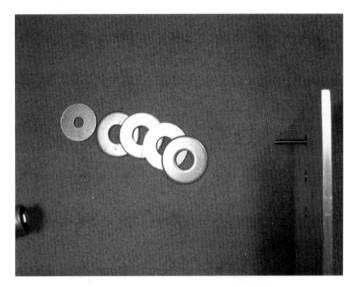

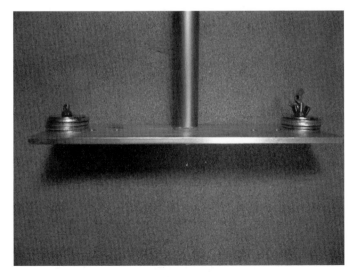

Stack 'em and put them on the outermost holes with a bolt and a wing nut.

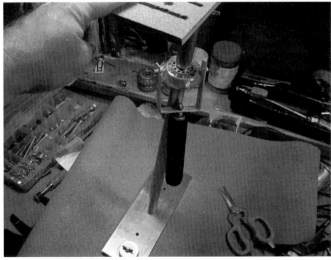

Congrats! You're done!

Let's go over some groovy stuff in the next bit.

Make It Groovy!

In this section I'm going to show you how to build a base from channel aluminum with a few more balance holes. The channel aluminum simply allows you to set the rig on the ground without it falling over. It can be convenient, but it's not necessary.

The second thing we'll be doing is making the camera plate from aluminum instead of wood. Sure, it's a little more difficult, but if you're using a heavier camera this mount might be a good idea, but again, not totally necessary. I've used the wood plate on the heavier cameras with great success, but I just prefer the metal. It has a better feel on the larger cameras.

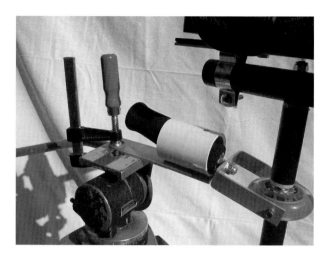

We'll also be making this little jig to help you balance your stabilizer. Again, not necessary, just damned handy. (In fact, the commercial versions don't come with anything like this. But for the price, I really think they should!)

How to Make the Camera Plate from Aluminum

Trim a ¹⁄₁₆" to ⅛" (1.5 mm–3 mm) thick by 3" to 4" (76 mm–100 mm) wide piece of aluminum to 10" (25 cm) long.

Put a grinding bit in your drill, or use a metal file and smooth out the freshly cut edge. I like using a file for this, but whatever floats your boat.

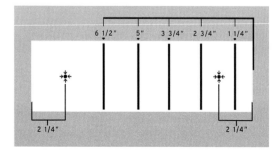

Mark up this base just like the wood one. Keep in mind, most cameras will work on the center slot, the next one to the right, or the far right. Start with these, and if your camera won't balance on the forward/back axis, make another where it will (this is usually somewhere between the two middle ones). It might be to your advantage to make the wood base first, find where your camera balances, then make this metal camera plate with only one slot for your specific camera. In the end, it would save you a lot of work.

As an alternative to the steps coming up, you can use a router to cut these slots. If you have a router, I'll assume you know how to use it.

Killer Camera Rigs That You Can Build

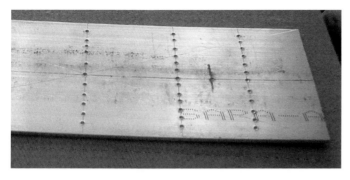

Remember, since this is metal, scratch your lines in with a prick punch. Then along the lines, take your center punch and hammer dimples along the line at about an ⅛" apart. Don't forget to make the dimples for the conduit hangers as well.

Use a ¼" (6 mm) drill bit to drill a hole in each of the dimples. Don't forget to use drilling oil! I know, it doesn't look pretty, but we're not done yet!

Note: If you're going to use cork instead of a mouse pad, you'll have to countersink the conduit holes and use a flat-head machine screw. Just get a big ½" (14 mm) bit, or countersink bit, and slowly grind away until you get something like what's shown in the photo.

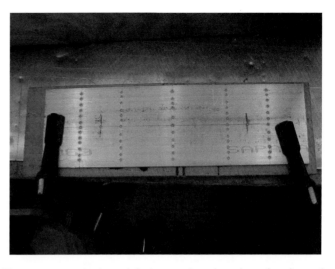

Clamp your marked up plate to your bench on top of a piece of scrap wood.

Now drill the holes for the conduit hangers. You want to use a bit slightly larger in diameter than the screw. In this case, I'm using a ⁷⁄₃₂" (5.5 mm) bit. So if you're copying my rig down to the last nut, you should too. But if your bolt is a little bigger that's just fine, too.

Now we need to make all of those holes into a slot. Clamp the plate in your vise, and grab the drill bit that acts like a saw.

Start in the top hole and use a little force to cut away the aluminum between the holes. Obviously, the closer your holes are to one another, the easier this part is.

Once you've got your slot cut, take a metal file and file down the rough spots.

You'll have a couple of choices on files: a single-cut or mill file makes a smooth finish but will take longer than a double-cut file. If you want to spend the money, get both. Start with a double-cut and finish up with a single-cut. It really doesn't matter in the operation of the stabilizer.

Now, don't go grinding this file back and forth. Use both hands and file away from your body, Take off the pressure, bring the file back and go again. Make sure you wear safety glasses!

Ohh, pretty. Now finish up the rest of the slots the same way.

Grab your conduit hangers and the nuts and bolts to attach them. Unlike the wood platform, we're going to attach these babies permanently with J-B Weld. I love this stuff!

By the way, you might notice slots in different places in some of these photos. Just ignore that. I can't tell you how many slot places these camera platforms went through before deciding on the placement I've finally given you! I really do test these things out with tons of different cameras.

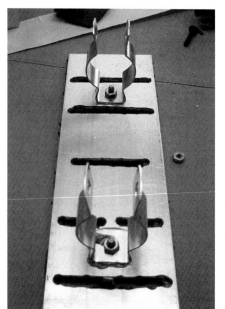

Mix up the two parts of J-B Weld.

Spread a thick layer on the top of the conduit hanger.

Take your nut and bolt and tighten the conduit hanger down on the plate. Do this with the second hanger as well.

Take a length of the large 1¼" (32mm) OD tube and tighten it into the hangers. We're doing this to make sure that the hangers are straight with one another. You obviously want to do all of these steps fairly quickly, before the J-B Weld dries.

While the camera base is drying, let's make the counterweight base.

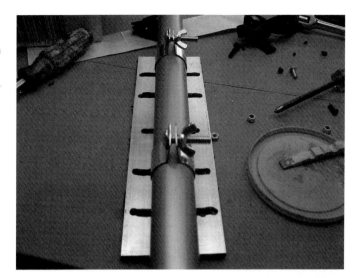

As you can see (at left), there are a lot more holes for your counterweights. 99% of the time, you'll use the ones in the center, but the side ones can come in handy if you, say, add a big mic to the camera and just can't get the thing to balance.

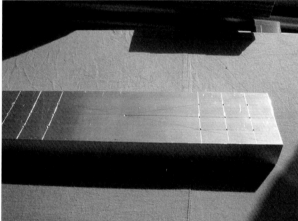

First, use your prick punch to mark up your aluminum. Do the same measurements for your holes as the flat base and use your combination square to draw a line across each of your middle hole marks.

Measure in about ½" from the side and make another mark on the line. Do this on each end and on each side.

Take your punch and hammer and make dimples on each of those marks. It should look something like the last photo, below.

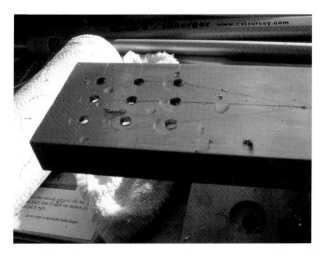

Use a ¼" (6mm) bit to drill the holes for the counter weights. Use a ⁵⁄₁₆" (8mm) bit for the center hole where the base attaches to the rest of the rig.

Once your holes are drilled, load a grinder bit into your drill and smooth out the holes on both sides of the base. The burrs from the drilled metal can be really nasty on your fingers. If you don't have a grinder bit, you can use your metal file.

Slide the base onto your rig and mark the threaded rod, leaving enough room to add your nut, but not so much that it extends beyond the sides of the base. Remove the base and trim off the excess rod with a hacksaw.

You'll probably have to smooth out the end cut rod with a file to get the bolt on. The rest of the steps is just like the basic rig.

Making the Mouse Pad Padding

If you're making the metal camera plate, you've got to use something thick like this. Why? Because on the wood, we could countersink the holes that hold the pipe brackets to the wood plate. You can only countersink holes on a thin bit of metal so far. That means the little bolt head will be making little bumps on our plate. We don't want that, so by using a thicker material like this mouse pad we can avoid that messy business.

Go to your computer and grab your mouse pad. Come on, you wanted a new one anyway. I'm using a circle, but the rectangle ones are easier to deal with.

Start by ripping the cloth cover off the rubber part.

It's really easy once you get it started.

Lay the plate on the pad and trace around it. You might have to make two pieces if your mouse pad isn't long enough.

Take a pair of scissors and trim the pad to size.

OK, here's that troublesome little screw head. A flat head machine screw is a great alternative for this, but I always have trouble finding them this small.

Killer Camera Rigs That You Can Build

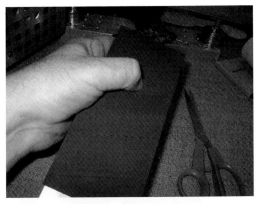

Lay your pad on the plate and feel around for it.

Then mark that spot. I just used a pencil to punch a hole in the pad. Do this on the other screw head as well.

Cut a hole in the pad where you made your marks big enough to surround the bolt head.

The thing I'm using is a cutting tool that comes with a grommet kit.

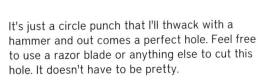

It's just a circle punch that I'll thwack with a hammer and out comes a perfect hole. Feel free to use a razor blade or anything else to cut this hole. It doesn't have to be pretty.

Remember the epoxy you used on the wheel part of this rig? Mix up a good-sized batch and spread it over your camera plate.

Line the hole up over the bolt heads, and set the whole business aside to dry.

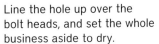

The Handle Cradle

The handle cradle is a very simple device to hold the rig between shots, to help adjust the balance, and anything else you can think of. Keep in mind, you don't absolutely need this little gizmo, but it's so easy to make, why the heck not?

☐ You're going to need a piece of wood or aluminum to attach the PVC pipe to. It should be around 6" to 8" (152mm–203mm) long × 1.5" to 3" (38mm–76mm) wide. I'm using aluminum simply because I have some left over from the pooper-scooper cam.

☐ This is a connector piece to link two pieces of PVC pipe together. It's in the plumbing section. You need to get one just large enough to fit your handle in. This one is 1.5" (38mm) in diameter × 3" (76mm) long.

☐ A flat or round head bolt with nut ½" (14mm) long.

☐ A screwdriver.

☐ A bit large enough to fit the screwdriver through.

☐ A bit the same size or a little larger than your bolt.

☐ A ruler of some sort.

☐ A vise or clamp for your work.

Let's Build It!

Clamp down the PVC pipe, take your small bit for the bolt, and drill through both sides of the pipe.

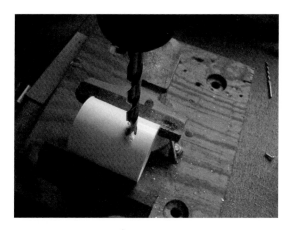

Load up your larger bit, and make the top hole a little larger.

Use the smaller bit to drill a hole in your aluminum or wood strip. This goes dead center and about 1" (25mm) from the end.

Stick the screwdriver down through the larger hole and screw the bolt into the smaller hole.

Then run it through the hole on your wood or aluminum strip and tighten the nut on and you're finished.

See how easy that was?

How to Balance Your New Stabilizer

A word of warning: Until you get used to this process, the first few times will probably be frustrating and take forever. This is a very sensitive device, and unlike some of the commercial versions, this one has a rotating handle, which makes it a little tricky to balance, but isolates movement much better when you're actually using the thing. In other words, be patient!

This first little trick isn't absolutely necessary, but it'll make things easier in the long run.

Because the camera plate is on conduit hangers, the plate can tilt left or right. Which is great for dutch angles (remember the old "Bat Man" TV show?), but most of the time we want the camera plate to be dead level.

Grab a compass—the pointy dangerous ones we used in grade school are just fine for this—and put the pointy end against the side of the top rig tube. The pencil end should rest somewhere near the top center.

So pop off your camera plate and lay the rig down on its side.

Pull the compass along the tube. The pointy end along the side of the tube will help keep your pencil mark on the same plane.

Next, hold a ruler or straight edge along the pencil line and mark a permanent line with a Sharpie.

Put your camera plate back on your rig, Then set the whole thing upright on a *level* surface.

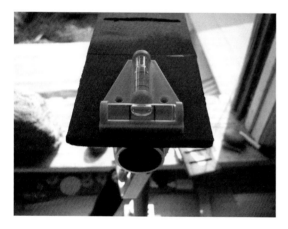

Next, set a level on the camera plate. I'm using this little combination level that gives me all directions at once. This works like the square bubble level with a circle in the center, but this one is only $3 and is really easy to find. I got mine at Lowe's Home Center. If you're doing anything where the camera is mounted on something (tripod, car mount, etc.) you need a level that works in all directions.

Loosen the hanger nuts and adjust the camera plate until you have it perfectly balanced with the bubble dead center on your level, then tighten the whole thing down.

Take your Sharpie and draw a line on each of the conduit hangers matching the line you marked on the aluminum tube.

Now all you have to do from now on is line up the marks, and your camera plate is level.

All righty then. Take your camera and attach it to the plate with your camera bolt. I like using an Allen head bolt or a hex bolt. This makes it easy to get a tool in there to tighten it down. Into which slot you attach your camera depends on the type of camera, the size of the battery, etc. This one is a Sony PD-100, so the slot I'm going to use is the second one from the rear conduit hanger, near the right side of the plate. Don't tighten the bolt down too much at this point. We'll be shifting the camera left and right.

Now let's see how we're doing, balance-wise, that is.

Set the camera on a level surface. If you're using a flat piece of aluminum for the base, you'll need to set it on a couple pieces of wood so the bolt heads that hold the weights don't touch the ground.

Killer Camera Rigs That You Can Build

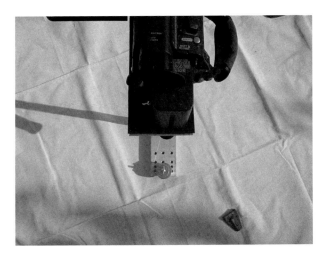

1.5 to 2.5 seconds

Take a close look at the photo. Make sure your base and the camera plate are in line with one another.

If you're using a camera with a fold-out monitor, open it. Also, take off any hanging lens caps and straps, and put on the battery you'll be using. I *strongly* suggest you use the smaller battery. The long-range batteries are a killer to haul around (even though I'm using one here!).

Now lift the rig by the handle (just a bit) and see which way it falls on the left/right axis. If it falls to the left, move the camera right and visa versa. Monkey around until you're close. It doesn't have to be perfect... yet.

Hey! How much weight do I put on the base?

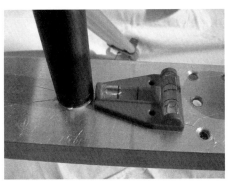

Glad you asked. Pick up the rig by its handle, and hold it in front of you. Grab the center column tubing and move it so it sits horizontally.

Let go of the center column.

It should take 1.5 to 2.5 seconds to right itself. Keep in mind, we've only sort of balanced the left/right axis, so your camera may fall a little wacky. That's OK. We're just checking to see how long it takes to drift upright before the camera reaches the top. If it moves too fast, you'll need to take off some of the weights (equally on front and back, please). If it doesn't move at all, or too slowly, you'll need to add more weight to the base. The bigger your camera and battery, the more counterweight you'll need. Which in turn, will wear you out much quicker. Try to keep things as light as possible.

Take your handy handle cradle, and clamp it to a tripod, table, "No Parking" sign... whatever is handy. (If you didn't make this, you can have a friend hold it by the handle.)

Slide the handle into the PVC pipe. Stand behind the rig while it's in the handle, and make sure it matches the same angle as if you were holding it. Take a look at the photos under the section, "It's balanced. Now what?" and match this angle. Set your level on the base as close to the center support as possible.

So, how does it look? Pretty out of whack, right? OK, let's get the left/right axis perfect. Shift your camera right or left until your bubble level reads dead center. You'll be moving the camera in tiny, tiny, increments. This rig is beautifully sensitive. Once you've got it, tighten the camera bolt down a bit—not too tight, you'll throw the balance off. Keep in mind that you are only adjusting the rig for the left and right at this point: that means the bubble level going across the base.

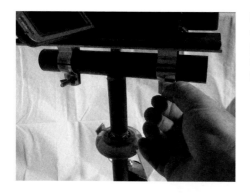

Loosen the wing nuts on the camera plate. Not too much! We want it to be just loose enough to be able to slide the camera plate forward or backward with a bit of pressure without the whole thing falling to one side or the other. Make sure you keep the plate itself level.

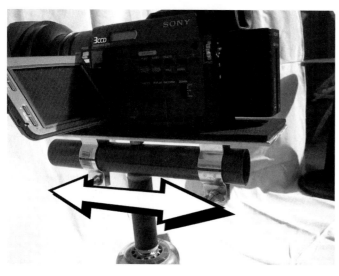

Push the plate forward or backward until your level reads level (duh!).

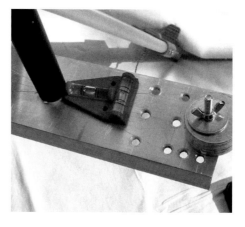

A thing of beauty! Tighten down wing nuts and make sure the camera plate is still level—aren't you glad you took the time to draw that line?

Other little tricks: You can shift the weights around as well. The more holes you have, the greater control (but don't get carried away). Also, most of the time it's not necessary to move the washers to a different hole. The inner diameter of these heavy washers is so big that you can shift the stack around the bolt without moving things to a different hole on the base.

If you're using a separate LCD monitor, use one of the weight holes on the front of the base to attach it. The better monitors come with a mount for this purpose. This is where the placement of the bottom weights—and the ability to move them around—is crucial.

Once you have the thing balanced in the handle cradle, take it out and see if it stays balanced while holding it. You might have to make some minor adjustments. It's important to make these adjustments holding it in the exact way you do when operating the rig.

If you're not using the handle cradle, you can still balance the unit. In fact, the commercial versions don't even come with one. Simply set the stabilizer on a flat surface (and I do mean flat!) and lift it slightly off the ground. Observe which way the base

goes on your left/right axis and adjust accordingly. Then do the front/back axis. You'll probably be lifting–adjusting–lifting–adjusting until you're ready to scream. Be patient. You'll get it.

It's balanced. Now what?

As I said in the introduction to this chapter: Stabilizers take practice! I'm amazed at the amount of filmmakers that run off to the rental house, pay $35 to $200 a day, and think a Steadicam™ or Glidecam™ is going to do all the work for them. Let me clear up this misconception right now about these devices: that you can move around like a mad man and the camera will stay rock solid. Not so! The idea is to not add any *extra* movement to the device.

Another mistake I see being made quite a bit is single-handed operation. A stabilizer is a two-handed job! One hand supports the unit by the handle, the other stays on the center column, either above the gimbal unit or below. Below is usually the preferred method because it makes tilting shots a little easier (or if you want to start the shot upside-down). But I've used both, above and below, from time to time. There is no hard-and-fast rule here. Just use two hands!

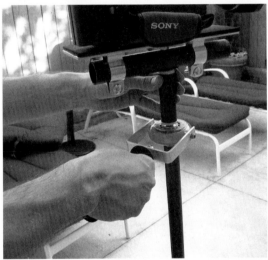

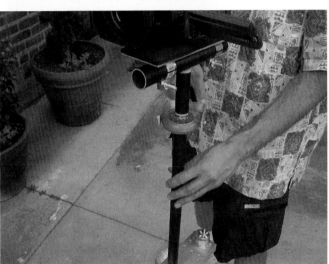

Your dominant hand holds the rig by the handle. If you're right-handed, you'll see that the handle unit angles off toward the right from the center column. If you're using your left hand, obviously it will angle off to the left. This is the same angle you must use in the handle cradle while balancing the unit.

Your other hand guides and steadies the unit by lightly holding the center column above or below the gimbal unit. Use this hand for panning and tilting—getting the lens where you want it.

Walking and Chewing Gum at The Same Time

A friend and mentor of mine, Kris Malkewicz (who has written a number of books on cinematography, now classics that you probably already have), is an amazing camera operator. Kris is a human Steadicam. His recommendation for becoming a great operator is to learn Tai Chi. And you know what? It's incredible. Tai Chi and this stabilizer make a killer combination. The Tai Chi movements are a perfect way to keep from adding any extra movement to the stabilizer. It keeps the body weight centered, lessens fatigue, and trains you to keep your movements controlled and even. Go out today and buy a Tai Chi video and learn at least some basics, then apply that to your camera work. This is highly recommended!

But until you get that video, do this: Go right now to your sink and fill a glass with water right to the brim. Now, try to walk

briskly without spilling a drop. This is basically how you want to walk with the stabilizer. Knees bent, body centered over your feet, walking heel-toe-heel-toe. Work with this a lot. You might be able to get perfect shots for the first three minutes, then fatigue will set in. You have to work on your endurance as well as your camera work. Practice in five-minute increments every day. And you might try switching hands. Practice letting that nondominant hand do some of the work. Once you're able to do that, no sweat, add another five minutes. When you are on a shoot, practice the shot over and over again long before you have to actually do the shot. Take a long rest (scheduling stabilizer work after lunch is a good idea), then do the shot.

Here are a few photos to clarify what I've been talking about.

Tilting down: Pull back on the center column.

Tilting up: Push forward on the center column.

Walking: Keep your knees bent, and use them as shock absorbers. If you want this to look like a dolly, you *must* keep your movement even and the lens at the same height. Heel–toe–heel–toe helps to keep things smooth.

Panning Using Your Body

Keep your back straight, your knees bent, and your arms in the same position.
Keep the lens on the same plane of the arc as you pivot your body.

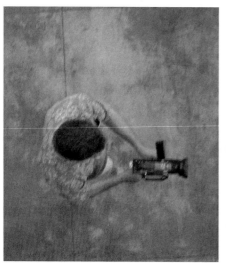

Killer Camera Rigs That You Can Build

Panning Using the Gimbal Unit

Your body stays still, and you simply turn the center column with the control hand.

One Last Word on Stabilizers

Focal length of the lens also has a lot to do with the steadiness of a shot. The wider the angle, the easier it is to keep things looking smooth. Some of the commercial versions even recommend using a wide angle adapter on your lens. Although that will keep the shot looking smooth, I think it's a bit of a cop out. The film should dictate the shot, not the device. I've used my stabilizer with much tighter focal lengths with good results,

but it does take practice. Start wide, and as you get better, try zooming in a bit. All of your small movements will be horribly obvious (but more obvious to you, than to anyone else!).

Now that you have your very own stabilizer, please practice. You'll be happy you did.

The *Sweet Smell of Success* Pooper-Scooper Cam

This rig has changed a bit for the third edition of this book. First, it's a bit more sturdy since everyone has started moving to the larger HD cameras (including me!). And second, it's a lot easier to build than the Pooper-Scooper cam of the first two editions.

With a little practice, the shots you can get with this rig are amazingly smooth. If you need any shot that rides low to the ground, this is a rig that can get it for you. Need to follow those footsteps of the killer up the stairs and down the hall? How about following a dog that simply can't hit a mark? (My last dog, Monk, could hit a mark. Silvie, my new dog seen in the photo, follows her nose and not much else.).

Also new from the previous rig is the use of an aluminum cane to hold the camera. The cool thing about this is it's better balanced, and you can adjust the length just in case you're seven feet tall.

Materials List for The *Sweet Smell of Success* Pooper-Scooper Cam

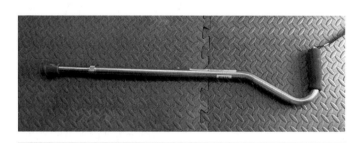

☐ An aluminum cane. Check out the way the handle bends on this cane. Try to find one like this. The balance is much better than the curve of a traditional cane.

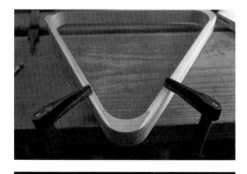

☐ A wooden rack for pool balls. You know those triangles you use to rack pool balls? Most cameras will fit inside this rack. I use a Panasonic HVX-200 HD camera, and it's not small by a long shot! I've tried tons of different things for this part of the rig, including bending aluminum into a triangle. This rack is my favorite, and you can find them for less than $10.

DOI: 10.1016/B978-0-240-81337-0.00012-4

☐ ¼" (7 mm) threaded rod. This is simply a bolt without the head on it. Threaded rod comes in different lengths. A 6" (15 cm) long rod is plenty, and probably the shortest you'll find.

☐ (2) ¼" (7 mm) bolts for the threaded rod. I'm using cap nuts simply because they look nicer on the finished rig. It makes no difference at all otherwise.

☐ Aluminum plate, ¹⁄₁₆" (1.5 mm) to ⅛" (3 mm) thick and 3" (76 mm) to 4" (100 mm) wide, or ¼" (7 mm) thick oak or other hard wood. The length depends on your camera. Get a piece as large as the base of your camera. Alternatively, it can be about as long as the distance between the camera screw hole to the front of the camera base plus 1" as a minimum.

☐ *Note*: You may not need the plate! To find out, place the pool ball rack on one of its edges. Place your camera inside the triangle. Line up the camera screw hole on the bottom of your camera to the center of the bottom of the triangle. Can you still open the camera's LCD viewer and twist it up so you can see it while operating? If so, you do not need the camera plate. If not, you need a way to move the camera a little bit forward. That's what the plate is for. Alternatively, if you are using a small monitor attached to the top of the cane, then you won't need the plate in that case either.

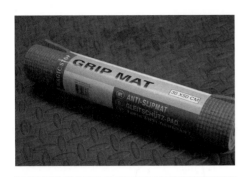

☐ Padding for the camera plate. I'm using this stuff I found for 99 cents called Grip Mat. Your padding needs to be thick like this. A mouse pad works really great as well.

☐ (2) round head ¼" (7 mm) machine screws with nuts. The length needs to be long enough to go through your camera plate (whether wood or aluminum), the thickness of the pool ball rack, and enough left to add the nut to.

Tools List for The *Sweet Smell of Success* Pooper-Scooper Cam

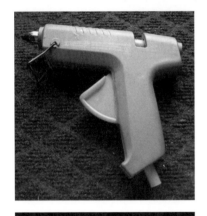

☐ An adhesive to glue the padding to the camera plate. I'm using a hot glue gun.

☐ A combination square.

☐ A drill.

☐ A ¼" (7 mm) drill bit.

☐ A drill bit the same diameter as the lower tube of the cane. Mine is ¾" (19 mm).

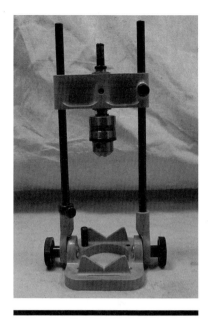

☐ A drill guide or drill press. Either of these works great for drilling a hole through round aluminum tube so that it's straight and true.

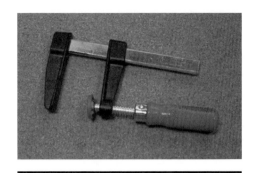

☐ A couple of C-clamps big enough to clamp the pool ball rack to your bench.

☐ A vice.

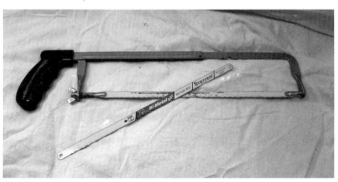

☐ A hacksaw.

☐ A screwdriver.

☐ A wrench.

☐ A utility knife.

☐ A grommet kit. This is an optional thing to buy. Actually, you'll only be using the hole cutter of the grommet kit on this project (see step 6).

☐ Masking tape. If you're making your camera plate from aluminum you'll also need the following.

☐ A hammer.

☐ A center punch.

☐ A metal file. Make sure you read the appendix, *Working with Metal*!

Let's Build It!

1 Determine the top of the pool ball rack. (Hey, it's a triangle. Any corner will do!) Draw an X dead center at the top of the rack. Clamp the rack to your bench with the top facing toward you.

Use the drill bit that is the same diameter as the bottom tube of the cane to drill a hole straight into the top of the ball rack.

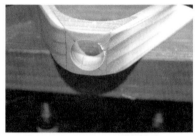

You should end up with something like this. Make sure you are drilling straight!

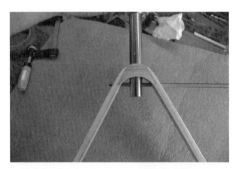

2 This is what we are working toward: The cane goes through the hole, then the threaded rod comes across, through a hole in the cane, and out the other side of the ball rack, attaching the cane to the ball rack.

Pull the rubber tip off the bottom of the cane, and insert the tube into the hole on the pool ball rack. It should be a snug fit.

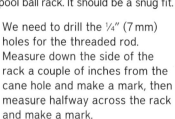

We need to drill the ¼" (7 mm) holes for the threaded rod. Measure down the side of the rack a couple of inches from the cane hole and make a mark, then measure halfway across the rack and make a mark.

This is where we will be drilling the hole for the rod.

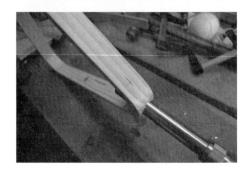

Here's where it makes my head a bit dizzy. This hole has to go straight—as in straight with the rest of the world, not on an angle *with* the ball rack. I find it's easiest if you clamp the rack to your bench on the bottom edge with the cane hole facing the ceiling. Ignore the angle of the rack and drill straight through. It's a big, big, help if your drill has a level on it!

Now we need to drill another hole on the opposite side in the exact same place. Take a piece of masking tape and tape it over the big top hole and the smaller hole on the side.

Use a ¼" (7 mm) drill bit to punch a hole in the tape where the drilled hole is on the side.

For the big top hole, I used a ball point pen to punch little holes to mark the edge of the hole.

Carefully peel the tape off and flip it around.

Line up the marks in the tape with the top hole and run the tape down the opposite side of the rack. Now the hole in the tape is exactly opposite the hole on the other side. I love not having to measure stuff like this! I always screw it up. This is pretty foolproof.

Now it's a simple matter to put the ¼" (7 mm) drill bit in the hole in the tape and drill your second hole.

Make sure your threaded rod goes through both holes. If it is a little off, you can drill out one of the holes a tiny bit larger to get the thing to fit. Not too big though!

3 Lay the cane over the rack so that the tip of it goes ½" (14 mm) to 1" (25 mm) below the threaded rod.

Mark the cane tubing where the threaded rod passes below it, and use a ¼" (7 mm) bit to drill a hole on that mark. It's best if you use the drill guide or a drill press for this.

Important! In some canes, the inside tube is adjustable up and down, but not side to side. If this is the case with your cane, make sure you drill the hole so that the handle points toward the back of the rig once it is put together.

As you can see, in the drill guide, there are these little V shapes that the tube rests in. This ensures that you'll go right down through the middle of the tube.

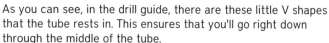

It's pretty easy to make sure you get the cane set up this way: Just stick it through the rack hole and lay the cane so that the handle is flat on top of your bench.

Once you have your hole drilled in the cane, run it down through the top hole in the rack, then run the threaded rod through the rack and cane.

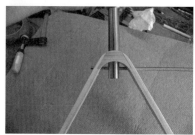

4 Screw the nut cap (or plain ol' nut) on the threaded rod. If you need more threaded rod to screw the nut on, just push a little more through the hole. If you have too much, pull the threaded rod back through the hole until the nut cap rests against the ball rack.

Remove the nut, and measure how much rod is sticking through the rack. That's how much you'll need sticking out of the other side.

Match the measurement of the rod on the other side, and mark where you need to cut it. I use a piece of masking tape because it's really easy to see.

Clamp the rod into your vice, and cut off the excess with a hacksaw. Don't use bolt cutters for this! You'll never get the nut screwed on.

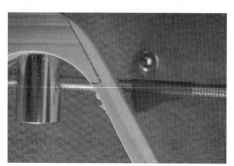

Killer Camera Rigs That You Can Build

Make sure you can screw the nut onto the cut end. If you can't, take a metal file and file flat on the cut end of the rod. It doesn't take much. A few strokes of the file can usually get rid of any stray bit of metal still stuck on there.

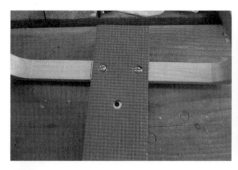

5 Now let's make the camera plate. You only need to make this if you can't open your LCD screen on your camera while it's mounted in the rig.

I find this part is easier if you drill a ¼" (7 mm) hole through the middle of the camera plate first. If you are making one out of metal, please read the appendix before you begin this part!

Most cameras use a ¼" (7 mm) screw. Run the camera screw up through the plate hole you just drilled and screw it to the bottom of your camera. Open the LCD screen on the camera and turn it so it's facing up. Coming from the back of the camera, lower the ball rack until it almost touches the LCD screen. This is where the plate needs to be mounted to the bottom of the rack.

Use a Sharpie to draw a line on the plate along the edge of the rack.

It might help to draw an arrow so that you'll know later that the line is the *front edge* of the rack.

Use a combination square along the line you just made to make sure it is square. Set the rack against the combo square and draw another line on the plate marking the outside of the rack.

So now you should have two lines going across the plate showing the width of the pool ball rack. Next, divide that width by half to find the center between those two lines, and draw a third line across the plate.

On that center line, measure in about ½" (14 mm) from the edge of the plate, and hammer a dimple on that point with your center punch. Go to the opposite edge and do the same thing. Drill ¼" (7 mm) holes on those dimples.

Now you should have three holes in your plate. One for the camera and two to mount the plate to the pool ball rack.

Measure halfway across the width of the plate and make a mark dead center. On the bottom of the pool ball rack, measure halfway across and make a mark. In the photo, I'm doing this on the top side because it's easier to understand what's going on. Again, you want to make your mark on the bottom. To be clear: if the pool rack is 10" across, your mark would be at 5". So we now have the center of both the plate and the rack.

Line up the two marks, then draw a line on each side of the plate. Again, this would be on the bottom of the rack.

So now you know the borders of the plate.

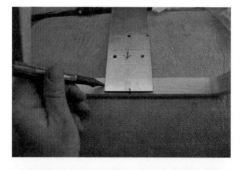

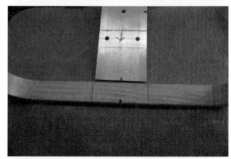

Now take the plate and line up the two lines on the plate you made when finding the edges of the rack and make sure the rack is on those lines. Use your combo square to make sure it's square. Line up the plate between the two marks you made on the bottom of the rack.

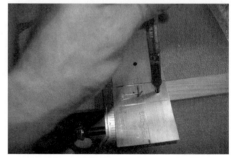

Now mark the holes in the plate to the pool ball rack.

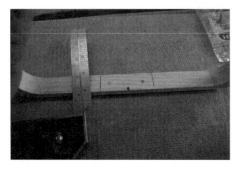

You should now have something that looks like this, except on the bottom of the rack.

Use a ¼" (7 mm) bit to drill out those holes.

ATTACH THE PADDING

6 Lay the plate on your padding and use a utility knife or scissors to cut the padding the same size as the plate.

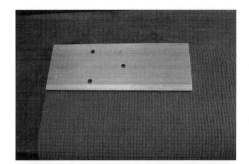

Lay the plate on top of the cut piece of padding and mark the holes with a Sharpie.

Set the plate aside.

Cut the holes in the padding. I'm using a hole punch from a grommet kit. You just center it over the mark and give it a whack with a hammer. Viola! Perfect hole!

Do all three holes.

The best way to glue padding to metal is with a hot glue gun. Do one half, let the glue set (about 15 seconds), then roll the mat back and do the other half. Make sure your holes line up!

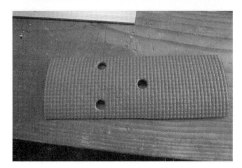

ATTACH THE PLATE

7 Use ¼" (7 mm) round-head machine screws and nuts to attach the plate to the rack. Now you can see why your mat has to be a little thick: so the head of the screws don't come in contact with your camera base.

Reattach the cane as you did earlier when measuring the threaded rod in step 4.

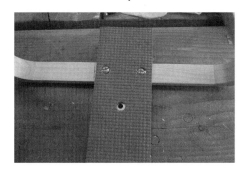

Use a short ¼" (7 mm) machine screw to attach the camera to the plate and you're good to go!

It's pretty easy to use this rig. You kind of want to pretend you are carrying a boiling cup of coffee filled to the brim of the cup. How smoothly would you walk if this were the case?

The *City Streets* Circle Rig

Over 10 years ago I was driving down Sunset Boulevard here in Los Angeles. As I sat at a traffic light waiting for it to turn green, I noticed somebody using a kind of rig I'd never seen before: a simple circle with a rail in the middle holding the camera. They simply held it like a steering wheel. I made one the next day out of a bicycle rim with the spokes removed. It worked pretty well, I must say.

About a year went by, and a movie by Mike Figgis called *Timecode* was getting a lot of press. As it turns out, Mike Figgis invented the rig because he wanted his actors to have an easy-to-use way of getting steady shots without a ton of camera experience. He dubbed it the *Figrig*. Now it's commercially available through Manfrotto (http://services.manfrotto.com/figrig/) for about $300.

Well, you can make your own really easily.

Materials List for the *City Streets* Circle Rig

☐ A metal circle. As I mentioned in the introduction, I made the first one of these from a bicycle rim. It worked fine, but my favorite thing to use is the foot rest off of a drafting chair. I don't know why, but I run across these everywhere in Los Angeles just sitting on the street or at thrift shops like the *Goodwill*. I think with a little effort, you can find a used chair with one of these on it for very little cash. To prove my "street gifting," I took a photo of this chair base on the street with the chair missing. But I didn't need the chair anyway! I just took out a screwdriver and removed the metal circle. Mine is 19" in diameter, but you can certainly go smaller, as long as your camera can fit in the middle of it! If you can't find one, I've also taken a trip to the junk yard where I found a large steering wheel that I cut the center out of with a hacksaw. As I mentioned, I've also built one of these out of a bicycle wheel with the spokes removed. You get the idea; just about anything big and round.

DOI: 10.1016/B978-0-240-81337-0.00013-6

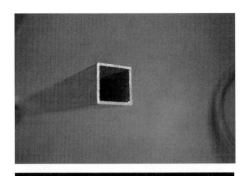

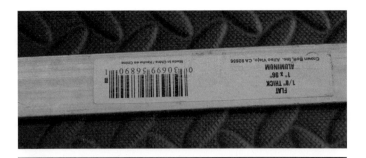

☐ Square aluminum tube, ⅟₁₆″ (1.5 mm) to ⅛″ (3 mm) thick tube long enough to go across your metal circle. I have also used solid bar aluminum. Either is fine. It needs to be ¾″ (19 mm) to 1″ (25 mm) square.

☐ Flat aluminum bar. This can be ⅟₁₆″ (1.5 mm) to ⅛″ (3 mm) thick. It needs to be the same width as your square tube. Mine is 1″ (25 mm) square, so I needed 1″ (25 mm) wide bar. It needs to be twice as long as your aluminum tube. Both these aluminum pieces are in every large home center I've gone into, so no excuses!

Tools List for the *City Streets* Circle Rig

☐ A combination square.

☐ A center punch or prick punch.

☐ A hammer.

☐ A metal file.

☐ 60 grit sandpaper.

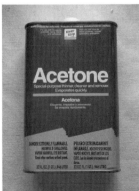

☐ Acetone.

☐ Shop towels.

☐ J-B Weld.

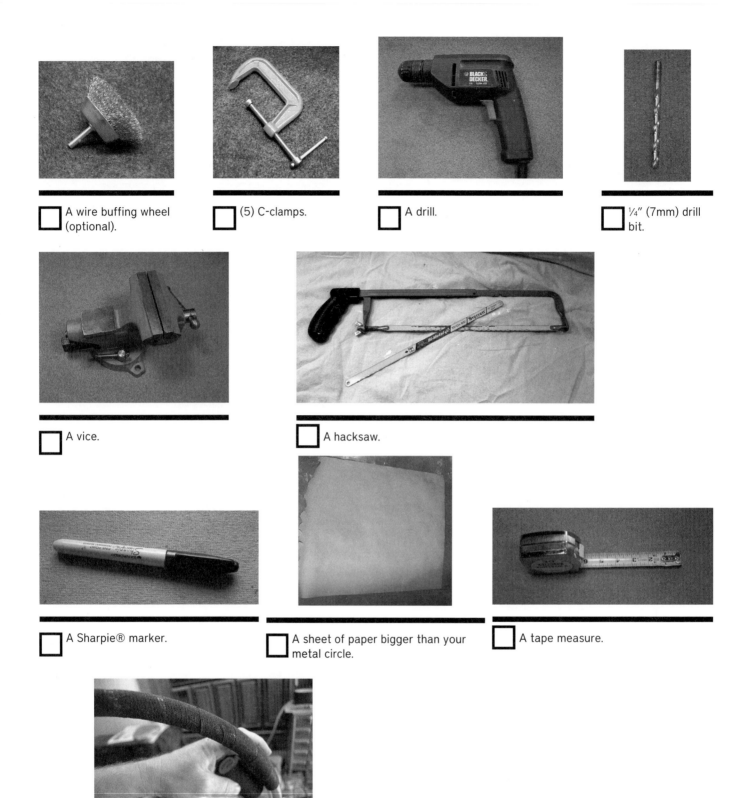

☐ A wire buffing wheel (optional).

☐ (5) C-clamps.

☐ A drill.

☐ ¼" (7mm) drill bit.

☐ A vice.

☐ A hacksaw.

☐ A Sharpie® marker.

☐ A sheet of paper bigger than your metal circle.

☐ A tape measure.

☐ Some kind of padded wrap. This is to wrap your circle in once the rig is done—and is completely optional, by the way. I've used bicycle handlebar tape, gaffer tape, duct tape, just about anything you can think of. For this one I'm using a self-adhesive wrap for injuries I found at a sporting goods store.

170

Let's Build It!

Before starting this project, read the appendix, *Working with Metal*!

We need to determine where to place the camera bar in our metal circle. Folding a big sheet of paper makes quick work of this no matter the size of your circle.

1 Cut your paper to the same size as your metal circle. Make sure it is square! I'm using a framing square to make quick work of this, but any measuring device will do.

2 Fold the paper in half. By placing the circle edge to edge on the paper, this gives you the exact center, but we need to put our camera bar a little lower than that.

Fold the paper in half *again*, make a good crease, then unfold it.

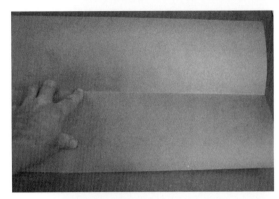

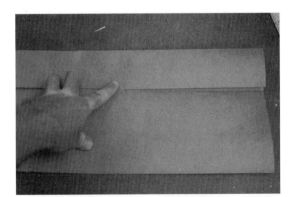

Now take the top edge and fold it down to that crease you just made.

Lay the circle on top of the paper. Make sure the edges of the circle are lined up with the edges of the paper. Where the top edge of the paper goes across your circle is where your camera bar will go.

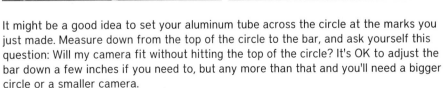

Use a marker to mark where the top edge of the paper meets the circle. Mark it on each side.

It might be a good idea to set your aluminum tube across the circle at the marks you just made. Measure down from the top of the circle to the bar, and ask yourself this question: Will my camera fit without hitting the top of the circle? It's OK to adjust the bar down a few inches if you need to, but any more than that and you'll need a bigger circle or a smaller camera.

3 Lay the circle on top of the square aluminum tube, being careful to line up the bar with the marks on the circle.

Use a Sharpie to trace the inside of the circle onto your aluminum tube.

Of course you need to trace both ends of the square tube.

Clamp the tube in the vise and cut along the line with a hacksaw. You don't have to worry about making a curved cut; a straight cut at that angle is fine.

Aluminum tube is super easy to cut with a hacksaw. You'll be surprised how quickly this goes! Cut the other end at the correct angle too.

Test it out in the circle to see if it fits. The top of the bar should match the marks on your circle you made earlier. If your bar is a bit too long, you can file it down with a metal file pretty quickly. If you want, you can mark the top of the tube at this point so you don't get confused later.

 Now we are going to drill some mounting holes for the camera through the bar.

Measure the length across the top of the bar. Make a mark at the halfway point. If your bar is 20" long, then the halfway point is 10", right?

Use a center punch or prick punch to mark a line across the aluminum tube at that halfway point.

Then make two marks on *each side* of the center mark 1" (25mm) apart. If your camera is a little out of balance for some reason, this gives you other holes for adjusting it.

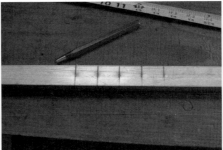

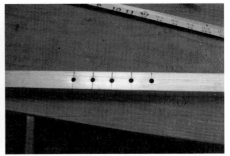

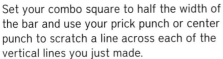

Set your combo square to half the width of the bar and use your prick punch or center punch to scratch a line across each of the vertical lines you just made.

Make a dimple in the metal where each of those lines cross with your prick punch.

Drill a ¼″ (7 mm) hole through the aluminum tube at each dimple. You don't have to worry about using a lubrication oil on thin tube aluminum like this. If you are using solid bar aluminum you *will* need to use cutting oil. If you don't know what I'm talking about, why didn't you read the appendix? Come on! It's important!

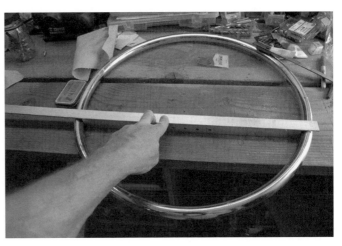

5 Lay the camera bar in your circle so the top of the bar is at the marks you made on the circle.

Take the flat bar aluminum and lay it on top of the camera bar. One end of the flat bar should be even with the outside edge of the metal circle.

Since the circle is, well, a circle, the bottom edge of the flat bar is going to extend out farther than the top edge. Don't worry about that. It's what we want.

Mark the opposite end of the bar where the top edge meets the outside edge of the metal circle. Cut two flat bars at that length.

Use a file to clean up the cut ends of the flat bar if you need to.

Use #60 grit sandpaper or a wire brush to clean and roughen one side of each of the flat bars and each side of the camera bar (the sides without holes in them). I prefer using sandpaper for this, because it gives the J-B Weld a good rough surface to adhere to. I usually use the wire brush for cleaning and shining up the sides that will be visible when the rig is finished.

Clean all the parts well with a shop towel and acetone.

6 Take your metal circle and roughen the surface p with sandpaper from the marks to about 1" (25 mm) below the marks on each side.

You should have two flat aluminum bars and the camera bar all clean and ready to glue.

Clean the circle at those points with some acetone. Be careful you don't clean off the marks you made!

Take a hammer and pound the ends of the flat bar around the metal circle. Remove the clamps, flip it over, and do the same to the second flat bar for the other side.

Set the camera bar in place, put a flat bar on top of the camera bar, and clamp the whole thing in place on your bench.

Remove the clamps and the flat bar. Mix up some J-B Weld according to the instructions on the package and spread it across the camera bar and the matching points on the metal circle.

Clamp the flat bar back in place. Use a shop rag with some acetone on it to clean up any J-B Weld that has squeezed out on the top and bottom of your camera bar. Let the J-B Weld dry for a few hours. Remove the clamps, flip it over, and J-B Weld the second bar to the other side. Clamp it down, and let the J-B Weld set at least overnight.

7 If you want, you can wrap your circle in gaffers tape, bicycle handlebar tape, or just about anything. I'm using a self-adhesive wrap for sports injuries.

I put black camera tape on the edges of the camera bar. None of this matters in the operation of the rig. It just looks nice.

8 You'll need a ¼" (7 mm) screw to mount the camera to the bar. The length depends on how thick your camera bar is and how deep your camera hole goes. If the bar is 1" (25 mm) deep and your camera screw hole is ½" (14 mm) deep, you'll need a screw 1½" (38 mm) or less. A little less is better to get a tight fit of your camera to the bar. You can always add a washer to the camera screw at the bottom of the bar if your screw is too long.

9 Try it out! Start by mounting your camera to the center hole, and see if you like it there. The balance should be pretty good, but if not, try a different hole. This is completely by feel, and how it feels to you.

...or down low with one. The use of this rig is completely what you find comfortable to get a steady shot.

You can either hold it like a steering wheel with two hands...

I've even tried hanging one from a crane. Use your imagination, and I'm sure you can find tons of uses for this rig.

The *Storm Fear* Shoulder Mount

There are a few things I hate about shoulder mounts. Most commercial versions are only minimally adjustable. The handles are short, which forces you to hold your arms up as opposed to locked at your sides. And the shoulder rest on many low cost units are far from comfortable. The designers of most shoulder mounts seemed to have designed them so that they are easy to ship and store, but less than desirable for actually using!

At the end of this chapter, you'll find cool and different ways of operating the *Storm Fear* shoulder mount, which will greatly reduce fatigue over most other shoulder mounts. Another great thing about this one is that the shoulder support piece of it is designed specifically for *your* shoulder.

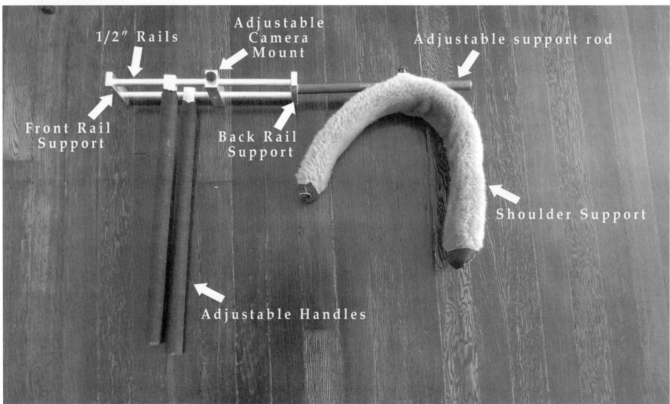

Before we get into building the *Storm Fear*, let's take a closer look. There are two ½" (14 mm) rails that the camera mount and handles ride on. You can adjust both the handles and camera mount along the length of the rails to give you a perfect view of your LCD screen (or adjust if for looking through the view finder if you'd like). Coming off the back of the rails is an adjustable support rod. Not only does this move the entire camera platform up and back, but can tilt the camera left or right. This makes it very easy to level the camera once you've set the shoulder support on your shoulder, and then lock it down tight. And lastly, the handles.

Yep, they *are* long! If you've ever used a commercial shoulder mount before, you'll be surprised at the ease of use these long handles will give you. You'll probably ask yourself why everyone doesn't do it this way.

As you thumb through the plans, you may think this is difficult to build. It's really not. Just take your time and it'll come out great!

Make sure you read the appendix, *Working with Metal*, before starting this project!

DOI: 10.1016/B978-0-240-81337-0.00014-8

Materials List for the *Storm Fear* Shoulder Mount

☐ (2) female clamping knobs size: #8-32 (4 mm approximately). Well, let's talk about the size, actually. This is what I used. And why? Because one of the things we'll be doing is tapping a hole in the aluminum. What a tap does is give a drilled hole threads, so that you can screw a screw or bolt into it. The most common tap I could find was #8-32, with #10-32 coming in a close second. You, on the other hand, can use any size *under* ¼" (7 mm) if you can't find the sizes listed here.

Note: For all of you in the land of Metric, I'll not keep listing the conversion for the tap size, because I know that some of you will not stop until you find the perfect conversion for #8-32. It's not that important. Really, it's not. Anything under 7 mm will do nicely.

Take a look at the tap and drill bit set in the *Tools List* section coming up. It's a good idea to buy this first, then buy all of your machine screws to fit that size. (By the way, tapping a hole is easy, and kinda cool). All the screws and knobs must match the tap size!

☐ (1) male clamping knob size: #8-32 × ⁹⁄₁₆" (length is not hugely important. About a ½" [14 mm] or more is good here). Again, this can be anything under ¼" (7 mm). Let me repeat this, because I know some of you just skimmed over what I just wrote in the previous paragraph and I'll get all sorts of e-mails about it. So pay attention: All the machine screws, knobs, and set screws in this project must match the size tap you bought. Mine is going to be listed as #8-32, because that's the size of my tap. Yours may or may not be different. Are we all clear? Or have I just confused the issue? Knowing me, probably the latter.

☐ (2) flat-head machine screws by 2" (50 mm) long, size #8-32 (or whatever your tap size is, right?). Chances are really good that you'll have to cut down the length later with a hacksaw. No worries. Better to have it too long than too short. And just in case you asked: yes, it does have to be a flat-head screw.

☐ Aluminum bar. In the end, you'll need (2) aluminum bars, 1" (25 mm) wide by ¼" (7 mm) thick by 4" (100 mm) long. My supplier carries this size in 12" (30 cm) lengths, which I simply cut to 4" (100 mm). It's much cheaper to cut your own aluminum than to have the supplier cut it. Often the cutting costs much more than the aluminum!

☐ Another size of aluminum bar. This is 1¼" (31 mm) wide by ¾" (19 mm) thick. Again, my raw stock is 12" (30 cm) long that I'll need to cut two lengths from: a 2" (50 mm) long piece and a 4" (100 mm) long piece.

☐ Plexiglass or acrylic sheet. You'll be making your shoulder piece out of this. I've made two sizes of shoulder support, and I tend to like the longer one just a tiny bit better. The thing is, you have to be able to fit this into your oven, so don't get it too long. Shorter is definitely easier to work with when making the support. So I'll give you a choice: 12″ (30 cm) × 24″ (60 cm) × 0.093″ (2.36 mm) thick, or 11″ (28 cm) ×14″ (35 cm) × 0.093″ (2.36 mm) thick. You can find this stuff in any hardware store. Don't worry too much about the thickness. It just needs to be around that thick. Also, you might see really expensive plexi products that look the same as the cheap stuff. Get the cheap stuff!

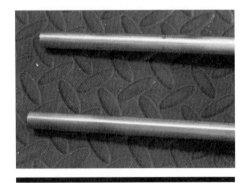

☐ ½″ (14 mm) round aluminum bar. Don't confuse this with round *tube* aluminum. Tube aluminum is hollow! You'll need two pieces, 12″ (30 cm) long.

☐ ¾″ (19 mm) OD (outside diameter) aluminum tube. You'll be cutting this to match your body and camera type later, but best to start with at least a 2′ long piece.

☐ (2) 1″ (25 mm) OD aluminum tube 17″ (43 cm) long. You can always get a long piece and cut it with the tube cutter or hacksaw you'll be needing. These make up the handles. I'm a pretty average size guy, but if you are a giant or a tiny person, you might need longer or shorter. If you get a few inches extra, you can always cut it down to size after you try the rig out.

☐ (2) square aluminum bars, ¾″ (19 mm) square × 3″ (76 mm) long. You'll need two pieces.

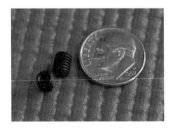

☐ (2) socket set screws, the same size as your tap. Mine is ⁸⁄₃₂″ × ¼″ (7 mm) long. As you can see, these are tiny! Don't forget to get an Allen wrench (also called a hex key) to fit these!

☐ A roll of athletic tape. This is sticky on one side and is usually used for wrapping ankles, wrists, and such. Get stuff that is at least 1½" wide (3.8 cm) and 12 yards (11 meters) long.

☐ Something to pad your shoulder support. I'm using sheep's skin. It's pretty cheap here in the L.A. garment district, and makes your shoulder support very comfortable. You can also use a thin piece of foam.

Tools List for the *Storm Fear* Shoulder Mount

☐ A bench vise. Most projects in this book need this, but you *really* need it for this project!

☐ A prick punch or center punch. Their use is explained in the appendix.

☐ A combination square.

☐ Cutting oil or some other lubricant for drilling into metal. See the appendix.

☐ Locking pliers.

☐ A variable speed drill or drill press. A drill press will make things *much* easier!

☐ A #8-32 tap and a drill bit to match. In automotive stores, you can find these packaged together. In hardware stores they are sold separately most of the time. Find the right size tap (just about anything under ¼" (7 mm) will do), and on the tap package it will tell you what size drill bit you need to buy. By the way, a tap is something that puts screw threads into a drilled hole.

☐ You will also need a bit that is only slightly larger than your tap. Size isn't terribly important as long as it's a tiny bit bigger.

☐ A tap wrench. This holds the above tap.

☐ A ½" (14 mm) drill bit.

☐ A tube cutter. This is for the aluminum tube. A hacksaw will also work.

☐ A hacksaw. Get a bunch of extra blades. They are dirt cheap, but wear out quickly. For faster cutting get ones that have 18 teeth to an inch; 24 teeth are about the most you want. The fewer teeth the faster you'll get the cutting done.

Killer Camera Rigs That You Can Build

☐ A hammer.

☐ A ¾" (19mm) hole saw and arbor. This is basically a big drill bit. The other thing in the photo is called an arbor. The hole saw screws onto this, then the drill holds the arbor. There are several sizes of arbors. Make sure you get one that fits this small hole saw!

☐ A flat metal file.

☐ A large round metal file (this one is shown without the handle). Don't think you can get away with a tiny flat file! You can't. It's gotta be round.

☐ A screwdriver.

☐ A Sharpie®.

☐ Scissors.

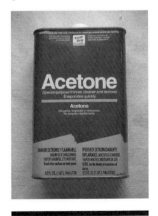

☐ Acetone.

☐ J-B Weld.

☐ A wire wheel brush for your drill. You don't *have* to have this, but it does a nice job of cleaning up aluminum.

☐ A countersink. A ½" (14mm) diameter one is plenty big enough for this project.

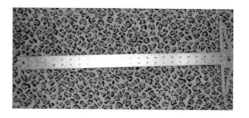

☐ A ¼" (7 mm) drill bit. Please don't get this bit mixed up with your tap bit. It's a real drag when you've drilled a hole too big.

☐ A straight edge of some sort at least as long as the plexiglass.

☐ Shop towels or old rags.

☐ #60 grit sandpaper.

☐ Thick white cotton gloves. You'll be handling hot acrylic, so don't skip these! You can get these for less than $2 a pair, so no excuses.

☐ Epoxy rated for plastic and metal.

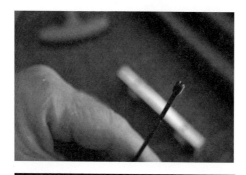

☐ An Allen wrench (also called a hex wrench). You need to get one that fits those tiny *set screws* in the materials list.

☐ Before we leave the hardware store: Does your tap size fit the flat-head machine screws, the set screws, and the male clamping knob?

☐ And does your arbor fit your hole saw? See the drill bit coming out the bottom? You need that. Don't get a cheap hole saw with an arbor "built in."

Killer Camera Rigs That You Can Build

Let's Build It!

Making the Shoulder Support

This thing is sweet! It'll fit you exactly, which makes it super comfortable. Many of you are probably not old enough to remember taking vinyl records and sticking them on top of a coffee can in the oven until they melted into the shape of an ashtray, plant pot, or the like. This is exactly the same thing, only slightly more difficult.

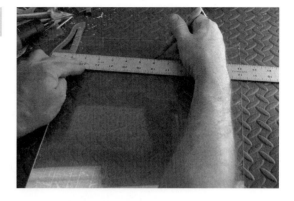

1 Measure halfway across the width of the acrylic.

Then draw a line down the middle with a permanent marker.

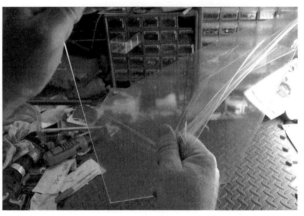

If you haven't yet, remove the protective plastic from the other side.

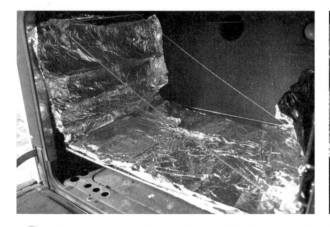

2 Line your oven with aluminum foil. Better make it a few layers up the side if you have to put your plexiglass at an angle like mine.

It's great if your plexi is small enough or your oven is big enough to lay it flat, but if you can't it's perfectly OK.

Close the oven door and turn the heat up to 350 °F (177 °C). It takes about 20 minutes for the acrylic to get soft enough to fold and bend. Don't worry though: if you can bend it only once before it cools, you can always stick it back in the oven.

While you're waiting for the acrylic to soften, lay out a towel on the floor. Once the 20 minutes are up, put on your cotton gloves.

You have to do the next steps very quickly before the plexi cools.

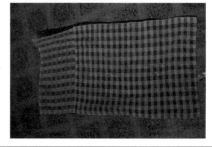

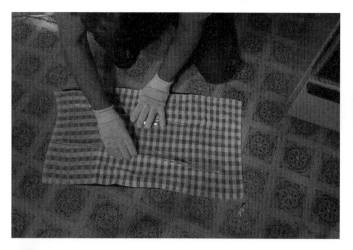

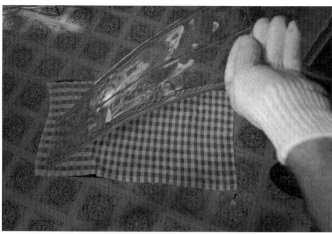

3 Lay the soft plexi on the towel. Quickly fold one long edge to the center line you made. Then fold the opposite edge to the center line. Press down on the folds as hard as you can and try to flatten them.

You should have something that looks like this.

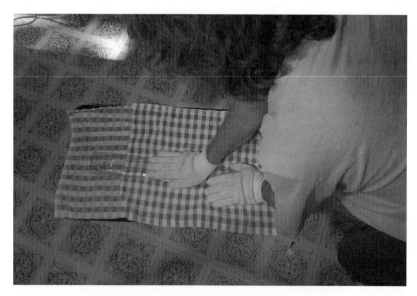

Fold one side over again at the center line so that the opposite edges meet. Press it down as hard as you can.

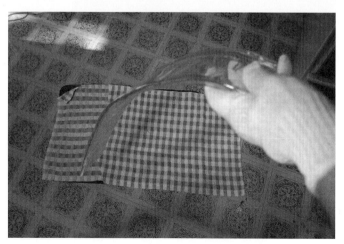

You should have one thick piece that looks like this. If you need to stick it back in the oven to soften it up again, go ahead.

Roll the plexi up in a towel and place it over your right shoulder. The narrow front edge of the plexi should be at least lower than your collar bone. Press your back and the plexi against a wall. Press your back hard against the wall and press the front part of the plexi hard against your chest. Hold it there for a few minutes until the plexi cools.

You should have something that looks like this.

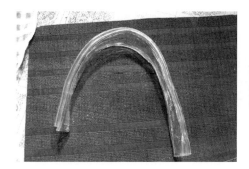

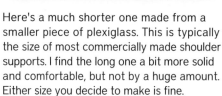

Don't be afraid to stick it back into the oven if you find it has cooled in a shape that doesn't seem comfortable. Just soften it up and do it again.

Set it aside while we make the support rod holder that attaches to the shoulder support.

Here's a much shorter one made from a smaller piece of plexiglass. This is typically the size of most commercially made shoulder supports. I find the long one a bit more solid and comfortable, but not by a huge amount. Either size you decide to make is fine.

THE SUPPORT ROD HOLDER
(You did read the appendix, right?)

4 This piece attaches to the shoulder support. It has two clamping knobs so that you can adjust the support rod, then tighten it into place.

Measure across the top of your shoulder support. It should be just under 3" (76 mm). You can make your holder anywhere from 2" (50 mm) to 2½" (63 mm) long. Mine is 2" (50 mm), so I'll be saying 2" (50 mm) in these plans.

Take the 1¼" (31 mm) wide × ¾" (19 mm) thick aluminum bar and measure 2" (50 mm) off of it. Use your prick punch to scratch a line across the bar at that point. If you are going to cut this with a hacksaw, make sure you put the aluminum tightly into the vise. Try to stay on the scratch line when you cut it to make sure it's nice and straight.

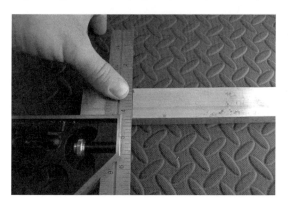

5 Scratch an X from corner to corner. This will give you the exact center of the block.

Use your prick punch to put a dimple into the center of the X. If you don't know how to do this, you didn't bother to read the appendix, *Working with Metal*. Go ahead. I'll wait.

6 Load the ¾" (19 mm) hole saw into your drill, and set the center bit tip into the dimple. Your drill should be going super slow, around 500 rpm. I confess, I'm using a drill press to do this, but I have done it with a hand drill.

In either case, it takes *forever* for the bit to make it through this thick bit of aluminum. Make sure you use tons of lubricant and clean the hole saw often. Let me be clear: A drill press will make this easier, but it won't take less time. On the bright side, you only have to drill two of these larger holes in this project, and the second one is through much thinner aluminum.

Now turn the block up on edge. Careful not to move the measurement of the combo square; set it against the right edge of the block and make a mark across the top edge. Do the same on the left edge. Now reset the combo square to half the thickness of the block. Draw lines across the marks you just made. You should have two little crosses on top of the block.

Use your prick punch to put dimples in the middle of the crosses.

Sure, it took forever, but look how pretty!

7 Next we'll be adding screw holes and chopping this thing in two.

Draw a line halfway up the piece so that it cuts it in two along the length of the block.

Next, measure from the edge of the hole to the nearest edge of the block. Cut that measurement in half, and set your combo square to that measurement.

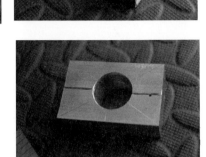

8 Grab the drill bit that matches your tap. It's a good idea to always keep your tap and its matching drill bit together. It makes it much easier!

Load the bit into the drill. Put the point of the bit in the dimples and drill all the way through the block. Don't forget the cutting oil! You should now have two holes going all the way through the aluminum.

9 Load the block into your vise. Make sure the center line you made earlier is outside the jaws of the vice so that you can cut down it.

Killer Camera Rigs That You Can Build

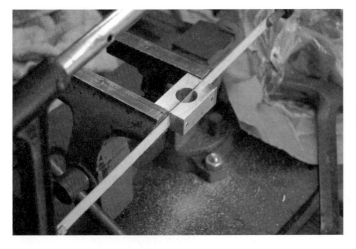

Cut the block in half along the line. It's OK if it is not absolutely perfect.

Sweet! See it didn't take long at all, did it?

10 Pick one piece of what you just cut. That will be the bottom from now on.

Load that piece into your vise, bottom pointing up.

Load the tap into the tap wrench.

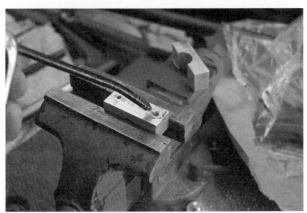

Soak the holes and the tap in oil (the same lubricant you are using on your drill bits when cutting metal).

Carefully twist the tap into the hole. This is just like screwing in a screw except for every two or three turns of the tap, unscrew the tap about one turn. Keep going like this until you are all the way through the hole, then tap the other hole.

11 This next part will be easier if you look in the mirror or get a friend's help. Take your acrylic shoulder support and place it on your shoulder. Find a good placement for the aluminum piece you just tapped: it should be on top of the shoulder support somewhere. Try to place it so it's facing squarely forward. Take a marker and draw a line on the acrylic marking the front of the piece of aluminum.

Remove the shoulder support and line the piece up with the mark you just made. Draw a line all the way around the piece with the marker.

You should now have an outline on top of the acrylic of the aluminum bit.

12 Take two machine screws and screw them down through the top of the piece. If you've never made threads in metal before, this is pretty cool. You only want the slightest bit of the tip of the screw poking out the bottom of the aluminum piece. It's important that they *are* sticking out though!

OK, let's head back to the kitchen. You'll need that aluminum piece, a pair of locking pliers, and your cotton gloves.

Clamp the piece into the teeth of the locking pliers as shown here.

Turn on one of the burners on the stove top, and set the aluminum piece right over the flame. (You can't see it in the photo, but the flame is on!) You'll need to leave it there heating up for about five minutes.

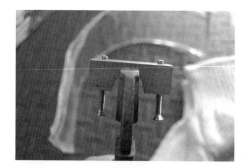

You should end up with something like what's in the photo. The reason the screws needed to be a bit out of the aluminum is so that they would melt little dimples in the acrylic so that you'd know where to drill your holes in the next step.

Once it's hot enough, press it down into the acrylic inside the marks you made on top of the shoulder support. If it's very hot, it will melt the acrylic. Just keep pushing until the piece has a solid level surface in the acrylic. If it's not hot enough, and just melted the acrylic a little bit, that's OK. Just heat it up some more and try again.

13 Find the drill bit that is a little bigger than the holes on the aluminum bit and load it into your drill.

Killer Camera Rigs That You Can Build

Put the drill bit into the dimples on the acrylic and slowly drill holes all the way through. Go easy. If you press too hard or try to drill too quickly, you may crack the plexiglass. Do the second hole as well.

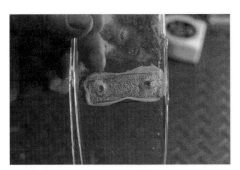

You should now have a nice secure place for the aluminum piece and two holes in the acrylic.

14 Remove the machine screws from the piece. If the piece is still hot, you may have trouble getting them out. Just let it cool. If they are still stuck, clean the bottom of the piece with a wire brush. Melted acrylic may have gotten in the treads of the screws.

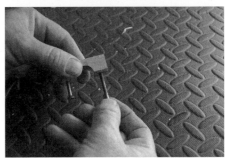

Load the countersink bit into your drill. On the underside of the shoulder support, drill out a countersink in each of the holes. Don't go too deep. You need only enough countersink to allow the head of the machine screw to be flush with the bottom of the support.

If you go a little deeper than you need, that's OK, just don't go too deep.

15 Put the bottom aluminum piece in your vice, and clean all sides of it. Be especially careful to clean and roughen up the bottom!

Use acetone and a shop towel to clean off all the grease and dirt still left on the piece.

16 Run the 2" (50 mm) screws up through the bottom of the shoulder support, screwing them into the aluminum piece. Don't screw it down tight yet! We are going to be gluing it, so you need to have enough room between the aluminum and acrylic to get the epoxy in there. And don't glue it, then add the screws afterward. Epoxy will get on the top of the screws and they'll be worthless.

Mix up the epoxy according to the instructions on the package.

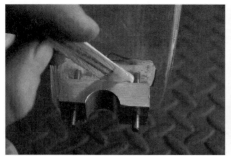  

Glob a bunch of epoxy between the aluminum piece and the acrylic.

Turn it over and glob a bunch in the countersink holes as well.

Screw the screws down tight so that the aluminum piece fits snug against the acrylic.

Use acetone and a shop towel to clean off any epoxy that may have gotten on the screws. Do this before it dries!

17 Remember the drill bit you used to drill out the holes in the acrylic? Use that to drill out the small holes in the second half of the aluminum piece that's been lying around doing nothing all this time.

Now the holes are big enough for it to slide onto the screws coming from its base. Go ahead. Try it out.

 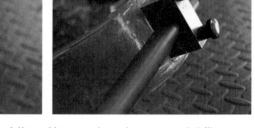

Slide the ¾" (19 mm) aluminum tube into the hole, and screw on the female clamping knobs to the screws. Are you able to tighten the clamping knobs all the way down so that the round tube doesn't move? If not, you'll have to use a hacksaw to cut a tiny bit off the tip of each screw. Two things: let the epoxy dry 24 hours before you do this, and make sure the top aluminum piece is on over the screws as it is now. It will help support the

screws as you cut them. You may have to use a metal file on the top of the screw after you've cut it to get rid of any stray metal. Otherwise, you might not be able to screw the clamping knobs on. As an alternative to cutting the screws, you can add a couple of tiny washers or nylon spacers to the top of the screws between the aluminum top piece and the clamping knobs.

18 Now let's make the rail supports and the camera mount.

THE BACK RAIL SUPPORT

We'll be making two of these. Since one piece has a large hole in the middle, I'm going to make them separately so that there's no confusion. But feel free to mark the aluminum at the same time and drill the smaller holes by clamping the pieces together in a vise.

Take your 1" (25 mm) wide × ¼" (7 mm) thick aluminum bar and measure off 4" (100 mm). For the rig, you'll need two 4" (100 mm) long pieces. Use the prick punch to mark the aluminum and cut it with a hacksaw (or if you have a chop saw or band saw, even better!).

Once your 4" (100mm) long piece is cut, measure halfway across the width. Since my aluminum is 1" (25mm) wide, that would be ½" (14mm). Set your combo square to ½" (14mm) and make a mark with the prick punch (or center punch).

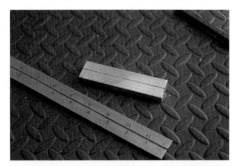

Do this all the way across. I've made a line with a Sharpie so that you can see it. Using your prick punch alone is just fine as long as you can see the mark.

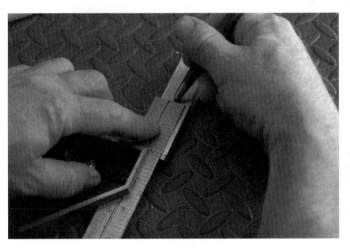

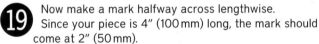

19 Now make a mark halfway across lengthwise. Since your piece is 4" (100mm) long, the mark should come at 2" (50mm).

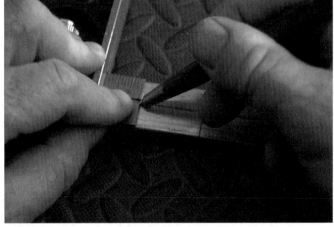

Next, set your combo square at ¾" (19mm). Measure from the left edge and make a mark across the piece at ¾" (19mm). Move to the right edge and repeat.

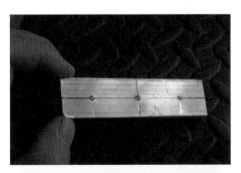

Take your prick punch and hammer and make a dimple at each point the lines cross. That's a dimple in the center and one ¾" (19mm) from each end.

20 Remember that ¾" (19mm) sized hole you made in that thick shoulder piece? Time to do it again. Only this time, the metal is much thinner so things won't be as nasty. Drill a ¾" (19mm) hole in the center with the hole saw. Just put the tip of the guide bit that's in the middle of the hole saw into the center dimple and drill away.

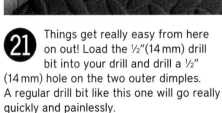

21 Things get really easy from here on out! Load the ½" (14mm) drill bit into your drill and drill a ½" (14mm) hole on the two outer dimples. A regular drill bit like this one will go really quickly and painlessly.

22 You'll need your ½" (14mm) solid rod for this step. If you haven't cut them into two 12" (30cm) long pieces, go ahead and do that now.

Clamp the back rail support (the thing you just made) into the vise, exposing one of the holes. Try to put the ½" (14mm) rod into the ½" (14mm) hole. It always seems to me that it should fit, but it never does. So we need to make the hole a tiny bit bigger.

Stick the round file into that hole and shave away the inside of the hole. Try to file evenly on all sides of the hole. This won't take long, I promise. By the fourth hole, it will only take you a couple of minutes, if that.

As you go, check to see if the rod can slide into the hole. Once it slides easily without a lot of movement within the hole, you're done. Do the other ½" (14mm) hole. Leave the middle hole for now. We'll do it later.

 23 Now lets make the front rail support. Just two holes in this one!

Line up the finished back rail support to the other 4" (100mm) long unfinished front rail support. Make sure you can see the scratched measurement lines from the back support.

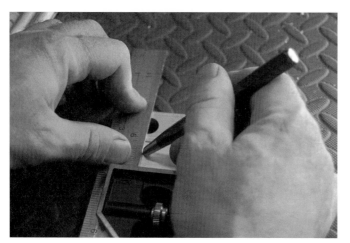

Match your combo square with the line on the finished support, and use your prick punch to scratch a line in the same place on the unfinished piece. Do this on each end.

Now measure halfway across the width and make a second line across the vertical lines you just made.

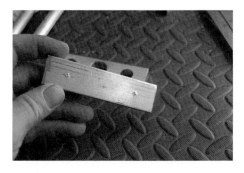

Use your prick punch to hammer dimples into those two points where the marks cross.

Drill ½" (14 mm) holes on those dimples.

Now all that is left to do is file out those holes so that the ½" (14 mm) rod fits.

Slip the supports onto the rails to see how they fit.

24 The best way to mark the camera mount piece is to use a rail support as a guide. I'm stacking them together so that the rail support will be even with the top of the camera mount piece.

25 Let's make our camera mount.

We need to go back to our big piece of aluminum that is 1¼" (31 mm) wide × ¾" (19 mm) thick.

We need a 4" (100 mm) long piece of this as well. The best way is to use one of the rail supports as a guide. Just lay it on top of the big piece and line up the edges.

26 The best way to mark the camera mount piece is to use a rail support as a guide. I'm stacking them together so that the rail support will be even with the top of the camera mount piece.

Use your prick punch to mark a line at the end of the rail support, then cut the camera mount piece the same size: 4" (100 mm).

Use your combo square to follow the lines you made on the rail support piece and transfer the line straight across to the camera support piece. (This is why it's a good idea to use a prick punch or center punch to scratch measurements into metal. A marker is wiped off too easily.)

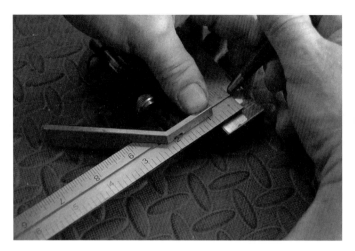

Use a hammer and prick punch to make dimples where the two lines cross.

Once you have the two lines marked that match the lines on the rail support, set your combo square to half the width of the camera mount piece. Scratch a line across the lines you just made halfway across the camera support.

Use a ½" (14 mm) drill bit to drill two holes into the piece at your dimples.

Use the round file to make the holes a tiny bit larger as you did with the rail supports. The rod should slide easily through the holes.

27 You have two more holes to drill in the camera mount piece, one for the camera screw and one for a locking knob.

Measure halfway across the length and make a mark.

Measure halfway across the width and make a mark across the one you just made.

Hammer a dimple where the two lines intersect.

This is for the camera screw: drill a ¼" (7 mm) hole though the camera mount at the dimple you just made.

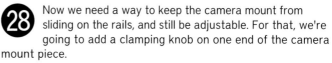

28 Now we need a way to keep the camera mount from sliding on the rails, and still be adjustable. For that, we're going to add a clamping knob on one end of the camera mount piece.

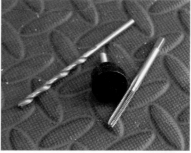

For this you'll need the #8-32 tap (or whatever size you're using), the matching drill bit to that tap, and the #8-32 male clamping knob.

Scratch an X from corner to corner on one end of the camera support piece. Make a dimple in the middle of the X and use the matching drill bit to your tap to drill a hole far enough to come out in the ½" (14 mm) hole that the rail goes through.

Tap a hole as you did with the shoulder piece. (You should be an old hand at this by now. Told you it was easy!) Screw in the knob to make sure it fits and you're done.

29 As long as you have your tap and drill bit handy, let's make some set screw holes in the front rail support (the front support only has two holes in it). Just so you know, you can make both rail supports like this if you want. I'm going to use J-B Weld on the back support and set screws on the front, just in case there comes a time I have to take the camera mount off the rails for some reason.

Transfer the lines you made for the ½" (14 mm) holes to the top (or bottom) of the front rail support piece. You want the set screw going up the bottom edge of the ½" (14 mm) hole.

Again, use your prick punch to scratch that line into the aluminum.

Then measure halfway across the width, make another mark across the first marks, and hammer a dimple into the metal.

Use the drill bit that matches your tap to drill two holes on those dimples. Use the tap to make threads in those holes.

Put a set screw on the end of your hex wrench.

Screw the set screws into the holes. Don't go all the way in at this point.

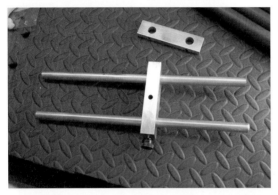

30 Slide the rails into the camera mount holes.

Take your front rail support and feed the rails into the holes. Make sure the rails are flush to the front of the rail support. Tighten down the set screws.

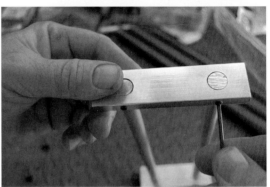

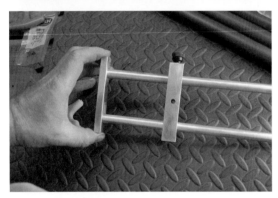

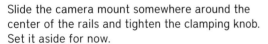

Slide the camera mount somewhere around the center of the rails and tighten the clamping knob. Set it aside for now.

31 Take the ¾" (19 mm) OD round aluminum tube and some 60 grit sandpaper. Really roughen up one end of the tube with the sandpaper. Do the same on one end of each of the ½" (14 mm) rails.

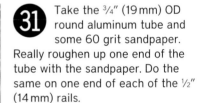

The more scratched up, the better! Take some acetone and a shop towel and clean the end of the tube, the end of the rails, and also clean out all three holes on the rear rail support.

Mix up some J-B Weld according to the instructions on the package. Glob a good bit on the end of the aluminum tube.

Twist the rear rail support onto the aluminum tube. Use acetone and a shop towel to clean up the J-B Weld that oozes out.

Killer Camera Rigs That You Can Build

Apply J-B Weld to each of the ½" (14 mm) rails.

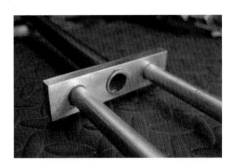

Push them into the opposite side of the ½" (14 mm) holes on the rear rail support. Again, clean any J-B Weld that oozes out before it dries.

Put it in a safe place to dry for 24 hours. You might use your combo square to make sure that the aluminum tube is square with the rear rail support.

32 Could we be almost done? Yep. Let's make the handles!

You need two ¾" (19 mm) square aluminum bars, 3" (76 mm) long. So go cut those. I'll wait here.

Set your combo square to ½" (14 mm). Make a mark ½" (14 mm) from one end of the aluminum bar. Repeat this step on the second bar.

Make a mark across the line you just made, halfway across the width of the bar. Use your prick punch to bang a dimple where those lines intersect. Repeat on the second bar.

Use a ½" (14 mm) drill bit to drill a hole through the bars at the dimple.

As with the other holes in this project, use a round file to make them big enough for the rod to slide through.

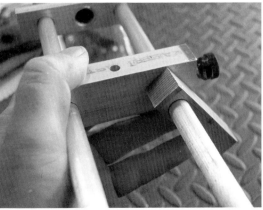

33 Before we start shaping these bars, there are a couple of things to be aware of. First, remove the front rail support by unscrewing the set screws and taking it off. Slip the ¾" (19 mm) bars on the rails. When you rotate the bar, does any corner of it go *above* the top surface of the camera mount piece? It shouldn't, but if it does, you'll have to file it down.

Next, slip the front rail support back on. You don't need to tighten it down, we're just going to use it for reference. Rotate the bar parallel with the rail support. When we put the aluminum tube handle onto the bar, it can't go any farther onto the square bar than where the edge of the rail support meets the bar. So take a Sharpie (yep, it's OK to use a marker for this part) and mark on the square bar where the end of the rail support meets the bar. Do this on the other bar as well.

Despite what your father told you, you can fit a square peg in a round hole. And that's exactly what we are going to do.

Set the bar in your vise so that the teeth of the vise grab two corners of the bar. Take a file and file down the top corner. You may think this will take forever. Not so! Aluminum is very soft, and you'll be done with all the corners in under five minutes.

You only need to file the corners up to the Sharpie mark. Test the piece out as you go to see if it fits into the 1" (25 mm) OD aluminum tube.

You can even pound the aluminum bar into the tube as you go. You'll never get the bar back out of the tube, so clamp the whole thing into the vise.

File down the bits that are giving you trouble...

If you want, you can file the head of the handle until it's all shiny.

...until you can hammer the piece into the tube up to the Sharpie line.

Killer Camera Rigs That You Can Build

See? Pretty. Do the other handle (this one will go much faster now that you've had a little practice).

Take some kind of tape and wrap your new handles with it. I'm using an athletic tape that is sticky on one side for mine.

Sweet! Let's put the rig back together and try it out before the final steps.

34 First, slide the camera mount on, then the handles, then the front rail support. Use the hex wrench to tighten down the front rail support. Use a ¼" (7 mm) bolt to attach the camera to the camera mount. I'm using a hex screw for this, but you can use any type of ¼" (7 mm) bolt or machine screw. It has to be long enough to go up through the camera mount plus a little extra. If it's too long, you'll never be able to tighten the camera down onto the mount! Feel free to use a hacksaw to cut the tip off the bolt if it's too long.

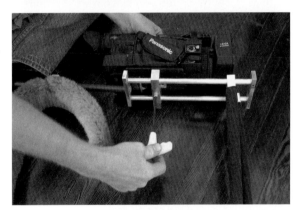

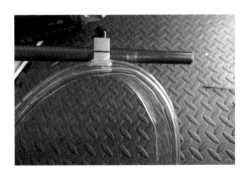

Slide the shoulder support onto the aluminum tube and tighten down the clamping knobs.

Put the rig on your shoulder and loosen the clamping knobs slightly. Adjust the front part of the rig by pushing or pulling it forward or back. Once you have a good position to shoot from, lock the clamping knobs back down. (Remember, the camera mount is also adjustable for fine tuning, so don't get too hung up on where the aluminum tube adjustment falls.)

Take the rig off and remove the camera. Make a mark on the aluminum tube about 4" (100 mm) or 5" (12 cm) to the rear of the shoulder mounting piece.

Cut the excess tube off with a hacksaw or tube cutter.

Now let's put some padding on the shoulder piece, and we're done!

This is why I had you get tube that was a little long: to give you plenty to play with at this point.

35 About padding; I'm using sheepskin because it's really comfortable. You can use thin foam, fake sheepskin, lime green fake fur... whatever floats your boat, really.

If you're using the real thing like me, you'll have to monkey around with it a bit to get an angle on the skin that covers the entire length of your shoulder mount. Use a grip clip to clamp it at one end, and smooth it around the underside of the shoulder piece.

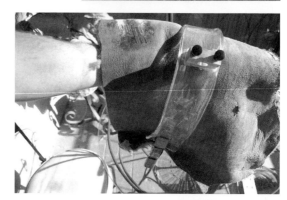

Use a Sharpie to draw around the edges of the shoulder mount piece onto the sheepskin.

Measure the width of the shoulder piece at its widest point. Add a ½" (14 mm) to that measurement (to allow for the thickness of the piece). Whatever that measurement comes out to be, cut it in half. So if the measurement is 4", half that would be 2".

Lay it flat on a table. Don't start cutting yet!

Killer Camera Rigs That You Can Build

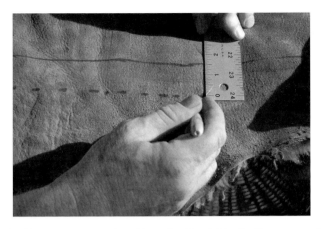

Take that measurement and transfer it outside the line you made on the sheepskin, all the way around on each long side. If you don't have a big enough piece of sheepskin or whatever you're using (like me), it's OK if it's a little narrow. You'll just have a gap of no material at the top of your shoulder piece when you're done. No big deal.

So you should have something that looks like this.

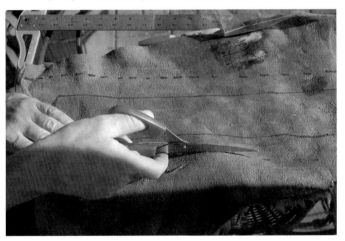

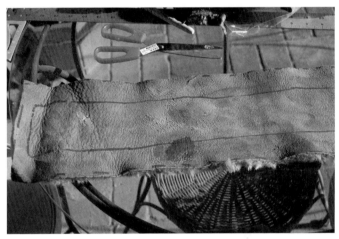

Cut along the outside lines.

Set the cut sheepskin aside for a minute.

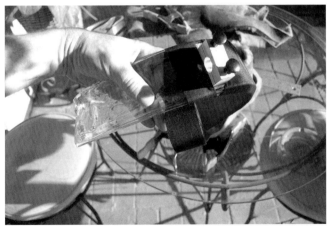

36 Now we need to find a way to stick the sheepskin onto the shoulder piece. You could sew it or glue it. I'm a bit too lazy for both those. Remember the athletic tape you may have used on the handles? This is how I'm going to use that stuff to stick the sheepskin onto the shoulder piece:

Take the tape, and wrap it tightly around the shoulder piece *sticky side up*. Overlap the edges as you go.

Carefully line up the outline you made earlier with a marker on the sheepskin to the underside of the shoulder piece. Stick it on there, pulling the sheepskin around the top of the shoulder piece.

My sheepskin was just a little too narrow at one end to go all the way around the shoulder mount, but I decided to cut it evenly so the gap at the top side of the mount looks like I did it on purpose.

Connect the shoulder piece back on the aluminum support tube, and you're done!

It sticks really well, is super easy, and if you make a mistake, it's easy to correct.

Adjusting and Using Your New Shoulder Mount

Screw the camera to the mounting plate.

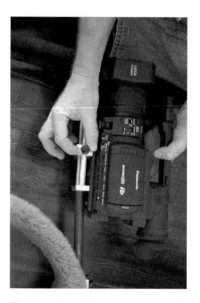

Tighten down the camera mount adjustment screw.

Set the shoulder piece on your shoulder, and hold the top of the camera. Don't worry about the camera at this point: it will probably be wonky. Just make sure the shoulder piece is comfortable on your shoulder.

Loosen the shoulder clamping knobs slightly.

Adjust the camera by twisting it to the left or right until it's level. Then adjust it forward or backward to your personal taste and comfort. Then tighten down the clamping knobs.

Now you can grab the handles. By pushing slightly forward on the handles, they will lock themselves into place. It takes almost no pressure at all. If you want to adjust the handles—even in the middle of a shot—simply let off on the pressure and move them. To get very steady shots, the best place for your arms is to hold them against your sides. Most shoulder mounts force you to hold your arms up. Now you know why I made the handles so long.

Here's a front view. You can adjust the aluminum tube forward or back, or the camera mount itself, so it's pretty easy to get the LCD screen right where you need it.

If you want to have a hand on the camera for zooming, etc., hold both handles in one hand and the other hand on the camera. Because the handles swing over without having to unlock and adjust them, you can do this in the middle of a shot if you need to.

If it's more comfortable for you to have one handle forward or back from the other handle, again, the design allows you to do this quickly and easily.

Even shooting from a seated position is easy and comfortable because you can immediately adjust the handles to wherever you need them.

Not to beat a dead horse here, but play around with handle positions!

I've used a lot of commercially made shoulder mounts, and the one I made is my favorite. I'm passing the plans along to you in this new edition. I hope you'll find the time to build this rig! I'm sure you'll be as happy with it as I am.

Cranes are like dollies: everybody wants one. Well, here are three. The photo shown here is the first crane described in this section: the *Killer's Kiss* crane. It's a short jib I use more than any other in this book (yes, I do use the equipment in these pages for my own films just in case you were wondering).

In earlier editions of this book, I used only one type of mount to attach the crane (or more accurately, a jib) to a tripod. On the last crane in this section I've added a different type of mount. It's much more difficult and expensive to make, but if you live outside America, you may not have a choice. Both mounts work great, but the mount for the *Double Indemnity* crane looks more professional if that's a concern for you (as for me, I couldn't care less what a rig looks like as long as it works).

I would really encourage you to make the tripod later in this book for your crane. It is a very inexpensive surveyor's tripod that is altered to hold a heavy crane. It's really nice to have a tripod devoted to a crane even if you already have a tripod. Cranes take a little time to set up and break down, so you won't be wasting a lot of time on a shoot to change from a crane shot to a tripod shot if you have two tripods.

I get asked a lot if the camera can pan and tilt on these cranes. The answer is yes and no. I typically operate the *Killer's Kiss* from the camera end with the camera mounted on a fluid head. So you'd be physically moving the camera as you would if it were on a tripod. The *Big Combo* has a static mount and a tilt mount, as does the *Double Indemnity*. It's very difficult to build a system that allows you to pan and tilt the camera remotely, but there are a few companies that make motorized pan and tilt heads that you can put on these cranes (very expensive!).

In Chapter 18, you'll find helpful hints for working with a crane. This applies to all the cranes in this book, so read it!

The one is very easy to make. I think if you can open a jar of peanut butter, you can build this crane. You don't even have to drill into metal for this one! Tons of film schools all around the world have built this one.

You'll have a couple of choices in the counterweight arm for the *Killer's Kiss*, so go through the plans carefully!

This is a much longer crane that has a static mount and a tilt mount. It's more difficult to build than the *Killer's Kiss*, but is still quite easy.

This uses a different type of mounting system. But if you live in say, the United Kingdom or Australia, you won't have a choice! Don't worry, it is still a pretty easy crane to build and breaks down into smaller bits for easy hauling.

Important stuff here like safety and attaching a monitor.

A quick and easy way to make a rig to haul all those weights around.

The *Killer's Kiss* Crane

This crane is made out of plumbing pipe and is super fast and easy to make. It's a perfect complement to the *Dark Passage* dolly. On cameras over 7 lbs, you can get a little vibration at the end of a boom up or down. But since you typically operated this crane from the camera end, either by holding the camera or fluid head *or* the top or bottom boom, this vibration is eliminated. So no worries, really. Just to be clear; the vibration is very slight and is hardly a concern even if you operate the crane from the weight end.

There are two slightly different versions, the A version and the B version. Let's look at what makes them different before you go buy materials.

Version A has a longer counterweight pipe, and the weights stack on one vertical pipe. What the counterweight does is act as a counterweight to the camera. It's sort of like a playground teeter-totter. If a 100 lb child is on one end and a 50 lb child on the other, it's not going to be much fun. But if both children are 50 lbs, there will be a perfect balance, and they will be able to push each other up and down very easily. But if you move the center balance point toward one end of the teeter-totter, the child that is closest to the pivot point will have to be much heavier than the child on the opposite end to bring the teeter-totter into balance. Same with a crane—any crane. The longer the counterweight pipe is on the *Killer's Kiss*, the less weight you have to haul around because the pivot point between the counterweight and the camera has been shifted. The closer the weights get to that center pivot point, the more weight you have to add.

Version B uses a shorter pipe for the counterweight boom, with two horizontal pipes coming off a T to hold the weights. The advantage of a shorter pipe allows you to use your jib in tight places. The disadvantage is that you have to haul around more weights. And the heavier the crane is, the more problematic it can become with vibration, but as I mentioned, it's not a huge problem.

The other thing about Version B is that I'm using a big 2″ (50 mm) pipe attached to the dolly. If you have a smaller camera, under 5 lbs, you can use a 1″ (25 mm) pipe to attach it to the dolly in the same manner.

DOI: 10.1016/B978-0-240-81337-0.00015-X

Did you make a camera pedestal for your dolly from the Dolly Section? If so, you can use this 2" (50mm) pipe as a way to mount it to your dolly. (You'll notice as you build the rigs in this book that I try to cross-purpose tools and materials so that you don't have to haul as much to a shoot or spend a fortune on different tools and materials).

You can also use the tripod mount found in Chapter 16 to mount the *Killer's Kiss* to a surveyor's tripod (see Chapter 21 to find out how to adapt a surveyor's tripod into a cinema tripod). In other words: two cranes, one mount!

Hey, Dan! Which one do I build? I'm really confused.

No worries. Let's figure that out right now. First, how heavy is your camera? Keep in mind that on a shoot you may be putting all sorts of stuff on that camera; matt boxes, focus pullers, big fat batteries, a fluid head, a 35 mm lens adapter. Take a look at the very first photo at the beginning of this chapter. There is a ton of crap on that camera! So when I ask "how heavy is your camera?" I mean with everything you plan on using with it. You can easily double the weight of a camera without even thinking about it. And just so you know, even if you mount a heavy camera on a tiny 1" pipe, it's not the end of the world. In the first photo, that mass of camera is still being supported by a 1" (25 mm) pipe and a ton of sandbags

on the dolly. Was that the best for that camera? Heck no! But by operating from the camera end, it all worked just fine (although that *is* Hollywood cameraman Mike Ferris operating, which doesn't hurt!).

So, if your camera is under 5 lbs, you can easily support it with a tripod or a 1" (25 mm) pipe coming off the dolly with a 30" long counterweight boom. If you want to use a shorter 24" (60 cm) counterweight boom, it's a good idea to use a tripod or the 2" (50 mm) pipe coming up from the dolly.

If your camera is over 5 lbs with a short counterweight boom, you'll need a 2" (50 mm) pipe or a tripod. If you are using the longer counterweight boom, it's still a good idea to use a 2" (50 mm) pipe or tripod.

So Version A (that was in the first two editions of this book) will be for lighter cameras and Version B will be for the heavier stuff.

Materials List for *The Killer's Kiss* Crane

This section for the *Killer's Kiss* is going to be a little different than other plans in this book. Instead of giving you a straight materials list, we'll just build the thing step-by-step for the crane part. For the camera mount, we'll go back to the old way. Here's why: Over the years, I've gotten e-mails from filmmakers that couldn't find the exact lengths of pipe I used. That's perfectly fine as long as certain bits of pipe are the *same* length. I've been known to put the crane together in the hardware store to make sure I have all the right stuff. One day, a plumber looked at me and said "That makes no sense at all." I told him I lived in a house designed by M.C. Escher. He didn't get the joke.

If you're looking at the step-by-step photos, you'll just need to reach into the bin at the hardware store and pull that part, and it will be a lot less confusing if my lengths and the lengths available don't match. And you'll also know immediately if length even really matters; like the pipe that holds the weights. If they don't have a 6" pipe, but do have a 9" pipe, you'll know that in this case, it just doesn't matter how long it is, just so it's long enough.

With that in mind, and before we head off to the hardware store, let's look at what needs to be the same on either version of the crane.

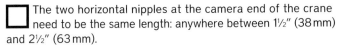

The two horizontal nipples at the camera end of the crane need to be the same length: anywhere between 1½″ (38 mm) and 2½″ (63 mm).

The two horizontal nipples at the center post need to be the same length: anywhere between 2″ (50 mm) and 3″ (76 mm).

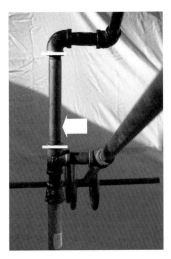

The pipe separating the two booms must be the same length as...

...all the little pieces put together at the camera end.

So the 1″ (25 mm) long (or so) nipples, the T fitting, and the union, when screwed together, equal the length of the one back piece. Feel free to mix different sizes of nipples until you can match the long single pipe.

If you are going to mount this crane on the dolly via the pipe method, you'll need to attach a 1″ (25 mm) or 2″ (50 mm) floor flange on top of the dolly deck. Please see the dolly section on how to do this.

One more thing about the plumbing pipe used on this crane: It doesn't matter whether you get the black or galvanized stuff, just make sure it has threads on each end.

For now, we are just going to screw all this together by hand. Some of the parts need to be tight and some need to be just a tiny bit loose. It's better to get an idea first about how this crane works, then take the crane apart and tighten down the bits that need to be tight with a pipe wrench.

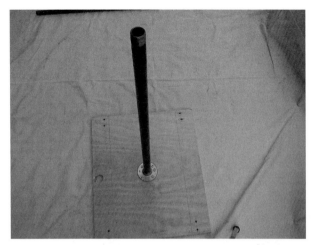

2 For Version A: 1" to ¾" (25 mm to 19 mm) reducing adapter.

Screw the reducing adapter onto the 1" (25 mm) pipe.

For Version B you will *also* need a 2" (50 mm) to 1" (25 mm) reducing adapter (unless you can find a 2" [50 mm] to ¾" [19 mm] reducing adapter; I've never been able to find one).

Screw the 2" (50 mm) to 1" (25 mm) reducing adapter onto the 2" (50 mm) pipe. Then screw a ¾" (19 mm) to 1" (25 mm) long nipple into the top of the adapter. Next, screw a 1" (25 mm) to ¾" (19 mm) reducing adapter onto the nipple. And finally a ¾" (19 mm) diameter by ¾" (19 mm) long nipple into the top of the second reducing adapter. All we are trying to do here is go from a 2" (50 mm) pipe down to a ¾" (19 mm) pipe.

Until I tell you otherwise, everything from this point is for both A and B versions.

1 On Version A, this piece is the pipe that comes up from the dolly. It can be 1" (25 mm) plumbing pipe by 36" (1 meter) long. (This is only if you're going to mount the crane on the dolly in this fashion.) Get a 6" to 12" (15 to 30 cm) long pipe for tripod mounting. On Version B for heavier cameras, you'll need to get a 2" (50 mm) diameter pipe by 36" (1 meter) long. You'll probably need to get the hardware store to cut and thread a 2" (50 mm) pipe, so if you don't see it in their bins, be sure to ask.

Screw this piece onto the floor flange on the deck of the dolly.

3 Screw a ¾" (19 mm) T fitting onto the nipple with the bottom of the T pointing to one side.

4 Next, let's figure out how long our rear pipe needs to be by putting together the camera end connections. All of these pieces are ¾" (19 mm) in diameter. Starting at the bottom: find the shortest nipple you can, hopefully under 1" (25 mm). Next screw that into a T fitting with the bottom of the T pointing to one side. Next, screw another short nipple into the top of the T. Then screw a union fitting onto that. And finally, screw another short nipple into the top of the union.

Now find one ¾" (19 mm) nipple that is as long as all the bits screwed together.

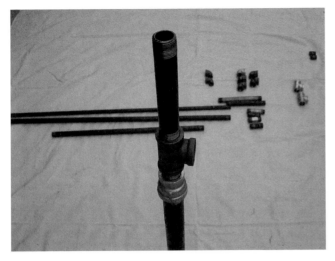

5 OK, back to the crane. Screw that long piece onto the top of the T.

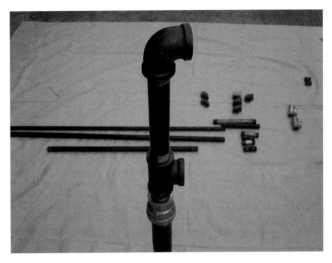

6 Screw a 90° elbow on top of that. Make sure that the mouth of the elbow is pointing the same direction as the T fitting below it.

7 Screw a 2½″ (63 mm) nipple into the elbow. It doesn't *have* to be 2½″ (63 mm); it can be less. It's not a good idea to go much longer though.

8 Screw another 2½″ (63 mm) nipple into the T. This is one of those points that this nipple and the one you just put in above it have to be the same length!

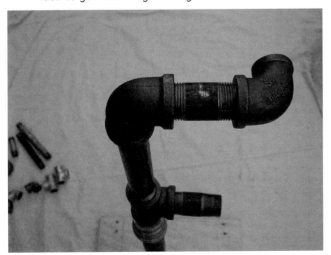

9 Screw a ¾″ to ½″ (19 mm to 14 mm) reducing elbows onto the top nipple.

10 Screw a ¾″ (19 mm) T onto the bottom nipple.

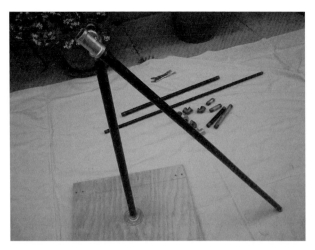

11 Screw a ¾" by 48" (19 mm by 1.23 meter) long pipe into the bottom T fitting.

12 Screw a ½" by 48" (14 mm by 1.23 meter) long pipe into the top elbow. This pipe has to be as long as the pipe below it! So if you used, say, a 40" pipe in Step 11, you have to use a 40" pipe here as well. Remember, too, that you put a reducing elbow from ¾" to ½" on top to take a ½" pipe.

13 Take a ½" to ¾" (14 mm to 19 mm) reduction elbow and screw it to the end of the ½" (14 mm) bar that is screwed into the top elbow.

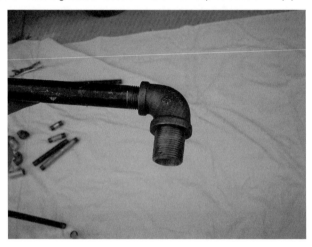

14 Add a ¾" (19 mm) long nipple to that elbow.

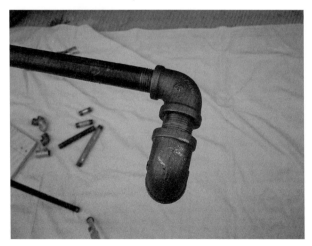

15 Add an elbow to that nipple. Are all of your bits pointed in the same direction as mine?

Here's a front view.

Killer Camera Rigs That You Can Build

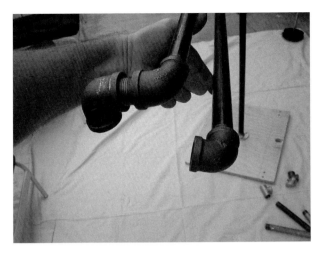

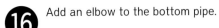

16 Add an elbow to the bottom pipe.

17 Then another nipple into that. This nipple *must* be the same length as the one you put in the top elbow.

18 Then add another elbow pointing up.

19 Remember all the front bits screwed together? Grab that now.

Unscrew the big bolt looking thing on the union. Now you'll have two pieces. Screw the top nipple above the union into the elbow coming off the top pipe on your crane. Next, screw the bottom nipple below the T into the elbow coming off the bottom pipe. (Actually, it makes no difference what part of the union pieces you make the "top" and what you make the "bottom." If you flip it so the T is below the union, your camera will be able to get just a tiny bit closer to the ground.)

20 Screw the union back together.

21 Screw a 9" (23 cm) long nipple into the T. This can be between 8" and 10" if you can't find a 9" nipple. Some of you may have noticed that the union joint disappeared from this photo. Don't panic! This photo is from the second edition of the book, when I didn't use a union. You don't have to use one either, it's just *so* much easier if you do!

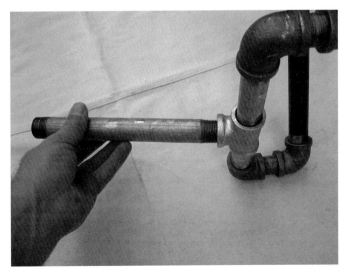

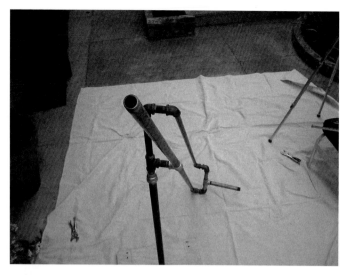

 OK, let's move to the back of the crane.

If you're making Version A:

Take a 30" (76 cm) pipe and screw it tightly into the T coming off the center column.

If you're making Version B:

Use a 24" (60 cm) long pipe.

 If you're making Version A:

Screw an elbow on the end of the 30" long pipe.

If you're making Version B:

Screw a T onto the end.

 If you're making Version A:

Add a 6" (152 mm) pipe onto the elbow. (Pointing "up" please! Because as you can see, you'll be stacking weights on here later!)

If you're making Version B:

Add a 6" (152 mm) long pipe to each side of the T fitting. If they don't have a 6" long nipple, you can go longer. By the way, the two big knobs holding the weights together is a PVC pressure fitting cut in two I was trying out. I found them too difficult to get off and on, but if you'd like to try them, feel free!

Now, before we make the camera plate for this thing, I need you to do something. Grab the boom arms and move the crane up and down. Don't put any weights on it yet. This crane works by rotating on the threads of the nipples. Every joint that does *not* move on these nipples needs to be tight! For every part that *does* move, do this: tighten the nipple by hand all the way in, then unscrew it one turn. Take a look at the following photos.

Killer Camera Rigs That You Can Build

 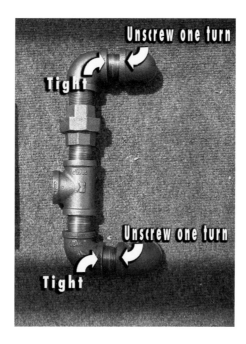 

If you've got a stack of reducers and nipples coming from the 2" (50 mm) pipe, pick one point that is unscrewed one turn and tighten down the rest. I tend to keep where the crane attaches to the top nipple of this stack loose one turn.

Got it? Now I'm going to make you take the rig apart and tighten everything that needs to be tightened with a wrench. It's a drag, I know, but it is really the best way to go about

it. But *before* you do all the tearing apart and reassembling of the crane, make the camera plate for it. It will be much easier to do fine adjustments once you have a camera plate on there.

OK, back to the way we normally do things. We're now going to build the camera plate so you can mount a camera or fluid head to your crane.

Materials List for the Camera Plate for the *Killer's Kiss* Crane

☐ ½" to ¾" (14 mm to 19 mm) thick piece of plywood around 7" by 9" (178 mm by 23 cm).

☐ (2) ¾" to 1" (19 mm–25 mm) grounding clamps. You'll find these in the electrical department. The bolt below replaces the bolts that come with the clamp—make sure you find ones that fit. They are usually ¼" (7 mm) bolts.

☐ (4) 1 ¾" (44 mm) long bolt with nut. These bolts replace the bolts that are in the grounding clamp above. I'm using a ½" piece of plywood for the camera base. If you're using a ¾" (19 mm) thick plywood, add ¼" (7 mm) to the length of this bolt.

☐ Mouse pad or cork for padding for your camera plate. You can use any kind of rubber or nonskid mat.

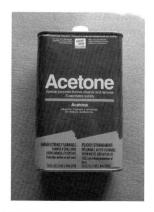

☐ Acetone. The pipes are pretty filthy as you may have discovered. It's a really good idea to clean them with a little acetone—especially if you plan on painting the crane later.

☐ Glue of some kind. This is to glue the padding to the camera plate. Hot glue, spray adhesive, or even wood glue will do the job.

☐ Baby powder. Since this is great for silencing squeaky dolly wheels, I'll assume you have some.

☐ (1) conduit hanger if you're making Version A; (2) conduit hangers if you're making Version B. These aren't for the camera plate, but make sure your weights stay and don't rattle during a shot. These need to be ¾" (or #2 conduit hangers).

Tools List for the Camera Plate for the *Killer's Kiss* Crane

☐ A drill.

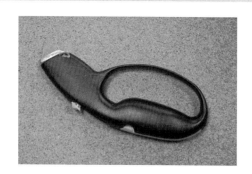

☐ A utility knife.

☐ ⁵⁄₁₆" (8 mm) drill bit.

☐ ¼" (7 mm) drill bit.

Killer Camera Rigs That You Can Build

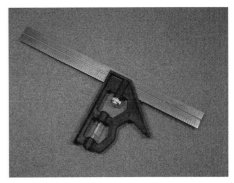

☐ Screwdriver. Get a head that matches the screws you bought (usually Philips).

☐ Channel locks or vice grip pliers.

☐ A ½" (14 mm) grommet kit. We'll only be using the hole punch part of the kit. This is a great tool for punching holes in padding for the camera plate, and these kits are so inexpensive, that it's well worth it.

☐ Combination square.

Let's Build It!

ATTACHING THE GROUNDING CLAMPS

1 The goal here is to mount the grounding clamps in the middle of the plywood so that we can run the ¾" pipe through them.

Draw a line down the middle of the length of the plywood.

Center the grounding clamp on that line, about 1" (25 mm) in from the edge of the plywood. Mark where the bolts from the grounding clamp come into contact with the plywood. Make sure your grounding clamp is square with the edge of the plywood.

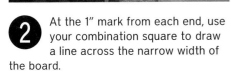

2 At the 1" mark from each end, use your combination square to draw a line across the narrow width of the board.

Adjust your combination square to run down the length of the plywood. Line the straight edge up with the mark you made where the grounding clamp bolt met the wood and draw a line across the four marks that represent the bolt placement.

You should end up with four points to drill your holes for the grounding clamp bolts.

3 Now let's figure out where we can drill some holes to mount our camera or fluid head. Frankly, I'm going a little overboard here, because I use a lot of different cameras. If you're going to be using the same camera, all you need to do is to make sure that you have enough room between the crane and your mounting hole. You don't want your camera so close to the crane that it rubs up against it, or if you're using a fluid head, that you have enough room between the crane and the base of the head to be able to mount it. With that in mind, one or two mounting holes near the center of the platform is plenty.

Measure halfway down the length of the plywood, and use your combo square to draw a line across the plywood. We'll be putting some holes along this line.

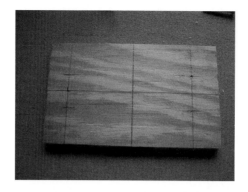

Since it would be difficult to get a bolt up through the plywood to mount your camera where there's this big pipe in the way, it would be pointless to drill holes there. So lay the 9" (23 cm) long pipe down the center of the plywood.

You can put as many camera mount holes as you want. Use the ¼" (7mm) drill bit for the four grounding clamp holes. Use the ⁵/₁₆" (8mm) bit for all the rest (camera mounting screws are ¼" [7mm], but fluid head bolts are larger, so it's a good idea just to make them big enough in the first place).

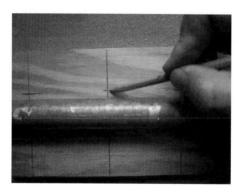

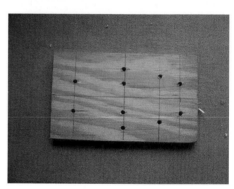

On each side of the pipe, make a couple of marks on the center line. Since these are for the camera bolts to hold the camera to the platform, make sure they are just far enough away from the pipe so you'll have room to screw a screw or twist a bolt.

4 Look on top of your grounding clamps. There are a couple of little screws holding a little clamp. You don't need these, so just take 'em off.

Take out the bolts that came with the grounding clamp and replace them with the longer ones.

Run the pipe through the grounding clamps.

Then run the bolts up through the holes you drill for them.

Killer Camera Rigs That You Can Build

Add the nuts. Make sure that the bolts don't extend too far above the nut once you tighten the nuts down. If you have an extra bolt, you can use a hacksaw to cut off the end of the bolt. Don't worry about the nuts making an uneven surface. The padding will take care of that.

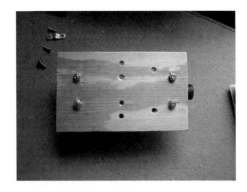

ADDING THE PADDING

Now we need to figure out where to make the holes in the mouse pad to match the holes in the camera plate. A good way to do this is to sprinkle some baby powder into the holes and carefully lift off the camera plate from the pad. Alternatively, you can use a drill bit to poke little marks where each hole is.

5 Take all the hardware off your camera plate. If you're using a mouse pad for padding, you can rip the cloth cover off of it if you'd like. Lay the camera plate on the mouse pad. The pad probably won't be big enough to cover the entire surface; that's OK.

I overdid it a little with the baby powder so you could see it clearly. Where each pile of baby powder is, put the punch from the grommet kit over it and punch a hole in the padding by thwacking the punch with a hammer.

Follow the directions on whatever adhesive you're using to glue the pad to the plywood. Make sure you carefully line up the holes on the pad with the holes in the plywood.

Once it's dry, trim off the excess padding and reattach the pipe and grounding clamps.

ASSEMBLING THE CRANE... AGAIN

 6 Clean all the pipe with some acetone. We'll be using a lot of acetone, so it's a good idea to wear rubber gloves.

Reassemble the crane making sure that the pieces that need to be a little loose are just that, and the pieces that need to be tight are tight.

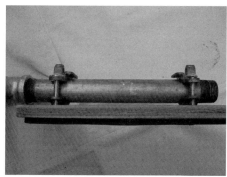

When you get to the camera plate pipe, screw it in tight. If your camera plate ends up in an awkward position, loosen the nuts on the grounding clamp and adjust it so that it is perfectly level, then tighten it down in that position.

Add just enough weights on the back until the camera end floats up a bit. If you put too much weight, the crane will go to its highest point and stop. You want it to stop midway.

Weight Warning: I used to never have this problem when the pipe was made in America. Now that it is mostly coming from China, I see this all the time: sometimes the weights don't fit on the ¾" (19mm) diameter pipe (that's not a comment on either country, it's just the way it is). If you find that your weights don't quite fit on the pipe, it's an easy fix:

This is a little grinding stone that fits into a drill. Make sure you get one that is smaller than the hole on the weight. They are really cheap, so you might pick up a couple.

Stick the stone in the hole of the weight and grind down the sides a bit. It really doesn't take much.

Sometimes, just grinding off the paint from the hole will allow it to fit.

Once you have the weights on your rig, push the conduit hanger up against the weights, then tighten the screw down with a screwdriver.

ADJUSTING THE CRANE

Since everything is connected by threads, you might find that the crane is out of whack. I've greatly exaggerated the "out of whackness" to get the point across. (In fact, if your pipe is not tight enough, the crane will fold in on itself. Make sure everything is nice and tight).

Simply grab the top and bottom booms, and push one boom while pulling the other until the camera platform is level.

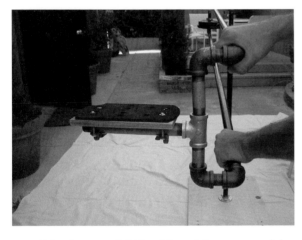

It's a good idea to use a fluid level to get the camera plate perfect. Keep in mind that the dolly or tripod you are using is level *before* you level the camera plate!

If you try and try, and still can't level the camera plate, you still have an option; remove the top of the grounding clamp, run the bolts down through the top of the camera plate, and tighten the bottom part of the grounding clamp against the pipe. This will allow you to use a shim in-between the pipe and the bottom of the camera plate. There is no shame in doing this. You can buy camera shims by the truckload at grip supply houses. The pros use them, so you can too.

Using your New Crane

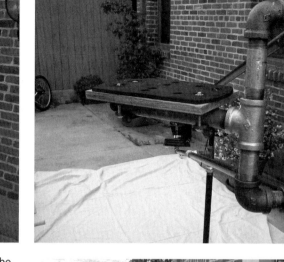

One of the great advantages of this crane is that you can tilt the camera bracket on the threads of the pipe and it will stay at that angle throughout the move.

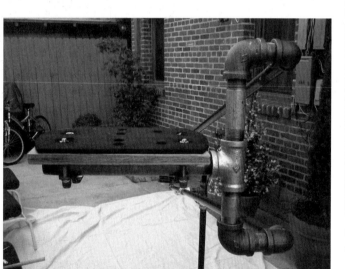

Or you can go along the horizontal axis (something most cranes can't do).

Or, like all the cranes in this book, you can attach a fluid head. This is a small camera with a small fluid head, but as you saw in the first photo of this chapter, you can go big!

Before using your crane, please read Chapter 18, *Working with a Crane*.

Killer Camera Rigs That You Can Build

The *Big Combo* Crane

I like this crane a lot, if I do say so myself. If you want something fairly long, this is a good way to go. You can make the bottom boom up to 18' if you're adapting a surveyor's tripod to hold the thing. It has two different mounts: a static mount that you can bolt a fluid head to, and a tilt mount that allows you to tilt the camera up or down, which can be found in the *Make It Groovy* part of this chapter. If you want even more control, there are a few companies out there that make motorized pan and tilt mounts that you can mount on this crane. They are expensive though, around $1,500.

I like having a tripod devoted to the crane. There is no need to spend a fortune on one. I'm using a surveyor's tripod, but you'll need to butch it up. (See plans in Chapter 21 for the *Third Man* tripod.) Surveyor's tripods are pretty cheap—around $80—and work well for these lighter rigs. Just make sure the legs are held down by a spreader and sand bags and you're good to go. It's a good idea to get a surveyor's tripod before you build the crane so you'll have something to put it on. I'm using a Berger Surveyor's tripod that can be found in most large home centers.

To mount the crane to a tripod, there is a very easy-to-make mount in this chapter. The mount works by using threaded pipe that screws into a flange on the tripod. The crane moves to the left or right by riding on these threads, and it works great! Unfortunately, if your country doesn't use this kind of plumbing pipe (the United Kingdom and Australia don't) you won't be able to make this mount. All is not lost, though; I've designed another mount for the last crane in this section. It's a little more difficult to make and a little more expensive, but certainly not out of reach.

Important: Before starting work on building this crane, please read the appendix, *Working with Metal*!

After you've built the *Big Combo* crane, please take time to read Chapter 18, *Working with a Crane*.

DOI: 10.1016/B978-0-240-81337-0.00016-1

Materials List for the *Big Combo* Crane

I've broken down the materials list a bit so you don't have to buy all this stuff at once if you don't want to. The first chunk is for the body of the crane bits. Then the tripod mounting parts. Then the weight end, and so on.

Materials for the Crane Body

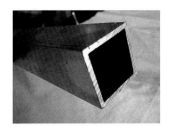

☐ 1" (25 mm) diameter × 24" (60 cm) long plumbing pipe with threaded ends.

☐ A length of rectangle or square aluminum tube. This is the bottom part of the boom and supports the full weight. This one is ⅛" (3 mm) thick and 1" × 1 ½" × 9' (25 mm × 38 mm × 2.7 meters). Nine (2.7 meters) or 10' (3 meters) long is plenty, but if you want to make a longer one, you might get aluminum that is more of a rectangle like 1" × 3", or thicker stuff if you're making a crane that is closer to 15'. Don't go much smaller than these width measurements unless you're making a very short one, otherwise it will bounce.

Note: The bolt lengths in these plans are based on the width of my aluminum of 1" (25 mm). If your aluminum is 1 ½" (38 mm) for example, plan accordingly.

☐ A length of square or rectangle aluminum tube. This is the top part of the boom and supports no weight. To give you an idea, the aluminum tube on the left in the photo is the top boom. On the right is the bottom boom listed earlier. The top one keeps your lens on the same plane as you boom up or down. This one is 1" × 1" (25 mm × 25 mm) square aluminum tube and is only ¹⁄₁₆" (1.5 mm) thick. Make it easy on yourself and make sure the width (1" (25 mm) in this case) on this arm is the same as the width on the bottom arm—1" (25 mm). You can do it with different widths, it just takes a little futzing to get them exactly even on assembly. When you're done, this piece will be shorter than the bottom boom arm, but it's a good idea for now to get a piece that is as long as your bottom boom arm and cut it later. I can't tell you how long it needs to be, because I don't know how big a boom you're making and where you'll be putting your pivot point.

☐ Channel aluminum about 30" (76 cm) long and ¹⁄₁₆" (1.5 mm) to ⅛" (3 mm) thick or better. The channel on this piece must be slightly wider than the width of your boom arms. If your boom arm is 1" wide, the channel needs to be at least 1⅛" wide. The sides of the channel need to be at least 1 ½". And 2" will give you more room to work. The booms have to have room to move inside this channel, and to understand how that works, you'll need to read the chapter before buying these materials.

Killer Camera Rigs That You Can Build

☐ *Option*: If you can't find channel aluminum, angle (L-shaped) aluminum will work fine—heck, maybe even better. If you use angle aluminum, get stuff that is ⅛" thick or better.

☐ ⁵⁄₁₆" (8 mm) bolts in these lengths (or longer). We'll be chopping them off if they're too long, so don't worry about exact lengths on any of the bolts. The length will also depend on the thickness of your aluminum bar. (2) 2¼" (57 mm), (1) 2" (50 mm), (1) 1½" (38 mm), (1) 3½" (89 mm).

☐ ½" (14 mm) bolts in these lengths (or longer): (1) ½" (14 mm), (1) 4" (100 mm).

☐ (12) Nylon washers. Get two to fit the ½" (14 mm) bolt, ⁵⁄₁₆" (8 mm) on the rest.

☐ (5) ⁵⁄₁₆" (8 mm) lock nuts, (2) ½" (14 mm) lock nuts. Lock nuts have a little nylon ring at the top of the nut that keeps them in place.

☐ (1) 3" (76 mm) Simpsons Strong Tie L-bracket.

Materials for the Tripod Mount

☐ (4) ¼" nuts (7 mm).

☐ (1) floor flange for 1" (25 mm) pipe.

☐ (4) ¼" × 1" (7 mm × 25 mm) long bolts. These attach the flange to the plywood.

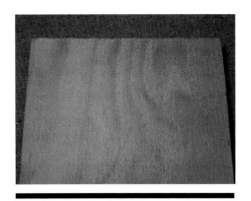

☐ ¾" (19 mm) thick plywood. A 4" (100 mm) square.

☐ (1) bolt ½" × 3" (14 mm × 76 mm) or a ⁵⁄₁₆" (8 mm) bolt. This mounts the crane plate to the tripod. ½" (14 mm) is best; ⁵⁄₁₆" (8 mm) is the absolute minimum. If the bottom boom of your crane is over 10' long, use a ½" bolt.

☐ Wing nut for holding your mounting plate to the tripod. ⁵⁄₁₆" (8 mm) to ½" (14 mm), depending on how big a bolt you get. Again, a ½" (14 mm) is best, and ⁵⁄₁₆" (8 mm) is the absolute minimum. If the bottom boom of your crane is over 10' long, use a ½" bolt.

☐ An assortment of washers: (2) fender washers (fender washers look like regular washers, except the hole is smaller), a large mean lookin' washer (take a look at how this mounts on a surveyor's tripod before buying this big one), and a regular washer that is just small enough to fit inside the pipe hole on the floor flange.

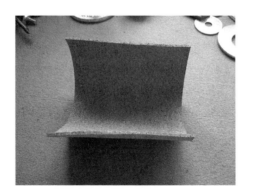

☐ A small square of thin cork. This will be glued to the 4" × 4" plywood, so get some at least that large. A big roll of this stuff is really cheap, and you can use it for other things.

☐ (1) ½" (14 mm) jam nut. Jam nuts are narrower than regular nuts.

Materials for the Weight End

☐ 1″ OD (25 mm) aluminum tube, 12″ to 24″ (30–60 cm) long (12″ is minimum). If you've made the stabilizer, you've got this already. You can also use an electrical conduit: Take a weight to the hardware store and find the size that fits into the hole on the weight exactly.

☐ An assortment of weights, around 20 lbs total. This is just a good start. Depending on where you put your pivot hole, you could need more or a little less. Better to get a bunch of lighter ones than one heavy one.

☐ (2) Conduit hangers. This will hold your weights steady. Get hangers for ¾″ to 1″ pipe (these are smaller than the stabilizer ones). If you live outside North America, you'll have to hunt around for something similar. You can do it!

☐ Cotter pin with a Clevis pin. These come in the same package, about 2″ to 3″ (50 mm–76 mm) long and around ⁵⁄₁₆″ (8 mm) diameter. This goes through the above aluminum tube.

☐ A nylon spacer, about ¾″ to 1″ (19–25 mm) long. This goes at the end of your cotter pin. If you can't find a spacer, that's OK. You can bunch up five or six washers.

Tools list for *The Big Combo* Crane

☐ A good assortment of clamps—at least four of the style here would be helpful.

☐ A combination square.

☐ A drill; we'll be drilling metal, so no battery operated drill here! Get one with a cord and variable speed ability.

☐ Drill bits. You'll need the following: ½" (14mm) bit, ⅛" (3mm) bit, and 5/16" (8mm) bit.

☐ Locking pliers.

☐ Safety glasses. *Always* use these when drilling into metal. I can't tell you how many times I've had a little metal shard hit these glasses. Avoid blindness: use 'em.

☐ Cutting oil. As you learned in the appendix, *Working with Metal*, you use this when drilling into metal. You might want to pick up a little oil can to put it in.

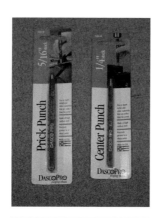

☐ Center punch and prick punch. *Officially,* a center punch is used to put a small dimple in metal where you're going to drill a hole. You have to have this or your drill bit will "walk" across the metal, and that's not good at all. The prick punch scratches into the metal for marking (a pencil comes off too easily). *Unofficially,* I use these two tools interchangeably. If you want to do things "right," buy both. If you don't have the extra $4, just buy one or the other.

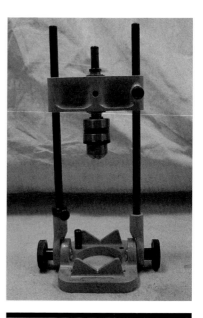

☐ If you don't have a drill press, I really encourage you to get one of these. It's a handy drill guide, and will keep your holes straight and true—very important in this type of work. It also has a V in its base to hold a round piece of pipe for perfect center drilling (something we do a lot around here). It runs about $35. A good investment if you build more than one project in this book. On the other hand, a pretty decent drill press can be found for around $100 and is much more useful if you decide to build a lot of these projects.

☐ Vise. Gotta have it. Mount it on your bench or a heavy piece of plywood.

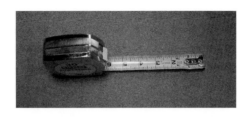

☐ A tape measure.

☐ Hacksaw. Get extra blades that have 14 to 16 teeth per inch. (A soft metal like aluminum doesn't like any more than 16 teeth, 18 per inch on the outside.)

☐ A hammer.

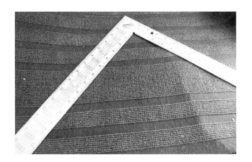

☐ A framing square. Helpful, but not totally necessary.

Let's Build It!

1 Take your bottom boom arm and the top control arm and clamp them side by side. By clamping them together, we can mark for the holes that need to be drilled at the same time, since all the holes must be in the same position on the top and bottom booms.

First, let's take a look into the future; see the holes at the end of both booms in the photo? We'll be marking where to drill those holes.

There. Now we're going to do the same thing for the center support holes that the entire crane pivots on, so leave your pieces clamped together.

On my two boom pieces, I'm going to drill a hole as close to the edge as I can, without compromising the strength of the aluminum. So with that in mind, use your square to draw a line straight across the two pieces about ¼" (7 mm) from the end. Be aware that if your aluminum channel has short sides or you are using a large rectangle for your bottom boom, that these holes may be too far in for the booms to rotate freely without hitting the bottom of the channel when you operate the crane. We'll figure that out later. Just know that you *might* have to trim a bit off the end of your booms to get the holes closer to the edge. It's a really easy fix.

2 In the photo, the lower boom is longer than the top boom. It extends beyond the center column, and counterweights go on the end of it. Take a close look at the photo; you'll see two holes in the bottom boom. I found that I wanted a little more reach out the crane, so I set the pivot hole back toward the weight end about 6" from where I decided to put it the first time. If I had put it back 12" instead of 6", that would almost *double* the amount of weight I need to add to the back of the crane! That's a lot of weight to haul to a shoot! So the pivot hole placement is important, but it isn't a do-or-die situation either. You can always drill another hole.

Let's talk a little about where to put the holes for the center column. As a rule, you want to put the center support at about ⅓ the length of your boom. On our 9' (2.75 meters) boom, that would be at 3' (91 cm) from the *weight end*. This is a good general purpose point, but I want just a little more reach for my camera, so I'm going to back up to 2' 6" (76 cm). If you have a camera more the 7 lbs, I wouldn't recommend backing up more than this. Also, the farther you are from dead center, the more weight you're going to have to haul around.

All of this is relative. If you have a 2-lb camera, you can get away with a lot more reach on the boom end than if you have a 10-lb camera. If you're using a 12' (3.6 meter) boom arm, staying at the ⅓ mark is a very good idea regardless. Or if you have a

big camera and don't want to carry a bunch of weight around, even a little more toward dead center would be a great idea.

In other words, give this some thought, and experiment a bit by clamping some weights at one end the same weight as the largest camera you'll use, and some counter weight at the other and lay it across some kind of support like a saw horse. Try different points along the boom to see what you can easily control. Of course, this isn't ideal, but it will give you some idea.

Killer Camera Rigs That You Can Build

3 So with all of that in mind, mark the booms for the center column. Measure from the opposite (what will be the weight) end and draw a line straight across both pieces as you did on the camera end. As you can see, I'm making my mark at 2′ 6″ (76 cm) from the back of the crane instead of the ⅓ mark of 3′ (91 cm).

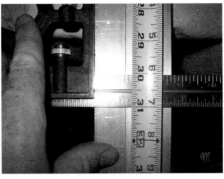

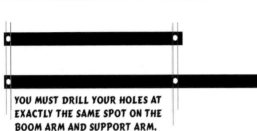

YOU MUST DRILL YOUR HOLES AT EXACTLY THE SAME SPOT ON THE BOOM ARM AND SUPPORT ARM.

4 Now you can unclamp the two arms from one another.

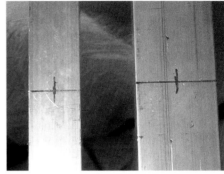

You should have two lines marked across each boom: the camera end, and the pivot point. At each of those lines, measure halfway across the width of the aluminum tube, and draw a line across each line you made earlier, forming a kind of cross.

5 Use your center punch to make a dimple on each of the four crosses.

The point of your drill bit goes in this little dimple to keep it from walking.

6 Drill the holes. You can do this by hand if you're sure you can go straight. Or if you bought the drill guide, this is a good time to use it. Ultimately, a drill press would make your life very easy here.

I'm using my drill guide, but I've modified it a bit by attaching it to a piece of plywood with

a big hole drilled in the center. Attaching it to the plywood gives me more surface for clamping, but you can use it without the plywood without too much trouble.

First, I'm going to use a scrap piece of aluminum the same thickness as my boom arm to support my drill guide.

Then I'll clamp the drill guide, the metal, everything, to my bench. You do *not* want anything moving when you start to drill. For the holes on the camera end of both the top boom and the bottom boom, I'm going to use a ⁵⁄₁₆″ bit. Add a little lubricant to the dimples and drill your holes.

Of course you want to get a bit that is rated for metal, and the more you spend on the bit, the easier drilling and longer lasting it will be. Make sure you get the point of the bit into the dimple you made.

Here are the two holes for the camera end. Next we'll do the holes for the center column.

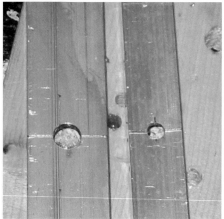

Do these just like the others: Clamp your work, use lubricant, and get the point of the bit in the dimple. For the big boom arm, use a big ½" (14 mm) drill bit. For the smaller top support arm, a ⁵⁄₁₆" (8 mm) bit will do.

Make sure your holes are even with one another by running a bolt through both sets of holes. (In this photo, I've already cut my top boom arm. Feel free to wait until you're sure you've got your pivot holes in the right place.)

Can you get a bolt through both sets of holes with the booms side-by-side? If so, great. If not, leave the bolt in the middle hole, and cut the aluminum tube off at the end trimming off the camera end holes and drill those end holes again.

7 If you're fairly sure that you won't be moving your pivot hole back toward the weight end later, you can trim the top boom now. Cut off the excess from the top arm a few inches behind the hole for the center column. You don't need this piece of aluminum to run the entire length of the bottom main arm.

8 Now let's make the part that will keep your camera on the same plane as we boom up and down.

Grab your piece of channel aluminum.

The channel has to be big enough to fit around the width of your boom arm with a little breathing room. The measurements for my channel aluminum are 1½" (38 mm) deep and 1½" (38 mm) wide. You really don't want to go smaller than this if you have the same boom measurements as I do; 2" (50 mm) sides are plenty deep.

Killer Camera Rigs That You Can Build

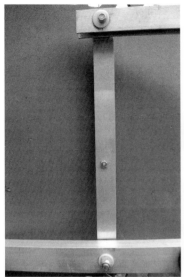

The amount of space that we keep between the top boom arm apart from the bottom boom arm dictates how high you can boom before the two arms touch. The wider the placement, the higher you go (not withstanding other factors like tripod height and boom length). Don't space your arms any closer than 8" or so. And don't go too far apart unless you have one massive tripod to hold your camera going into the stratosphere. Keeping the arms at 12" (30 cm) apart is perfect.

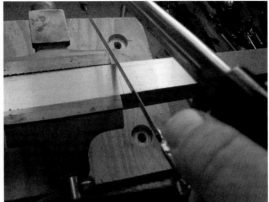

So at 12" (30 cm) apart, I'm only going to need about a 13" (33 cm) length of aluminum channel. In other words just add an inch to the spacing you want between the top and bottom arm. If you're building one just like mine, cut that baby at 13" (33 cm).

9 Now we need to drill some more holes to attach the boom arms to the aluminum channel that will hold your camera. If you'll take a close look at the photo, you'll see that our mark is *not* dead center this time. The reason for this is to leave the boom arms enough room at the front of the channel to be able to move freely as we boom up and down.

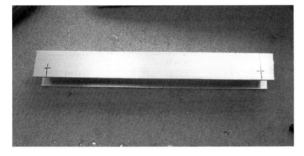

I've put my mark ½" (14 mm) in from the open edge of the channel. I've also gone down ½" (14 mm) from the end. Do the same on the other end as well, *making sure the marks are in perfect alignment to one another.*

Use your prick punch to put dimples in these marks. Since you'll be hammering at the edge of the channel, you might want to put a piece of wood inside the channel to support it while you are thwacking it with a hammer. You don't want to bend it.

You should be an old hand at drilling in aluminum by now. Remember: Wear safety glasses, set the work on a piece of scrap wood, clamp everything, add a little oil to the dimple, and drill away. For the holes on the channel, use a 5/16" (8 mm) bit. As in life, make sure you go straight and true.

Once your holes are done, run a bolt through them to make sure it's straight. If not, you've got to redrill some new ones. Sorry. Very Important!

If your holes are straight, take your boom arms and line up the end holes with the holes you just drilled in the channel. Make sure you've got enough room to pivot the arm without hitting the front of the channel.

10 Grab what's left of your aluminum channel (should be about 17"—it can be as long as 20"; if it's longer than 20", you should probably cut the excess off) and set it next to the channel aluminum you just drilled.

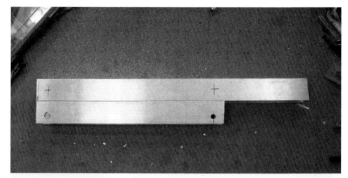

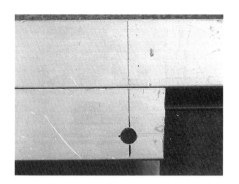

Take your combination square and line up the straight edge with the old line you made on the finished front piece and make a new line across the longer piece of channel. Do this on both holes. This is why it's important to use a prick punch for marking.

Next measure halfway across the piece and put your cross mark. Next, hammer your dimple. Do this on both ends.

For the mark at one end of the channel (we'll consider this the top) drill ⁵⁄₁₆" (8 mm) hole. For the mark you made that will fall about 12" below that, drill a ½" (14 mm) hole, but take a look at this first:

When you have a big drill bit like a ½", it might be a good idea to drill a small pilot hole like the one in the photo. As the name suggests, this hole helps guide the larger bit, and makes getting things straight a little easier.

Once you have your perfect ½" (14 mm) and ⁵⁄₁₆" (8 mm) holes, drill another ⁵⁄₁₆" (8 mm) hole at the bottom. It doesn't have to line up with anything; we'll be using this to bolt the channel onto our center shaft.

11 Now we're going to bolt our channel aluminum onto a 1" (25 mm) diameter steel plumbing pipe. The pipe is used as a connector to the tripod, and to give the center column a little more strength. The crane will rotate left and right on the threads of the pipe, so don't bang them up by accident.

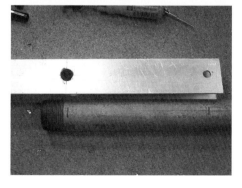

You'll need about 24" (61 cm) of the 1" (25 mm) pipe. Line the pipe up in the channel aluminum: the top of the pipe should be a little higher than the half inch hole in the channel at the point just below the pipe threads. We'll be drilling into the pipe, and we want a clean place on the pipe for that—not into the threads.

If the channel is a little snug for the pipe, take a hammer and pound the pipe down into the channel. Of course, pounding won't be necessary if you're using a wider channel or L-shaped aluminum for this.

Once you have the pipe pounded all the way in, you'll need to drill holes in it (if the pipe is loose in the channel, use clamps to keep it in place). Simply use the holes in the aluminum channel as your guide. The only difference here is this: drill through one side of the pipe, then flip it over and drill through the other. Obviously, use a ½″ (14 mm) bit on the ½″ hole and a 5⁄16″ (8 mm) bit on the 5⁄16″ hole. This is a harder metal than aluminum, so use a slower drill speed, plenty of lubricant (add more as you go), and sharp bits.

And there it is. You don't need to pull it back out of the channel like I did. This just makes it easier for you to see the holes in the pipe.

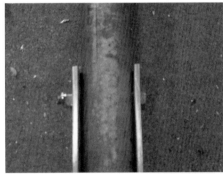

Put a 5⁄16″ bolt in the bottom hole and tighten it down with a lock nut.

THE BASE

12 You have to have a good-sized tripod, and a good-sized head plate on that tripod for a crane. That's why I like the butched up version of the surveyor's tripod as a cheap alternative. But if you've got a better tripod, by all means, use it!

Here's how to make a base for tripods of the surveyor variety. This is pretty much the same as mounting a floor flange on the deck of a dolly.

1. Cut a square block of ¾″ (19 mm) plywood about the size of the tripod base or larger.
2. Draw an X from corner to corner of the wood. The center of the X is the center of the board.
3. Take a 1″ (25 mm) floor flange and line it up dead center on the plywood. Mark on the board where the holes are on the flange.

4. Drill four holes to hold your bolts (don't use screws here!). Countersink the bottom side bolt holes. All countersinking does is get the head of the bolts flush with the surface of the plywood. You'll need a drill bit larger than the head of your bolt. Drill just deep enough into the plywood to get the head of your bolts just below the surface of the plywood and no deeper! I'm using carriage bolts. If you are using regular bolts, make sure to put a washer on the bolt before threading up through the hole.
5. At the center of the X drill a ½" (14 mm) hole. If you're using a ⁵⁄₁₆" bolt, drill a ⁵⁄₁₆" hole.
6. Run the bolts up through the plywood, and attach the floor flange with nuts.

Here's what you should have so far:

The pipe flange is bolted to the top of the plywood. If the bolts extend beyond the nut, take a hacksaw and cut them off.

On the bottom, the four bolts holding the flange should be countersunk below the surface of the plywood, and a hole in the middle for the bolt to hold the whole thing onto the tripod.

The next step is optional, but it's a really good idea. You'll need some cork or thin hobby foam. The thin cork from a cork roll is perfect. You may have already purchased this for some other mounts in the book. do not use a mouse pad for this part.

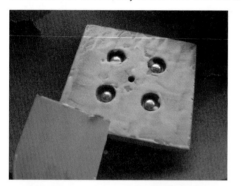

Spread some wood glue evenly over the base.

Weight it down and let it dry for a few hours.

Flip the flange unit over onto a sheet of cork.

Trim off the excess cork.

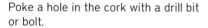

Poke a hole in the cork with a drill bit or bolt.

Drop a washer in the flange hole and run a bolt through.

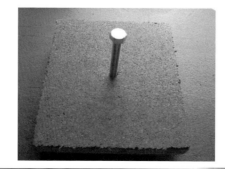

Killer Camera Rigs That You Can Build

Add a fender washer on the cork side.

Use a jam nut to attach the bolt to the base.

If you can't find a jam nut, don't use any nut at all. You need a narrow jam nut.

Turn over your tripod and look underneath. You'll see one of two things: If you're using a $5/16$" bolt for the crane mount, you probably left in that oval thing that looks a bit like a giant paper clip, or you took it out altogether. First, let's mount it with the "paper clip."

It is very helpful, well... necessary, to have a level that works in all directions. I found the "multilevel" at the home center and bought a few of them. I attached one of them to the top of the crane mount and you should too. You can also use a bubble level.

Normally, you'd screw this mount onto the threaded pipe that is the center column of your crane and tighten it down by hand. Then unscrew it one or two turns, and then mount it to your tripod. That's a little awkward for the first time you do it, so let's put it on without the crane attached so you can get an idea of how this mount works.

Run the platform bolt through there, add a washer or two, and tighten the whole thing down with a wing nut. Even though you can tighten the wing nut with your fingers, use pliers to get it super tight.

If you're using a $1/2$" (14 mm) bolt to mount your crane, it is too big to fit through the paper clip thing, so it's gone, baby, gone.

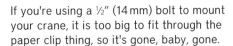

Instead, use a big washer. It has to be big enough to touch the edges of the hole in the tripod, with a hole big enough to take the $1/2$" bolt. I found this square steel washer that works great. I didn't have any trouble at all finding this washer, but if you do, you can take a thick (at least $1/4$" thick) piece of aluminum and drill a $1/2$" hole in it to make your own washer.

Take some pliers or vice grips and tighten the wing nut down.

Make sure the tripod is perfectly level and stays that way. And make sure the tripod is in a spreader (see how to make the Steel Trap Spreader in Chapter 23) at the very least. When you start using it for real, sandbag each leg of the tripod as well.

Now we'll loosely put the crane together, just to make sure everything is OK before we build all the mounts and weight holder for it. Screw the center support column in to the floor flange all the way, then unscrew it one turn.

Put a ½" (14mm) bolt through the bottom arm support hole and slide the large boom arm on to it. Don't worry about tightening anything down with nuts at this point, as we're going to be taking it apart soon. (I'm also using some extra long bolts here to make sure it doesn't slip while I'm moving it around.)

Take the large bottom boom and slip the ½" hole onto the bottom bolt.

Now move to the front of the crane with your aluminum channel. Set each boom inside the channel, line up the holes, and slip a bolt through each hole.

Slip a ⁵⁄₁₆" bolt through the upper hole on the center column, then slide the upper boom arm onto that bolt.

Now try lifting the crane or push down on the weight end forcing it to go up. Does it snag at any point going up? If so, one or both of your booms is catching at the front of the channel piece. Take a look. You might have to trim just a tiny bit off the front of each boom so that the booms clear the front of the channel aluminum. If it goes up smoothly, you're in business.

Try moving the crane to the left and right. It moves incredibly smoothly on the pipe threads, doesn't it? The other thing I like about the pipe threads is that the crane doesn't drift at all. It stays where you put it!

Take a look at the front bit. Does it stay on the same axis as you crane up and down? If so, good job. If not, your holes are off. Back to the drill press for you.

Killer Camera Rigs That You Can Build

13 OK. Back to the workshop. (You know, for the first two editions of this book the "workshop" was my kitchen. Yep, drills and hacksaws along side pots and pans. So if you live in New York City, all is not lost as long as you don't mind a little drill oil in your eggs.)

Now we need a way to put weights on the opposite end. The easy way, of course, is to drill a big hole in our large boom arm, put a huge bolt there, and throw the weights on it. But... I still have some of this 1" (25 mm) tube left over from the stabilizer project, and the weights I found at the sport shop have a hole that is just about perfect for the tube...

The problem is the tube won't fit inside the aluminum arm. Good thing I have a vise.

Stick the end of the tube in the vise and start squeezing. As long as it doesn't crimp, it'll be plenty strong enough. Squeeze it slowly until it fits inside the boom.

That's the ticket!

Add some washers or a nylon spacer onto the cotter pin. Slip it through the hole on the tube, then add the clip that came with the cotter pin.

Now, on the nonsqueezed end of the aluminum tube, drill a hole big enough for a cotter pin. Once again, I'm using a 5/16"(8 mm) pin, but a 1/4" (7 mm) will work too. This will keep the weights from sliding off the end if your conduit hanger fails.

Let's drill a hole through the back of the boom and through the round tube now stuck inside. Pretty much anywhere you'll drill through the round tube is fine, but near the back is best. Add a bolt with a lock nut. I used a 5/16"(8 mm) × 2" (50 mm) bolt here. That puppy is not going anywhere.

Use our friend from the stabilizer, the electrical conduit hanger, to keep the weights in place. Just slide it against them and tighten the nut. If you have two hangers, one on each side of the weights, that's the best, because you can then move the weights up or down the tube for fine-tuning adjustments.

The camera bracket. We're going to use a 3" (76mm) L-bracket to mount the camera on our crane. (Take a look in the section, "Make It Groovy," to give this bracket a little flare).

Arrange the L-bracket so that it just peeks over the top of the channel that goes on the front of the crane.

Mark the hole in the front of the aluminum channel and drill a ½" (14mm) hole.

Bolt the bracket on using a ½"(14mm) bolt about ½" to ¾" (14mm–19mm) long. Use a washer and lock nut on this one too.

Make sure the nut is on the front side.

Let's slap this thing together!

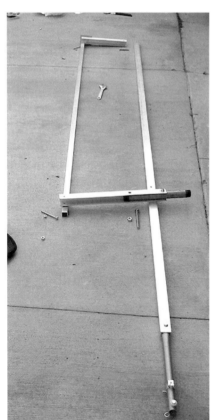

We're going to use nylon washers between all the moving parts: You don't want metal scraping against metal.

Put a bolt through the top of the support shaft and add a nylon washer.

Slip the top aluminum bar over the bolt, add another washer, and tighten on a stop nut.

15 Grab all your crane pieces and lay them out.

Do the same with the bottom boom arm.

Killer Camera Rigs That You Can Build

If you don't have a stop nut, make sure you use some Loctite or other thread-locking goo.

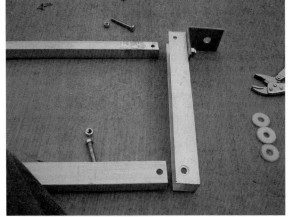

Do the same on the camera mount end, but this time put the bars inside the channel aluminum.

If you don't have enough room in the channel for two nylon washers, that's OK. Do the same on the bottom.

Now we need to make sure that the top and bottom bars are on the same plane. Take a big square and set it flush on the bottom bar. (Pay no attention to the cord for the tilt bar in this photo. We'll be getting to that.)

Does the edge of the square rest against the top bar like this?

Or does it look like there is a little gap? If there's a gap, you'll need to do a little adjusting.

Just add another washer or two to the top bar to move it out a bit until the framing square is resting against the top boom.

Screw your floor flange tripod mount onto the pipe that makes up the crane's support column. Remember; screw it on until it stops, then back off one turn.

Then mount the whole shebang onto your tripod. If you're using a surveyor's tripod, make sure you strengthen it by following the instructions elsewhere in this unbelievably fantastic book.

Did you level the tripod before attaching the crane? That's OK. This time, *before* you put any camera or weights on the crane, *make sure* it's level. Otherwise, things could get nasty in a hurry. By the way, if I didn't mention it before, an easy way to level the tripod is to put the crane mount on the tripod all by itself, then level it (of course, I'm assuming that you put this liquid multilevel or a bubble level on your tripod mount), then attach the mount to the crane.

Hey, it's really starting to look like something, isn't it? Let's take a look at our counterweight system.

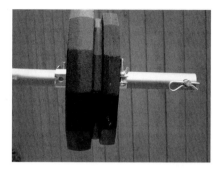

OK, here's what we have going on: On each side of the dumbbells I've put an electrical conduit hanger. If you built the Camera Stabilizer, you're already familiar with these babies. The only difference is that these are a little smaller to fit the smaller tube. These serve two purposes: to keep the weights jammed together so they don't clang around, and to allow you to move the weights as a group up or down the shaft for fine-tuning your balance.

Did you put the cotter and clevis in? It's there for safety. If the conduit hanger slips, this will keep your counterweights on the rig. Believe me, you *do not* want these weights slipping off the end and sending your very expensive camera crashing to the ground. I've seen it happen (not on one of my cranes of course)! Do not skip this step!!

Let's take it for a test drive. Put some weight on the front end (not your camera yet—better test it first). I'm just using a bunch of clamps, little weights, wrenches, and what-not. Just fly it around and put it through its paces. Make sure everything is hunky-dory before you stick a camera on there.

Once you've checked the movement, and everything is fine, take a hacksaw and cut off any bolts that aren't flush to the top of the bolt.

Keep in mind that you can add a fluid head to the camera mount instead of the camera directly. Whatever angle you put the camera at on the fluid head, it will stay at the angle throughout the shot.

Killer Camera Rigs That You Can Build

Make It Groovy

As you may have guessed by now, the crane you just made keeps the camera on the same plane. No tilting. For most people this is plenty of crane. Fact is, most commercially made booms in the $1000 to $3000 price range work this way. (Not too shabby for less than 200 bucks, huh?)

Dig a little deeper and for about another $25 investment and we'll put a tilt head on this puppy.

Here's what you'll need:

(2) 3" (76 mm) or larger garage door pulley. Some manufactures make them with holes, some don't. Try to find one with holes, or you'll have to drill some. This one is made by Prime Line.

(1) 3" (76 mm) Simpsons Strong Tie L-bracket. (Yep, that's two in all: there was one in the last section, remember?).

(1) Turn buckle. This one is 3/16", but anything up to 5/16" (8 mm) is just fine.

(4) ¼" (7 mm) flat or round head bolts × 1 5/16" (38 mm) long. These will go through the outer holes of the pulley. These measurements are for this pulley. Just try to find a bolt that doesn't wobble around in the hole.

(6) ¼" (7 mm) nuts for the preceding bolts.

(4) ¼" (7 mm) jam nuts (these also go on the preceding bolt). A jam nut is about half the thickness of a regular nut.

(2) Nylon spacers. These need to have a hole big enough to slip over the bolt and should be about ¾" (19 mm) long. You can also buy shorter ones and stack them.

Get a package of clothesline, the stuff that is plastic-coated with a wire core inside.

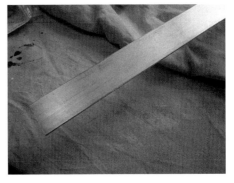

(1) flat piece of aluminum about 9" (23 cm) long × 1½" (38 mm) wide × ⅛" (3 mm) thick. These measurements aren't written in stone. This is going to be the arm to the tilt handle.

(1) 5/16" (8 mm) × 4" to 6" (100 mm–152 mm) long bolt for the handle. Or if you've made the stabilizer, you'll have some threaded rod left over. Use it. Speaking of handles... I'm making the same handle I use on the Stabilizer, but a handle can be a simple as a wooden dowel with a hole drilled down through it and slipped over a bolt.

(2) 5/16" (8 mm) lock nuts for the threaded rod. Lock nuts have a nylon ring that holds it tight to the bolt. (You might also see these called "stop nuts.")

(2) 3/8" (9.5 mm) bolts × 3" (76 mm)—or long enough to go through the wheel hub and the width of your bottom aluminum boom.

3/8" (9.5 mm) drill bit.

(2) in-line skate wheel bearings.

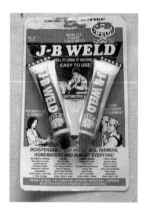

A package of J-B Weld.

A little bottle of thread-locking goo.

1" OD aluminum tube about 5" (127 mm) long. If you made the stabilizer, you'll have plenty left over for this handle.

Let's Build It!

On the bottom support arm, we're going to need to drill a hole to hold the wheel. I'm going to put this one about 3" to 5" (76 mm–127 mm) in front (toward the camera end of the bottom arm) of the support column. The hole in the center of the wheel is 3/8" (9.5 mm), so that's the size I'll drill through the support arm.

Make your dimple to keep the drill bit from walking!

Make sure you drill straight and true! If you have this very handy drill guide, clamp it right on the aluminum and drill away. (If you're using a drill press, you'll need to take the boom off. It'll probably be easier in the long run that way.)

Slip your ⅜" (9.5 mm) bolt through the hole and the pulley wheel. Add some Loctite or other thread-locking goo, and muscle a nut down on the whole thing—unless you're going to be painting the crane, then don't add the nut lock goo until after the *painting*.

Important: If your bolt extends beyond the top of the nut, take a hacksaw and cut it off.

On the second wheel for the camera end, take your bolt and slip it through the center hole in the wheel. Then take the L-bracket and slip the hole over the bolt.

Holding the wheel in place on the bracket, flip it over and mark the place of two holes that are opposite one another.

Your marks should look like this.

Make your dimples, clamp the bracket in your vise, and drill ¼" (7mm) holes for your bolts.

The second pulley wheel will go on the existing hole at the front of the crane. But you will need to take a ⅜" bit and drill out the ⁵⁄₁₆" hole so that it's big enough to take the new bolt size. You'll need a longer bolt to account for the thickness of the wheel and channel.

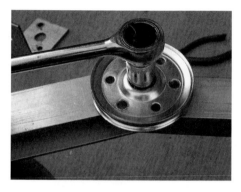

Bolt the wheel to the front of the bottom arm.

Slip your 1½" (38mm) long bolts up through opposite holes on the wheel.

Slip the nylon spacers over the bolts.

Slip the L-bracket onto the bolts, and tighten nuts down on the thing. For the love of God, man, don't add the thread-locking goo yet! We've got some checks to do in the next section! Didn't you read ahead?!!

Do the same to the wheel at the back of the crane, but instead of spacers, tighten nuts down against the wheel so that the bolts don't move at all.

Now let's make the handle unit. Ok, here's the deal: the handle can be something as simple as a wooden dowel with a hole drilled down the center. But I'm going to make mine from aluminum tube and bearings, just to be difficult! If you made the stabilizer, this is the same handle.

Killer Camera Rigs That You Can Build

Cut a 5" (127 mm) piece off the 1" OD (25 mm) tubing.

Roughen up the inside of the tube on each end with sandpaper.

Do the same on the outside of the bearings. Wipe everything clean.

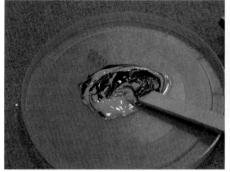

Squeeze an equal amount of J-B Weld onto a lid and mix it fully.

A popsicle stick works great (although, I prefer an Eskimo Pie stick).

Glob a thick layer of the J-B Weld all the way around the outside of the bearing. Be careful that it's only on the outside.

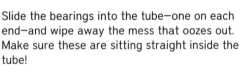

Now, these in-line skate bearings fit perfectly into this tubing. Coincidence? I think not!

Slide the bearings into the tube—one on each end—and wipe away the mess that oozes out. Make sure these are sitting straight inside the tube!

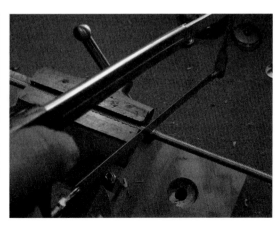

As you can see, on one end of the tube I've set the bearing flush with the top. On the other end I've inset the bearing just a bit. This is to hide the nut that will be on the bottom end of the handle. This isn't necessary, it just looks nice.

Cut the 5/16" threaded rod to the same length as your handle tube, plus ½" (14 mm) (or about ¾" [19 mm] if you didn't inset the bottom bearing).

Muscle the foam onto the handle and wipe away any lubricant that oozes out.

OK, set that aside for the moment and let's make the bar that holds this handle. You should be an old hand at drilling by now, so I'm just going to tell you where to place the holes.

If you want to add a foam grip to the handle, take some water-based lubricant and oil up the inside of the foam handle. Do *not* use a petroleum-based lubricant; it will eat away at the foam. If you can't find a foam handle, or don't want to use one, check out the shoulder mount handles elsewhere in this book. You can use sticky athletic tape as I did there.

Take your 9" (23cm) piece of aluminum and drill three holes. The two on the right should be the same distance apart as the bolts you just put in the wheel. Use a drill bit that fits the size of the bolts you used. The hole on the left will hold the handle. If you are making my handle, you'll need to drill a 5/16" (8mm) hole or a tad larger.

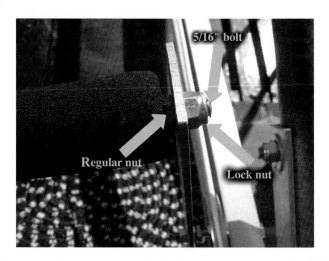

When you attach your handle to the bar, screw a regular nut a little way down on your threaded rod. Slip the end of the rod through the hole on the bar, then add a lock nut. Tighten the lock nut and regular nut against each other, then slip the handle on the rod.

Slip the handle on the bolt and add another stop nut at the bottom of the handle. A socket is a big help in tightening this down. Don't tighten too much. You want the handle to turn without moving up and down.

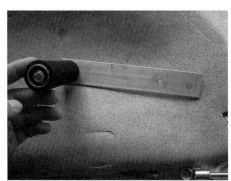

Oh, look how pretty!

Attaching the Handle to the Rig

Take a couple of jam nuts and screw them down even with the top of the nut that holds the wheel. I'm using the handle bar to make sure they're even.

Add some thread lock goo to the bolts above the nut.

Tighten a second jam nut against the first. Be careful not to let the bottom nut move from its position.

Slip the handle over the bolts and tighten some nuts over the handle arm.

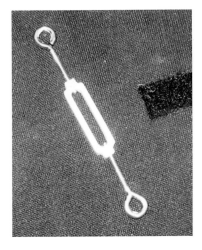

Take your turn buckle and unscrew the screw-eyes to their farthest extension. Tie one end of your clothesline through one of the eyes.

Loop the clothesline around the pulley wheels on each end.

Pull the other end of the clothesline through the other eye and pull it tight. Tie it down, keeping the line taught. Then turn the center buckle to take up any slack.

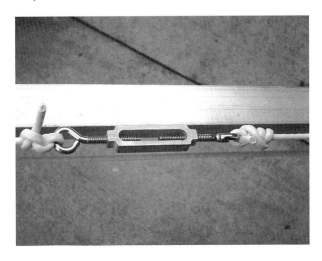

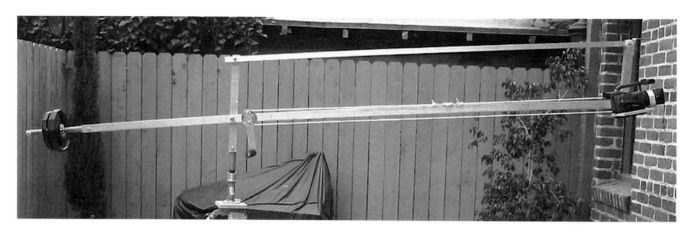

There ya go. Give it a turn. It should work quite smoothly.

Hey, I can't fit my camera on the L-bracket!

Yep, the smaller cameras fit nicely within the existing hole on the tilting L-bracket, but the larger ones need a little more room. You can also make a super-sized camera plate.

In this section we're going to be drilling another hole for the camera bolt, and checking out a flaw in the wheel the L-bracket is attached to. This is why I didn't want you putting any Loctite or similar product on to freeze those nuts in place. We're also going to build a little extension to make the bottom of the L a little longer. You can make this out of plywood, or better, aluminum. It's very important not to build this extension out farther than you actually need to hold the camera. You must keep this as light as possible. First, let's explore this little flaw in the wheel bearing.

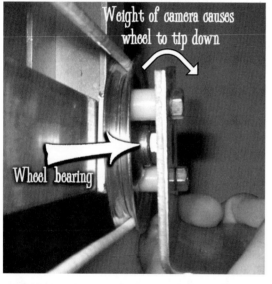

Weight of camera causes wheel to tip down

Wheel bearing

Take a close look at the photo. See the arrow that points to the bearing? Well, it's a little loose for our needs, so the weight of a larger camera causes the wheel to tip ever so slightly. If you can find a similar wheel and bearing that isn't a little loose, let me know, because I couldn't! Frankly, it's an easy fix, so let's get it on!

OK. Remove the L-bracket from the wheel and head for your workbench. Set your camera on the bracket, but leave a little space between the vertical part of the bracket and your camera. About ¾" (19 mm) should do it. You need enough room to clear the bolts that hold the bracket to the wheel. Now, turn the whole shebang over.

Take a look at where my forefinger is. That's the bolt socket on the bottom of my friend Scott's camera. (You didn't think I'd be experimenting with my own stuff do you?) Now, if we slide the bracket straight back, will the existing hole (huge as it is) match up with the one on the camera? Nope, not in this case. Not this fine Sony. If it did line up, you can go eat dinner. The rest of you, read on.

Killer Camera Rigs That You Can Build

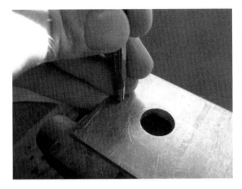 

Put a ¼" (7 mm) or a little larger bit in, add your oil, and drill away. Since this is a harder metal than aluminum, go a little slower. And don't forget the safety glasses!

Here's where things get really tedious. But a little care now will save you a ton of headaches later.

Set up your crane according to the earlier instructions. Make sure your tripod is level! If it's not, all your work from this point will be bogus!

Take your punch and make a dimple about halfway between the outside edge of the bracket and the existing hole, and dead center. If you've got a 2" (50 mm) wide bracket, that's 1" (25 mm) in, Junior.

Attach the camera through the new hole. It's ok that the camera doesn't rest entirely on the bracket. So do you notice that the weight of the camera is making our wheel tilt? Take a level and hold if flush against the bottom of the bracket. Not anywhere near level is it?

Tilt the level on one side until the bubble is in-between the two marks. See that gap between the bottom of the bracket and the top of the level? That's how much we've got to bend that bracket. So, take the camera off the bracket and the bracket off the crane and head back to the bench.

THWACK!

Bend the bracket until you've made up for the tilt in the bearing.

Clamp the bracket in your vice and give it a few good thwacks with a hammer. Once you've got the camera side of the bracket bent up a bit, take it back to the crane, reattach it, and put the camera back on. I did warn you this was tedious. Doing a bit at a time is the way to go here, though.

Darn. Close, but not perfect. If yours isn't perfect either, take the camera off the bracket, the bracket off the crane, and go do some more thwacking.

Just to give you an idea... This is how much thwacking I had to do before the camera was perfectly level.

Now, at this point it is possible to stop, even though your camera is hanging off the bracket a bit. Just glue some cork on the top of the bracket and you're done. You can't use the mouse pad trick here. Because the camera is resting only partly on the bracket, if you cushion it with anything thick and squishy, the camera will slowly go out of level as you tighten the camera bolt down.

If you want to make things even more groovy, keep going.

Take the camera off the bracket and the bracket off the crane ... you know the drill. We're going to add a camera plate to this baby.

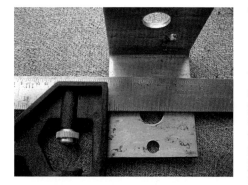

Take your square and draw a straight line across the camera mounting side of the bracket, about ¾" (19 mm) in from the crane mounting side.

Take a square of plywood or aluminum and center it on the bracket at the line you just made. I got this nice little piece of aluminum for nothing. It's ⅛" (3 mm) thick, super light, and measures 4" × 5" (100 mm × 127 mm). It's perfect for this job. Don't be too proud to beg at your metal supply shop!

Take your center punch and make a couple of dimples at the edge of your new plate. These should be placed just a bit narrower than the width of the L-bracket while the new plate is centered on the bracket as in the photo.

Clamp the plate to your bench on top of a piece of scrap lumber. Load up a drill bit that's just a bit larger than the bolts you're going to use. In this case, I'm using an ⅛" (3 mm) bit. Drill out the holes on your dimple.

BEE-U-T-FUL!

Line your freshly drilled plate on the L-bracket. Line it up against the straight line you made earlier. It *must* be straight on the bracket!

Take a marker (a felt tip works great) and mark through the two holes on your plate.

It should look a little something like this. The line above the two marker holes is a reference line I made to make sure the plate was straight and true.

Make dimples on the hole marks. Give the center punch a good whack or two. We're dealing with steel now.

Make sure you use some drill oil. You'll probably have to stop drilling a couple of times to add more oil because of the much denser metal. Your bit needs to stay wet.

Clean off the oil and metal shavings. Take a coarse piece of sand paper and roughen up the base of the L-bracket.

Do the same on the bottom of the plate.
Clean up the two pieces you just sanded. Acetone is great for this, but soap and water will work too.

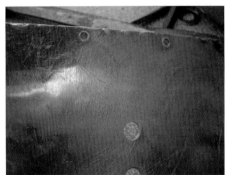

Mix up a bit of J-B Weld and glop some onto the top of the L-bracket.

Bolt the plate onto the L-bracket. Hurry, before the weld dries!

Flip the whole shebang over and clamp it to the piece of scrap lumber one more time.

Drill a ¼" (7 mm) hole through the plate, using the ¼" (7 mm) hole you drilled earlier as your guide (no need to make a dimple this time).

While we've got everything clamped down, let's make another hole just in case we need something farther out some day. Make a dimple about ¾" (19 mm) out from the hole you just drilled. Oil the dimple and drill another camera hole.

Oooh, look how pretty!

Ok, let's put a little pad on there.

I'm going to use an old mouse pad. Cut it to the size of your base plate. Hold it onto your plate and flip the whole thing over.

Mark the underside through the holes you just drilled. I'm marking mine with chalk or you can sprinkle some baby powder on there. It makes it super visible.

Cut holes on your marks. You can use a knife, razor, whatever. I'm using a cut punch that comes with Grommet kits for cutting round holes in fabric.

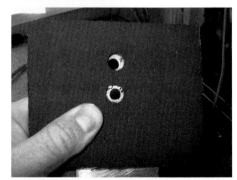

Glue the pad onto the plate. I'm going to use an epoxy. It seems to work best for gluing metal and rubber together. But feel free to experiment.

Attach the bracket back onto the tilt wheel on your crane, and you're good to go.

Killer Camera Rigs That You Can Build

HERE'S A GOOD THING TO DO ON BOTH YOUR CRANE CAMERA BRACKETS

You may have noticed that these big L-brackets have a big hole. It's a simple matter to slip a washer on the camera bolt before you attach the camera. But that can be a hassle, especially if you lose it on location.

Let's monkey around with the static camera bracket that's attached to the channel aluminum.

I'm simply going to J-B Weld a fender washer over the bottom side of the large hole. And Voila! A small hole. You can also leave the camera bolt in the hole by attaching a retaining ring on the camera side of the hole. I'm also adding an old mouse pad to cushion the camera, but that's not totally necessary.

Roughen up the bracket and fender washer.

Cut a mouse pad to size.

Cut a hole in the pad matching the hole on the bracket. I'm using a grommet punch.

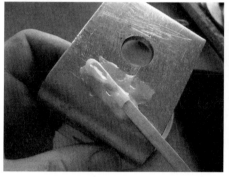

Spread epoxy on the bracket. (Remember, I'm doing this for the static bracket, so don't think I'm putting the pad on the wrong side!)

Stick the pad on. Make sure the holes line up.

Warning: Only do these next steps if you *never* plan on using a fluid head on your static camera plate!

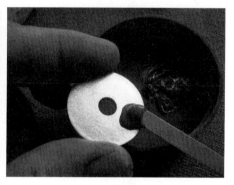

Mix up some J-B Weld and coat the entire surface of the washer.

Press it over the hole on the bracket and let dry 24 hours.

Put the camera bolt up through the hole and add a retaining ring. That's it!

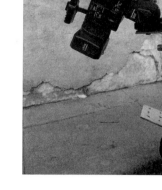

Oops. Did you do these steps by accident because you *do* plan on using a fluid head on your camera plate? That's OK. Just drill a ⅜" hole in the bracket next to the camera hole.

Be sure to check out Chapter 18, *Working with a Crane*, and Chapter 19, *The T-Men Crane Weight Holder*, later in this section.

The *Double Indemnity* Crane

The *Double Indemnity* is one huge crane. I've built mine with a bottom boom that measures 20' long. You can also make it so it breaks down into an easily hauled package as seen in the photo above. And just so you know, any longer than 20' (6 meters), and my modified surveyor's tripod wouldn't hold it, so don't get any bright ideas for a 30' crane unless you have a mount that can hold that kind of weight! Before we go any further, don't even think of putting this crane on a flimsy tripod! It's best if you modify the Surveyor's tripod from Chapter 21, *The Third Man Tripod*, *before* you start this project, and make at least four sandbags to boot!

If you live in Europe or Australia and a few other places around the world, you might not be able to find the materials for the tripod mount for the other cranes in this book. Not to worry! You *can* find the materials for this rotating cradle mount and use this mount for the other long jib in the book if you'd like, and you can get by with lighter materials for the cradle too. Just shoot me an e-mail at dan@dvcamerarigs.com with any questions.

Before we start to build, let's take a closer look at this crane.

Starting at the rear end of the crane we have a rod coming out the back of the boom that holds some counterweights. These are for fine-tuning the balance of the crane. By moving the rod and/or the weights along the rod, you can get a perfect balance that allows your camera to float just right.

DOI: 10.1016/B978-0-240-81337-0.00017-3

Next we have a big mass of counterweights at the end of that 20' (6 meters) boom. Just to give you an idea about how much weight you'll have to haul to a shoot: With a 20' boom and a Panasonic HD camera on the opposite end, I've had to put 167 lbs of weight on there. You can cut that considerably by making a 15' boom. Just something to think about!

Moving up the crane, you'll find the cradle that holds the boom and a monitor. The cradle sits on the tripod, and can rotate to the left or right. Since the monitor is attached to the cradle, it will move with the crane so that you can keep an eye on your shot as you move the crane.

Coming up from the bottom boom are two bars that hold a *top* boom. This top boom doesn't carry any weight, but by pushing it forward you can tilt the camera down. By pulling it back, you can tilt the camera up. (Sorry, you *cannot* pan the camera on this crane.)

See the section of the bottom boom that has knobs on it? That is where two 5' sections of the crane join together. I have three of these sections. If you want, you can certainly make one section to join two 10' (3 meters) lengths together (as long as you have a way to get 10' lengths to the shoot!). Or if you're making a shorter crane of 10' long, then one joined section is plenty. Get the idea? Just above the joined section, you'll see a cable with a turnbuckle. On a crane this long, you need a bit of counter-pressure working against gravity to keep the boom straight and to eliminate wobble. A shorter crane probably won't need this cable.

Around the middle of the boom, there is another set of bars joined to the top boom. The reason for this is that the top boom is made of very thin, very light weight aluminum tube. These bars simply help support that tube. If your crane is, say, 10′ (3 meters) long, you probably won't need these either. As with the cable, if you do find that you do need them, you can always add them later after you've finished building the crane.

At the front of the crane is the tilt bar that holds the camera mount.

The knob that holds the camera mount allows you to tilt the camera from the mount end as well so if you can't get enough tilt from the crane itself, you can add more of a tilt through the camera mount. If you'd like, you can also turn this mount around so that the camera is hanging directly under the boom. If you have a really heavy camera, this is probably a good idea.

That's it in a nutshell. Since this is such a big project, I'm going to break it down into sections; each section will have the tools and materials you'll need. First, we'll tackle the cradle and mounting it to the tripod.

Before you get started buying your stuff, please read the appendix, *Working with Metal*!

Killer Camera Rigs That You Can Build

Materials List for the *Double Indemnity* Crane Cradle

☐ A flange bearing: four bolt mounted. This is a bearing mounted into a flange, much like a pillow block bearing, but mounts horizontally instead. The bore (that's the big hole in the center) can be anywhere from 1" (25 mm) to 2" (50 mm). Try to get something with a bore a little bigger than an inch if you can. Mine is 1¼" (31mm). A hardware store isn't going to carry this, but if you look online, there are tons of parts suppliers that do. I got mine from Reid Supply Company (reidsupply.com).

☐ To mount the above bearing you'll need the following aluminum: (2) ½" (14 mm) thick pieces and (1) 1" (25 mm) piece. The size depends on your bearing flange. My flange bearing is 4¼" (107 mm) square. So each of those piece needs to be 4" (100 mm) square or larger (yes, 4¼" would be better, but the widest aluminum bar at my supplier was 4" (100 mm) by 12" [30 cm] long. It is perfectly OK to let the edges of the flange extend by an ⅛" [3 mm] on each side of the aluminum). Note: this is not all the aluminum bar you'll need for the cradle, but will take this one step at a time. There is some of the same stuff listed later for the U part of the cradle. Believe me, it's clearer this way in the end.

☐ Thick aluminum tube. Mine needed to have a diameter of 1¼" and a length of 3". Please read the instructions below to figure what you'll need to fit your flange bearing and the thickness of your aluminum piece.

This thick aluminum tube needs to fit into that bearing. Since my bearing bore is 1¼" (31mm) , that's the O.D. (Outside Diameter) my thick aluminum tube needs to be. If you bought a flange bearing that has a bore of 1½", your thick tube O.D. should be 1½". Make sense? Now the hole in the center of this thick aluminum tube needs to be slightly more than a ½" (14mm). I'm not going to make you scour the countryside for what I used specifically. It's not that important. Eventually, you will need to get a ½" (14mm) bolt through that hole in the center of the aluminum tube. With that in mind, find the thickest wall you can that will still fit into the bearing bore and take a ½" (14mm) bolt through the center. Now the length of the thick aluminum tube is a different matter. Mine needed to be 3" (76mm) long.

HERE'S HOW TO FIGURE IT

1 Your flange bearing will come with a retaining ring. You slip that retaining ring on, then slip the aluminum tube down into the bearing.

Flip the bearing over, and adjust the thick aluminum tube so that it is flush with the bottom of the bearing. There's a little set screw in the retaining ring. Once you have the bottom of the aluminum tube even with the bottom of the bearing, slide the retaining ring to the top of the bearing and tighten the set screw.

2 Measure the tube ½" (14mm) above the top of the retaining ring and that's your total measurement for the length of the thick aluminum tube.

So here's what it should look like once it is cut: The retaining ring holds the thick tube flush with the bottom of the bearing, then there is ½" of thick tube ABOVE the top of the retaining ring.

Note: Take a look at the photo above, on the right. This is part of the aluminum you'll be purchasing that's shown below. That top piece is ½" thick. This is why you need the thick aluminum tube to extend ½" above the retaining ring! Well, if you got something thicker, your aluminum tube measurement above the retaining ring needs to be that thick. I hope I'm not confusing things here, but I don't want you to get burned if you thought "hey, ¾" (19mm) thick aluminum bar will be even stronger!"

Yes, it will. And that's fine. Just get enough aluminum tube to deal with that extra thickness of your aluminum bar. So if that aluminum bar is ¾" of an inch thick, you need to measure your tube ¾" above the retaining ring to get the total length you need to buy. In the end, if you get at least 6" (15cm) of aluminum tube, that will be plenty long enough for any bearing and aluminum you get. Just go through the above steps for the length, and cut it.

One last thing about this aluminum tube and the flange bearing that I need to warn you about, and this has always driven me nuts: you buy a bearing with a 1¼" (31mm) bore, then you buy 1¼" (31mm) round tube to go in that hole... *and it doesn't fit*! Grrrrrrr! I'll never get why that sometimes it fits, and sometimes it doesn't. But not to worry! It's aluminum! Just make sure you pick up a metal file (it's in the tools list). You just need to shave a very small layer off around the bar and you're good to go.

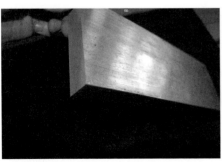

☐ OK, for that U-shaped cradle part you'll need two aluminum bars 1" (25mm) thick × 4" (100mm) wide × 12" (30cm) long and...

☐ (1) aluminum bar 1" (25mm) thick × 4" (100mm) wide × 4¼" (114mm) long and...

☐ (1) aluminum bar ½" (14mm) thick × 4" (100mm) wide × 4½" (114mm) long. In other words, the exact same size as the earlier one, just not as thick, right?

260

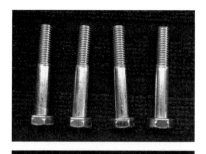

☐ (4) ½" (14 mm) bolts. These need to be long enough to go through an 1½" (38 mm) of aluminum, through the bolt holes on the flange, with a little left over to hold a nut. Mine are 3" (76 mm) long. Yours may be different depending on your flange.

☐ (4) ½" (14 mm) nuts for the above bolts. You can use regular nuts with some thread locking goo, or stop nuts, which have a little nylon ring at the top to hold the nut tight on the bolt.

☐ A washer. OK, this must be just large enough to cover the inner bearing's edge. There needs to be a ½" (14 mm) bore in the middle of this washer. If you find a perfect size for your bearing, but the hole is too small, you can always drill out the hole with a ½" (14 mm) bit.

☐ Also part of this is (1) ½" (14 mm) bolt the exact length to go down through your 1" (25 mm) thick aluminum bar, through the aluminum tube, then through the above washer, with enough room for a lock nut, *but no longer*. You might have to get a bolt a little too long and cut it with a hacksaw. This has to be exact, I'm afraid.

☐ (1) ½" (14 mm) jam nut for the above bolt. A jam nut is like a regular nut, but narrower. Please use a jam nut here. Once this thing is all together, you'll not have a lot of working room at the base of the flange bearing.

☐ (4) ⅜" (9.5 mm) socket head screws ½" (14 mm) to 1" (25 mm) long. You don't have to use socket head screws (the type that takes an Allen wrench) here—they just look cool.

☐ These will be going into our flange to solve a problem I'll talk about later. As you can see, mine could have been shorter, but I simply couldn't find shorter ones at my hardware store. A little longer is fine; they won't be in the way of anything.

☐ (8) socket head screws ¼" (7 mm) by 1½" (38 mm) long.

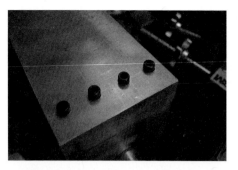

☐ These will help hold the side of your cradle to the base.

☐ A ½" (14 mm) bolt long enough to go through both sides of your cradle once it's finished. Mine is 7" (17 cm) long. If you're making a wider or narrower base, yours might be different.

Tools List for the *Double Indemnity* Crane Cradle

☐ Sorry about this, but you will need a drill press for this project. You don't need to spend a ton; around $150 will get you one good enough. By good enough, I mean that you won't be manufacturing film equipment for the masses in your garage. I have a Ryobi that has held up well for years of drilling into metal. It should have a couple of things though: a 12" press and the ability to change the bit speed. Metal needs a much slower drill speed than wood. And you don't need a fancy laser-guided unit either! Are there better things for drilling into metal? Yep. But the cost is enough to make you go blind! Next to the drill in the photo is a drill press vise. Many times these come with the drill press. But if not, it's a good idea to get one.

☐ You might need a metal chop saw. Now before everyone starts sending me e-mails about how this isn't the best thing at all for cutting big chunks of aluminum... I know. The idea is to get the job done as cheaply as possible without cheating too much! A metal band saw works much better with a price tag to match. They are easily three times the cost of a chop saw. You noticed I said you might need one of these. If you want, cancel your gym membership and use a hacksaw to cut all this aluminum, have at it.

As an alternative, you can head for a machine shop or have the metal supply cut all these bits for you. My metal supplier sells most of the aluminum used in this project in 12" (30 cm) and 36" (91 cm) lengths at a huge savings. On the other hand, they charge $8 a cut. In the end, it was just cheaper to buy this equipment than have my supplier cut it for me. If this is the only project you'll be building in this book, it might be cheaper for you to have someone cut all this stuff for you. Just remember, most of the measurements for the cradle are based on the size of the floor flange bearing. Buy that first so you'll know what size aluminum you'll need.

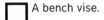

☐ A bench vise.

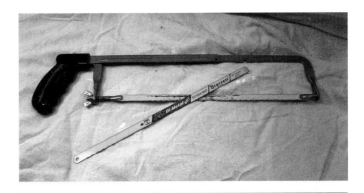

☐ A hacksaw. Get a bunch of blades with 14 to 18 teeth per inch.

☐ A prick punch and/or a center punch. Officially, a prick punch is used for marking metal and a center punch is used for making dimples in metal. Truth be told: I use one or the other for both marking and dimpling.

☐ A combination square.

☐ Cutting oil. This is very important when drill into metal. Don't use WD-40 or 3-in-1 Oil for this. They just aren't butch enough. Even cutting oil is a bit of a compromise; there are much better lubricants for this, but they are so darned expensive. You might get a little oil can to put this stuff in.

☐ A ½″ (14 mm) bit.

☐ A ¼″ (7 mm) bit.

☐ A hammer.

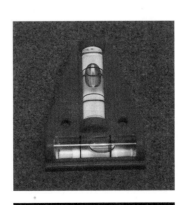

☐ A multilevel or bubble level.

☐ A wrench or a pair of locking pliers (actually both are good).

☐ Thread locking goo.

☐ A metal file. You want one that has around 20 teeth per inch. This makes very quick work of filing down aluminum. Now if you want a smooth pretty finish, get an additional file with around 60 teeth per inch to finish off the rough filing.

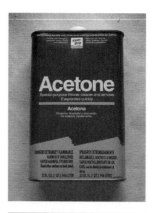

☐ Acetone. This stuff works great for cleaning metal. Get some rubber gloves too.

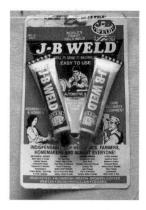

☐ J-B Weld. This is great stuff for gluing metal. You'll need about three packages before we're done with this project!

☐ Shop towels.

☐ 60 grit sandpaper.

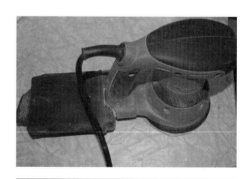

☐ A little power hand sander would be very handy too!

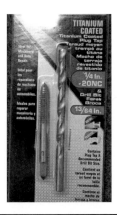

☐ A tap with matching bit.

OK, let's talk: A tap is something that puts threads in a hole you've drilled into metal. It's really easy to do and pretty cool. Sometimes you'll find taps that come with a matching drill bit (the drill bit has to be slightly smaller than the tap). Other times you'll buy them separately. It really depends on which store you're in. If you're getting them separately, pick up the tap first. On the package it will say "use drill bit 24" or something like that. Go to the drill bit section, and you'll find racks of drill bits with numbers on them. Pick the right number for that tap. Between you and me, this drives me crazy. Why not put the size of the drill bit on the tap package, as in, *use drill bit size* ¹³⁄₆₄". A good thing to do is to always keep your tap and the matching drill bit together. I have a plastic case with lots of little compartments, and each compartment holds the tap and its matching drill bit. There is nothing worse than drilling a hole for a tap, then watching the tap fall straight into the too big hole!

So, for this project you'll need a ¼" (7 mm) tap, and a ⅜" (9.5 mm) tap, both with matching drill bits. Try to get taps that are 2" (50 mm) long or better.

☐ A drill bit. Remember the ¼" (7 mm) by 1½" (38 mm) long socket head screws? You'll need a drill bit that is slightly larger than the *head* of that screw. So dig through your shopping basket and find those screws. Hold them up to the drill bits until you find one slightly larger.

☐ Allen wrench. You'll need three: one to fit the ¼" (7 mm) head, one to fit the ⅜" (9.5 mm) head and one to fit the set screw that came with your flange retaining ring.

☐ A tap wrench. This is a special wrench that you use to screw your tap with.

☐ A hole saw (this is basically a drill bit). What size aluminum tube did you get to fit your flange bearing? You need a hole saw this exact same size. Mine is 1¼" (31 mm). Make sure you get a hole saw with a guide bit in the middle of it.

☐ You will also need a 1" (25mm) hole saw.

☐ An assortment of clamps. You'll need at least four that can open to 7" (17 cm) or wider. The bar clamps shown will work fine, and are cheaper than big C-clamps. Get eight 3" (76mm) or better C-clamps too. C-clamps are a filmmaking tool. You'll use these on shoots all the time, so get a ton of them if you can.

☐ A wire brush for your drill. This is great for cleaning up aluminum. A 2" (50mm) or larger is fine.

Whew. I think that's it. Shall we build the cradle now?

Let's Build It!

First we'll make the bearing stuff, then the big U section.

1 Take one of the ½" (14mm) thick pieces of aluminum bar. As I mentioned before, because of the size of my flange bearing, mine is ½" (14mm) thick by 4" (100mm) wide by 4½" (114mm) long. Use a prick punch to draw a line from corner to corner, forming a big X. The middle of the X is dead center. Put a dimple on that X with your prick punch or center punch. In the photo, I'm using a marker simply because it's easier for you to see.

Killer Camera Rigs That You Can Build

Load the 1" (25 mm) hole saw into the drill press. When you're drilling this, it's a good idea to put the aluminum on top of a piece of scrap lumber so that the hole saw will have something to drill into instead of the top of your drill press platform! Set the guide bit that is in the middle of the hole saw into the dimple you made in the center of the aluminum. Once everything is lined up, clamp the metal and the wood to the drill press platform. If you have a drill press vise like in the photo, use that. Just make sure the metal is level in the vise. Use a very slow drill speed and as you go, clean the hole saw of metal chips, and use plenty of drilling oil. This will take a long time! Please be patient. It's not like drilling into wood.

2 Next, we need to figure out where to put ½" (14 mm) bolt holes so that we can bolt the pieces we are making onto the floor flange bearing. There are a couple of easy ways to do this: set the flange on top of the metal piece you just drilled the big hole into. Slip a prick punch down the bolt hole of the flange bearing and give it a good thwack with a hammer. Or, if you have some spray paint around, a tiny little mist of pain in the hole will mark the aluminum where the bolt hole is. Not too much paint, or it will just be a mess that's not at all helpful. In the photo, I've stacked this ½" (14 mm) piece on top of the 1" (25 mm) thick piece. There's no good reason for this, I just wanted to get an idea of things when I bolt the pieces together. Right now, we're just drilling the thinner piece.

Load a ½" (14 mm) drill bit into your drill press. Line the bit up over your mark and clamp the piece to your press platform. Drill away. Repeat for all four corners.

3 Take a look at the photo. Very soon now, you'll get to this point. This is another ½" (14 mm) thick piece of aluminum that will be on the bottom of our flange unit that sits on the tripod. We can't have the bolt heads resting on the tripod, so we're going to eat out each corner of this piece so that there is enough room for the bolt heads to be even or under that piece of aluminum.

Load the hole saw into your press. I'm using the 1" (25mm) one again. I've spray painted where the bolts are as before to give me an idea about how far to go, but this step really isn't necessary. You can just as easily trace around the bolt head with a marker, or just go for it! Just make sure you get the hole far enough in to allow that big bolt head room. Clamp it on some scrap wood and drill out the four corners.

4 Load the ½" (14mm) bit back into the press. Draw a big X on the 1" (25mm) thick piece to find the center and dimple it. Take the piece you just bit the corners out of and stack it under the 1" (25mm) piece on your press. Make sure it's lined up perfectly and clamp it down. Drill a ½" (14mm) hole straight through both pieces.

You should now have something like this.

5 Set the bottom "no corners" piece aside. Grab the other ½" (14mm) piece and put it on top of the 1" (25mm) thick piece. Using the ½" (14mm) holes in each corner as a guide, drill ½" (14mm) holes down through the 1" (25mm) thick piece. You won't need to make dimples this time. Just clamp the pieces together on the press, being careful to line up the drill bit with the holes you've already made in the ½" (14mm) piece.

When you're done, you should have five ½" (14mm) holes in all.

6 Let's glue these three pieces together.

Just so we're clear, on the bottom of the flange we'll first have the ½" (14mm) piece with the big hole in the middle of it, then the 1" (25mm) piece, and then the "no corner" piece.

We'll be using J-B Weld for the gluing. So have that handy, along with some acetone, shop towels, four 3" (76mm) C-clamps, something to mix the J-B Weld with (like a popsicle stick), and a ½" (14mm) bolt for each hole (length isn't important; we're just going to use them to make sure the pieces are lined up).

Killer Camera Rigs That You Can Build

Use 60 grit sandpaper to sand each side of the aluminum to roughen it up for gluing. Then use the acetone to clean all the dirt, oil, and metal dust from the pieces.

Mix up the J-B Weld according to the instructions on the package. Spread it on the top piece, being careful not to get too close to the holes. Run bolts through all four holes on the 1" (25 mm) piece, then slide this J-B Weld-coated ½" (14 mm) piece on to it. The bolts will act as a guide so you get this glued on straight.

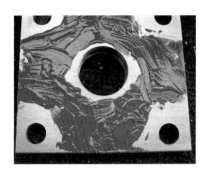

Coat the "no corners" piece in J-B Weld, and place that on top of the other two pieces.

Then run another bolt up through the middle.

Put a clamp on each side and remove the bolts. You can use an acetone soaked rag to clean any J-B Weld that oozes out before it dries.

OK, set that aside and let it dry overnight. Next we'll do the big U-looking part.

7 Using the skills you've already used, cut a hole in the ½" (14 mm) piece the *same size* as your tube aluminum. Drill a ½" (14 mm) hole in the middle of the 1" (25 mm) thick piece of aluminum, and have your aluminum tube cut to length as discussed earlier.

8 Sand and clean them as you did with the flange pieces. Have a ½" (14 mm) bolt and nut and washer ready that is long enough to go through the length of tube and the two metal pieces. Spread J-B Weld on one side of the 1" (25 mm) thick piece.

Spread some more J-B Weld along the outside of the top ½" (14 mm) of the tube. Place the tube in the hole that's in the ½" (14 mm) piece. Run the bolt through all three pieces and tighten it down with a nut.

Add a C-clamp to each side and let it dry overnight.

9 Fixing the flaw in the bearing.

The thing about a pillow block type bearing is that they are designed to give between the outside of the bearing and its casing. We don't want that. It's a really easy fix.

We'll be putting four screws in to hold the bearing in place.

There is sometimes a little oil valve in the casing. Simply unscrew that and remove it.

You'll need to twist the bearing out of the way. The easiest way to do that is to put your aluminum tube in the bearing hole and force it up or down. You might need to lock the casing in a vise for this.

10 Once the bearing is twisted out of the way, lock it into a vise on your drill press with one edge facing up. Find the matching drill bit for the ⅜" (9.5mm) tap and load it into your press. Around the center of the casing collar, drill a hole all the way through the casing. Do this on all four sides. *Note*: The existing hole for the oil valve may already be ⅜" (9.5mm), but if not, drill out that hole, too, to make it bigger. If it *is* ⅜" (9.5mm), but the threads aren't correct, you can simply tap that hole without drilling it out.

(12) Clean out the tapped holes, then twist the bearing back into place. Make *sure* that the bearing is sitting level in its casing! Twist four ⅜" (9.5 mm) bolts into your tapped holes so that they are holding the bearing tightly. I'm using bolts that need an Allen head wrench. You can use any kind of bolt you want. Also, mine are a touch long, but that's OK.

(11) Once you have a hole drill on each side, clamp the flange in your bench vise and tap a ⅜" (9.5 mm) thread in each of the holes.

ADDING THE SIDES ON OUR BIG U PIECE

(13) Has this part dried overnight? If so, let's get started.

You should have two big aluminum bars that are 12" (30 cm) long, 4" (100 mm) wide, and 1" (25 mm) thick. On one of them, measure 1" (25 mm) from the end and mark that measurement with a prick punch.

And then measure halfway across. Since mine is 4" (100 mm) wide, that's 2". Make a mark across your first mark.

Use your prick punch or center punch to put a dimple on the center of that mark.

Stack the other 1" (25 mm) thick bar under this one and clamp them together.

Put a ½" (14 mm) drill bit into your press, and drill a ½" (14 mm) hole through both bars at the same time. This won't take nearly as long as using a hole saw. Now you should have two bars with a ½" (14 mm) hole in exactly the same place on both.

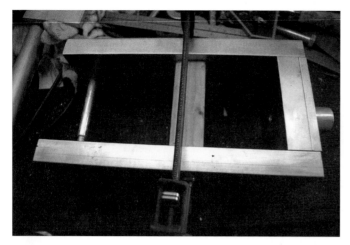

14 This is where we are headed. The base is 4" (100 mm) by 4½" (114 mm). These bars are 4" (100 mm) wide, so we will be attaching them to the 4" (100 mm) sides of the base. It's a good idea to cut a hunk of lumber at that width to support these heavy bars while the J-B Weld dries, and that you have a ½" bolt to go through both holes at the top.

Just like everything else, we use J-B Weld on around here, roughen up the bottom couple of inches on the two big bars on one side. Roughen up the sides of the base piece where the sides attach. Clean everything with acetone. Mix up some J-B Weld and smear it onto the sides of the base. Use the wood block to support your sides, and use the bolt to make sure the bolts holes are lined up, carefully setting them on either side of the J-B Weld smeared base.

Turn the cradle on one side and add a clamp at the wood support.

Use a couple of more clamps to tighten the sides to the base. Before the J-B Weld gets any drier, use a combination square to make sure the sides are square: line up the bottom of the combo square to the base, and the ruler going up one side. There should not be any gaps. The entire edge of the ruler should be touching the side of the cradle at all points. Check to make sure the opposite side is square too. If it's not square, you probably cut your lumber too short or too long. Just remove it now if that's the case.

I'm using three clamps on the base and one over the wood spacer.

Use acetone on a rag to clean off any J-B Weld that has oozed out. Let this dry overnight!

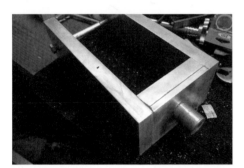

15 Remove the clamps once it's had time to dry.

This is what we'll be doing today: adding four screws to each side of our cradle to make it bombproof. You will need a ¼″ (7 mm) tap with its matching drill bit, a ¼″ (7 mm) drill bit, and a drill bit that is slightly larger than the head of the Allen bolt so we can countersink the heads. If you're not using an Allen bolt, just skip that last bit.

At the base of our cradle, we have a ½″ (14 mm) thick piece glued under a 1″ (25 mm) thick piece. Put your combo square against the bottom piece, then move the ruler up until you are halfway across the 1″ (25 mm) piece. In my world, that's setting your combo square to 1″ (25 mm) and locking it in place.

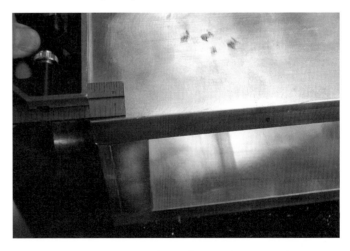

Turn your cradle on its side so that one of the 12 (30 cm) pieces is on top. Starting from the bottom, transfer the measurement you just took to the 12″ (30 cm) piece. Do the same on the opposite 12″ (30 cm) piece.

Set your combo square across that mark and draw a line with your prick punch all the way across the base of the 12" (30 cm) bar.

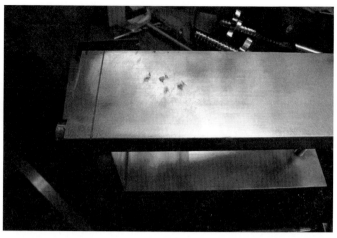

I'm using a marker here so you can see it, but you should have a line across your 12" (30 cm) bar that is halfway up the 1" (25 mm) piece of the base.

Set your combo square to ½" (14 mm). Measure in from the edge and draw a line across the long line you just made. Do this on the opposite edge as well, then turn it over and do it on the other 12" (30 cm) bar.

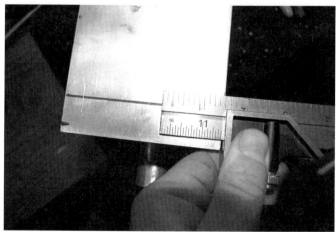

Then set the combo square to 1½" (38 mm) and repeat these steps, marking across the long line.

You should have four marks now. Take a center punch and hammer dimples into each mark. Do this on the other 12" (30 cm) piece as well.

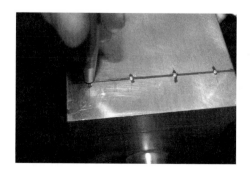

Killer Camera Rigs That You Can Build

DRILLING AND TAPING THE HOLES

16 Find the bit that matches your ¼" (7 mm) tap and load it into your drill press. You want the hole to go ½" (14 mm) deeper than the length of the screw (including the screw head). You can set up a *stop* on your drill press so that the bit only goes this deep and no further. I've never seen a drill press that didn't have a stop, so check the manual.

Drill out all eight holes (four on each side). Next load the ¼" (7 mm) bit into the press. Drill out the holes again with the ¼" (7 mm) bit, but only one inch down! Be very careful here: *only drill 1" or the thickness of your 12" side pieces!* If you go further, it will screw everything up! So seriously, you've gone too far now—be careful! Set the stop on your press so you don't go farther than 1" (25 mm) down.

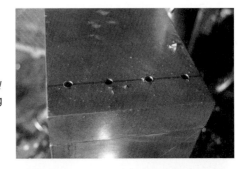

One more to go if you're using the Allen head bolts for this. Load the bit that is the same diameter as the head of the Allen screw.

Set the stop on your drill press so that you drill only as far as the screw head is long. This is probably going to be less than ¼" (7 mm).

Drill out each of the holes again, but remember, you're only going in a tiny bit so that you can countersink the Allen bolt.

Add some drilling oil into each hole.

Lower the tap into the hole (it will slide through the first inch of the ¼" [7 mm] hole, so don't panic). Now, if you read the instructions of a tap, you're told to twist it down two or three turns, then back off one turn, then proceed on like that. In this case, the odd bits of metal have no place to go; they can't drop out the bottom of the hole, because there is no open bottom. So for every three or four turns, back the tap all the way out, clean the metal off, and go back in. Repeat this until you've hit bottom. If you force the tap by turning it really hard, it is possible to break the tap off inside the hole! So be patient. I know it's a drag, but that's the way it's gotta be.

Once you have all the holes tapped, use some compressed air or a garden hose down in the holes to remove any metal bits that are hanging out in there.

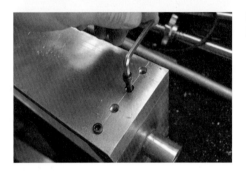

Use the Allen wrench to screw your bolts down.

Do this on both sides, and you're done!

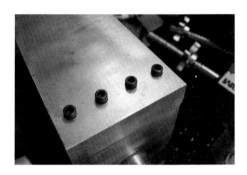

Putting It All Together

Just so you know, there are some photos in here after the rig was painted black. Don't panic. I just forgot to take these photos.

17 Slide the retaining ring that came with your floor flange bearing onto the aluminum tube that is now glued to the cradle and tighten down the set screw.

18 Make sure that the bearing is sitting levels in the casing, and that you didn't accidentally twist the bearing upside-down when seating it after you taped the holes. Make sure the set screws are nice and tight!

Slide the flange bearing onto the aluminum tube coming from the cradle. Your bearing should come up against the retaining ring, and the bottom of the aluminum tube should be even with the bottom of the bearing.

19 Run a ½" (14 mm) bolt up through the hole in the cradle, and all the way through the aluminum tube.

Add the washer that is the same size as the bearing.

Add a jam nut and tighten it down. You must use a jam nut because they are narrower than a regular nut. Also, the ½" (14 mm) bolt can't extend too far beyond the nut. If it does, cut it off with a hacksaw.

20 Take the bottom half (the one with five holes drilled in it), and run a ½" (14 mm) bolt down through it. The big hole in the center is to allow the bolt head room. If you can add a washer without the bolt head extending above the surface, do so. If you can't, that's perfectly OK too.

Here's the thing about the washer you may have just added: Bolts that have threads going all the way to the bolt head are getting near impossible to find (unless it's a carriage bolt, and you can't use that here). In fact, recently, even bolts of this kind are having their threads stop even lower than they used to! I guess it saves the manufacturer money, but does us no good. The problem is, we have to add a nut, but the threads stop short on the length bolt we need.

So even with the washer under the head of the bolt, I still have to add washers to the bottom so that the nut will have threads to grab. If you have to do this too, you'll need to use a jam nut, and not a regular nut. We just don't have much room to work here! So go ahead and tighten all this down really well.

Here's why we don't have much room: this part mounts to the tripod. The nut cannot extend beyond the collar in your surveyor's tripod. I've taken the legs off the tripod so you can get a better look. The ruler is sitting on the base of this collar. If your nut goes beyond the collar, the whole thing will wobble. Not good! So get away with whatever you can; no washers, washers and a jam nut, whatever. Just don't go beyond the collar base on the tripod.

21 Set this unit on top of the flange bearing and add your ½" (14 mm) bolts.

Add nuts to each bolt. I'm using stop nuts because once you put them on, they hold really well.

If your bolts are too short to take a stop nut, you can add jam nuts instead. Just make sure you use some thread-locking goo on them!

22 When you're ready to attach the cradle to the tripod, use a big washer or two. The washer needs to be big enough to grab the bottom of the collar on the tripod. I'm using a big steel square one with a smaller one on top of that. Then add a wing nut and tighten the pa-jeezus out of it.

If you want, you can add some padding of some sort to the base (like some kind of rubber). This will keep it really snug (though I've never had the base turn without the padding, so I guess this is more psychological than anything else). I used a spray adhesive from the automotive store to glue the padding on.

Killer Camera Rigs That You Can Build

And there you have it. We'll be adding the monitor mount in the section, "Make It Groovy" later in this chapter.

Making the Bottom Boom Arm

The bottom boom is that big thing that holds all the weight, so it needs to be hefty. Before we get into the materials you'll need, you should think some things out first. The total length of my boom is 20' (6 meters). That's really long. Really. Not kidding. Most commercial jibs don't even come close. With that in mind, how do I get 20' of crane to the shoot? You can break this down anyway you want. I've chosen to make four 5' sections. You can make two 10' (3 meters) sections and save yourself some time and money.

Each joined section looks like this. One end of one section slides into this big box-looking thing.

Since I have four sections of boom, I needed three box sections. It's also helpful to take a marker and write "Camera End" on one end of a piece of square aluminum tube and "Weight End" on another piece of square aluminum tube once all of your boom pieces are cut. This will really help if you're building sections like I did.

☐ If you're making a 20' (6 meters) boom like mine, you'll need some big aluminum tube: 2" (50 mm) wide ×4" (100 mm) tall × ⅛" (3 mm) thick. If you're making a boom under 13' long, you can get away with 2" (50 mm) × 2" (50 mm) aluminum tube that's ⅛" (3 mm) thick. Again, I have four 5' long pieces that require three joined sections.

☐ For each joined section you'll need the following.

☐ (2) aluminum bars 4" (100 mm) wide × 12" (30 cm) long × ¼" (7 mm) thick.

☐ (2) aluminum bars 2½" (63 mm) wide × 12" (30 cm) long × ¼" (7 mm) thick.

☐ (1) aluminum bar ¾" (19 mm) to 1" (25 mm) wide × 13" (33 cm) long × ¹⁄₁₆" (1.5 mm) thick. This is just a really thin strip of aluminum you'll be bending into a rectangle. Most hardware stores carry this in 36" (91 cm) long strips.

That's all the aluminum for each *joined* section. Remember, that's the list for one joined section. If you have three joined sections, multiply that by three. Two joined sections, multiply that by two. Get it?

☐ (2) aluminum bars 4″ (100 mm) wide × 12″ (30 cm) long × ¼″ (7 mm) thick. This is used to reinforce the pivot hole that the boom cranes up or down on. It's simply bolted to each side of the square aluminum tube. I point this out because if you're making a boom under 14′ (4.25 meter), you won't really need it, but it's still a good idea. On my crane, I've put two pivot holes 10″ (25 cm) apart just in case I simply have to have a little more reach out of the crane. Why not just put one hole with all the reach I can muster? Because that will add about 60 lbs to the counterweight I have to haul around! Yep, inches can add up to pounds just like my waistline.

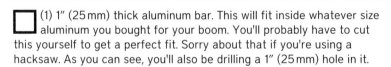

☐ (1) 1″ (25 mm) thick aluminum bar. This will fit inside whatever size aluminum you bought for your boom. You'll probably have to cut this yourself to get a perfect fit. Sorry about that if you're using a hacksaw. As you can see, you'll also be drilling a 1″ (25 mm) hole in it.

☐ (1) round bar aluminum. 1″ (25 mm) diameter × 36″ (91 cm) long. This is an adjustable bar that counterweights can slide along for fine-tuning the balance of the crane. You'll also see that the weights are held on the rod by a *shaft collar* on each side. You can also use conduit fittings that we used on the other cranes, but these look nicer. You'll find them a little later in the materials list. If you just happen to be using a 1″ (25 mm) floor flange bearing, you can use the thick aluminum tube that you have left over from making the cradle.

This is all the aluminum you'll need to build the boom. There is more aluminum to come for the camera mount and tilt mechanism later in the chapter, but as I mentioned, building this in sections is a little easier on you (I promise).

Remember, this is for *one* joined section. Multiply the nuts and bolts by the number of joined sections you have.

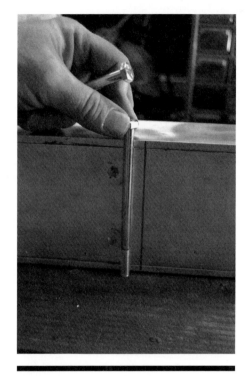

☐ *Note*: The length of the bolts is based on the size of my square tube aluminum and the ¼" (7 mm) bar. If you're going a different way, measure carefully! You need room for a stop nut and washer.

☐ (4) ⁵⁄₁₆" (8 mm) bolts by 3" (76 mm) long.

☐ (2) ⁵⁄₁₆" (8 mm) bolts × 5" (12 cm) long.

☐ (6) washers for the ⁵⁄₁₆" (8 mm) bolts.

☐ (6) ⁵⁄₁₆" (8 mm) stop nuts. Stop nuts have that little nylon ring that grips the bolt threads. You can use a regular bolt with some thread-locking goo if you want.

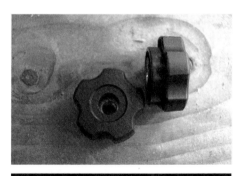

☐ (2) ⁵⁄₁₆" (8 mm) female clamping knobs. Just so you know, *male* clamping knobs have the bolt attached to the knob.

☐ (2) ⁵⁄₁₆″ (8 mm) bolts for the clamping knobs. These can be the same length or a bit longer than what's listed for the bolts that will be permanent. You'll be taking these in and out every time you build or tear down the crane, so because of the thickness of the knobs, you can go a little longer if you have trouble finding the exact length at the hardware store. You'll need one 3″ (76 mm) to 3½″ (88 mm) long, and one 5″ (12 cm) to 5½″ (13 cm) long.

Not to be a nag about it, but this completes the list for *one* joined section. I know how some of you like to skim when reading this stuff, and don't want to make you go back to the hardware store more times than you have to!

Now we're back to stuff that doesn't multiply depending on the sections.

☐ (4) ¼″ (7 mm) hex head (Allen head) screws, ½″ (14 mm) long. These don't have to be the hex head style at all. They just look nice.

☐ (1) ⅜″ (9.5 mm) clamping knob. This is a different size than the one mentioned earlier! It's for holding the fine-tuning weight rod.

☐ (2) shaft collars with a 1″ (25 mm) bore. These are the things that hold the counterweights on your rod. The bore is the size of the hole in the middle. It might be a good idea to go metric here because sometimes a 1″ (25 mm) bore fits a 1″ (25 mm) pipe, and sometimes it doesn't. An inch equals 25.4 mm exactly, so if you get a bore that is 25.5 mm to 26 mm, you'll be safe. If you can't find that size, go ahead and get an inch bore. I'll show you how to grind out the bore just a bit. There's also a little set screw in these shaft collars that you'll need to find an Allen wrench to fit. (An Allen wrench set is a good idea!).

☐ (1) ⅜″ (9.5 mm) jam nut. Remember these? They are narrower than a regular nut.

☐ (1) 36″ (91 cm) length of ⅜″ (9.5 mm) threaded rod. You'll be using a lot of this later, so you might as well get 36″ (91 cm) now.

☐ (2) weight lifting dumb bells. These are the short ones for pumping your arms. We're going to use them for holding our weights. You'll be taking the rubber grips off, so don't worry about that.

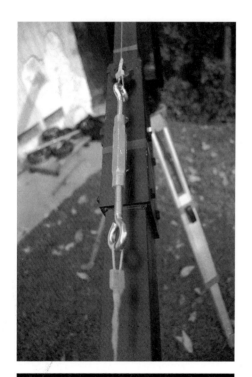

☐ How long is your crane? If it's over 12', you'll *probably* need to support it with some cable. Don't worry, you can always add this after the crane is completely finished. But if you're building a big monster like mine, let's get the cable stuff you'll need now.

☐ (1) ³/₈" (9.5 mm) turnbuckle by at least 7" (17 cm) long with the eyebolts completely screwed in.

☐ (2) ³/₈" (9.5 mm) eyebolts. These are not the eyebolts in your turnbuckle, but extra ones you'll also need. The length depends on the height of your boom. Since mine is 4", the bolt part of the eyebolt (not including the eye!) needs to be at least 4¹/₂" (114 mm) long.

Killer Camera Rigs That You Can Build

☐ (2) ⅜" (9.5 mm) stop nuts and (2) washers for the eyebolts.

☐ ⅛" (3 mm) cable. How long is your boom? Measure the length and add 2'. That's how much cable you'll need to buy.

☐ (4) ⅛" (3 mm) ferrules for connecting the cable.

Tools List for the *Double Indemnity* Boom

Most everything that's listed in the *cradle* section plus:

☐ A ⁵⁄₁₆" (8 mm) drill bit that is 6" (15 cm) long. Truth be told, I couldn't find one, but I know they exist. It has to be long enough to go through the width of the boom aluminum plus the two ¼" (7 mm) thick pieces. What I did was to get a long ¼" (7 mm) drill bit to go all the way through both sides of the boom, then I drilled out the ¼" (7 mm) holes with a ⁵⁄₁₆" (8 mm) bit by drilling out the hole on one side, then flipping it over for the other. Trying to measure out each side of the boom, then drilling the holes with a shorter bit, is a bad way to go. It's near impossible to get one hole to line up perfectly with the other.

☐ A couple of big shims will be a big help when building the connecting "box." I'm using shims that I usually use to level dolly track.

☐ A long level. If you use dolly track, you should have this already! If you use dolly track, and don't have a level, you need one.

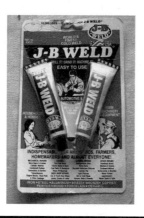

☐ J-B Weld. I know this is in the previous list, but I wanted to remind you here. You'll need at least one package. Do not get the quick drying kind! You need some time to work before it starts to dry.

☐ A Sharpie® marker.

Let's Build the Boom!

1 Let's look at the crane in its broken down state. The 5′ section at the bottom of the photo carries counterweight on the left side, there are two pivot holes around the middle to mount it to the cradle, and a clean right-hand side. The right-hand side slides into the box on the 5′ section just above it. Then that slides into the next 5′ section and so on. If this photo were in color, you'd see that I've used color tape to code the sections: blue goes into blue, red to red, and yellow to yellow. With the exception of the weight section, each 5′ piece of aluminum has a connecting box on one end and is clean on the other. The last boom section has a connecting box on one end, and holes for mounting the camera tilt mount on the other. If you're making a 10′ crane with two 5′ pieces, you'd only have one connecting box, right?

So let's build those connecting boxes.

The ¼″ (7 mm) thick aluminum bars that we will be using are 12″ (30 cm) long. 6″ (15 cm) of that mounts to one end of a boom section, and the other 6″ (15 cm) forms a box to slide the next section of boom into.

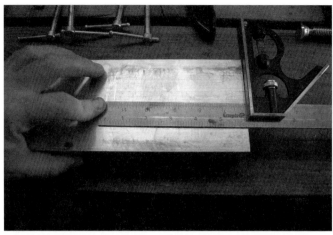

Set your combo square to 6″ (15 cm). Set the edge of the square against the end of a 5′ section and mark the square tube aluminum at 6″ (15 cm) in from the edge with a prick punch.

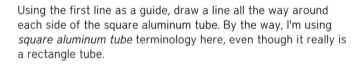

Use a Sharpie or other fine marker to draw a line across the piece at the 6″ (15 cm) point.

Using the first line as a guide, draw a line all the way around each side of the square aluminum tube. By the way, I'm using *square aluminum tube* terminology here, even though it really is a rectangle tube.

2 Use some 60 grit sandpaper and sand each side of the boom, up to the line you drew. If you don't have a sander, you can do this by hand, but this makes really quick work of it. When you're done with that, take the four pieces of aluminum bar that make up the box and sand at least one side and the long edges of all the pieces.

Clean the surfaces well with acetone and a rag.

Don't forget to clean the aluminum bar as well!

3 It will help if you use a block of wood or two to keep the first 6″ (15 cm) off your bench.

Mix up a big batch of J-B Weld.

Smear a thin layer of J-B Weld on all four sides of the tube. *Warning:* Stay back from the edge at least an inch! Two inches might even be better. You *do not* want this stuff oozing into the receiving part of the box! Really important!

Killer Camera Rigs That You Can Build

 4 Carefully line the edge of the aluminum bars to the 6" (15 cm) line you made. Have some clamps ready to hold the pieces as you go.

I'm using a scrap piece of aluminum from the boom to support the aluminum bar. You can use wood wedges or wood scraps cut to size. You can also just hold it with your hand. You need one free hand because I need you to coat the edges of the aluminum bar with J-B Weld. You need to put a little on the edges of the bar that make up the receiving box. Try to stay to the outside edge of the bar, and be very spare with the J-B Weld here. You don't want it oozing inside the box!

Get the sides of the box on there and clamp it as shown, the outside edges being forced up against the larger bars.

You can now add some clamps to the back end to hold the larger bar against the aluminum tube, and a couple on the front to sandwich the top and bottom against the larger bar as well.

Now look inside the box. If there is any J-B Weld that has oozed out inside, soak a towel in acetone, and clean it out before it dries. It might help to have a long screwdriver ready so that you can really force the towel into the edges to clean it. While you're at it, make sure that the edges of the wide aluminum are square against the edges of the narrower aluminum. You don't want them the least bit off kilter, making your box smaller!

Repeat these steps for each receiving box you need to make. Remember, the box will only be on *one* end of a boom section, *not* on both ends!

Let the J-B Weld dry overnight.

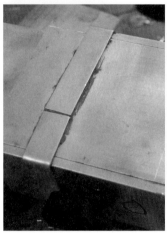

See this little aluminum band that wraps around the outer edge of our box? There's going to be a lot of pressure on the box, and this will help a lot. Within the next steps, you'll see that band in some of the photos. I decided that it's safer to do another step next and then the band. So don't panic. We'll get to the band a little later.

5 Now we're going to bolt the box permanently onto the tube aluminum in the first 6″ (15 cm). Use a Sharpie to draw a line on the outside of the box where the aluminum tube on the inside ends—in other words, 6″ from the edge of the box. By the way, you may ask yourself, "*Hey, why don't I just bolt the thing on there and forget about the J-B Weld?*" This has to be stronger than you think. Gluing and bolting is the way to go.

Bolt placement isn't critical here. You just need one in each corner. I'm measuring in 1″ (25 mm) from the top and side edges and marking it. I'm using a Sharpie here so that you can see the marks. You can use a prick punch or center punch.

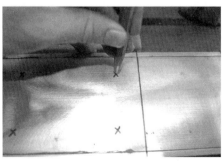

Use a prick punch to dimple your metal where the drill holes will be.

6 Load a ⁵⁄₁₆″ (8 mm) bit into your drill press. I'm supporting one end of this long piece with a light stand on one end, and a 2×4 block of wood on the drill press platform so that my bit will have some room underneath when it goes through the other side.

290

When working on one end of a long piece, you'll need to support the opposite end *and* make sure the piece is level. I'm using a level sitting on top of the aluminum piece and raising or lowering the ends until the bubble in the level is perfect. You simply cannot have wonky holes!

Drill out all four holes.

7 Now we need two bolts from top to bottom. Again, placement isn't a huge concern except that you don't want them over the bolt holes you've already drilled! So figure out where that is, and place a mark on top of the box, halfway across.

Dimple those two holes with a prick punch.

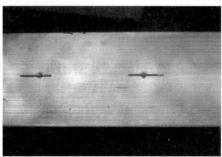

I couldn't find a ⁵⁄₁₆" (8 mm) drill bit that would go all the way though. My solution was to use a long ¼" (7 mm) bit to go all of the way through, then load up the ⁵⁄₁₆" (8 mm) bit and drill out the ¼" (7 mm) hole on one side, then flip the piece over and drill out the other side. *Note*: Depending on the reach of your drill press, you may find that you can't go all of the way through both sides even with this long bit. The solution is to drill one side, turn off the drill press, and crank up the drill press platform, letting the drill bit go into the hole you just made. Level your piece, and then continue on through the other side.

8 Add your bolts. Use a stop nut and a washer.

And tighten them down really well.

Bee-U-Ti-Ful! (And you thought this was going to be hard).

ADDING THE ALUMINUM BAND

9 Take that 1/16" (1.5 mm) thick piece of aluminum that is probably 36" long. Mark the band with a prick punch where the edges of the box fall.

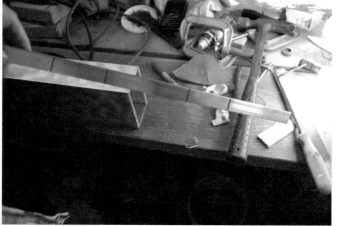

Once you have each edge marked on the band, you can cut it at the last mark with a hacksaw.

Killer Camera Rigs That You Can Build

10 Clamp it into your vise at one of the lines. Make sure the top edge of the aluminum band is even with the top edge of the vise.

Thwack that thing with a hammer until you have a nice square bend.

Move it to the next line, and bend it again. Keep moving and bending until you have a rectangle.

11 Scrape up the inside with some 60 grit sandpaper and clean it with some acetone. Sand and clean the box where you'll be putting this band too!

12 Mix up some J-B Weld and smear it on the inside of your band. Slip it over the end of the box. Again, placement isn't too critical; anywhere from ¼" (7 mm) to 1" (25 mm) from the edge. Add some clamps on the top first. Use caution when clamping the sides! If you push the edges of the box in, you'll never be able to slide another section of the boom into the box. As a precaution, it's a really good idea to put some shims or build up lumber scraps inside the box before you add the side clamps to keep the pressure from the clamps from folding in the sides of the box. The sides are really strong, but even if you push them in the slightest little bit, you will be in trouble later. Let it dry overnight.

13 Now we need to prepare the sections that slide into these boxes.

If you haven't already, it's a good idea to write "camera end" on the end of a 5' section and "weight end" on another. (And keep in mind, if you're copying mine exactly, the weight end section will *not* have a connecting box on either end.) Marking them in this way will help quite a lot. You don't want to go filing down a section by accident.

Now it seems like the clean end will just slide into the box, no problem. It just doesn't. Sure, you can get it in there, but it's a pain to get out again. We want something that is easy in and easy out. All we have to do is take a little metal off the clean end.

Measure down 6" (15 cm) from the edge as you did before, and draw a line around the tube with a sharpie. Then clamp it to your bench.

14 Use a metal file to remove the square edges up to the 6" (15cm) mark. You'll be surprised how easily the metal comes off, so don't get depressed. You'll be done in no time.

Then press the file flat against the surface and have at it again. You probably won't do much good in the middle, but the edges will start to go.

Here's a close look at the edge. I'm stopping at the 6" (15cm) line, but don't worry if you go a little over.

Load the wire brush into your hand drill and clean it up a bit.

Repeat the filing on each side. Don't forget to clamp it down!

 15 Sand it down really well with 60 grit sandpaper.

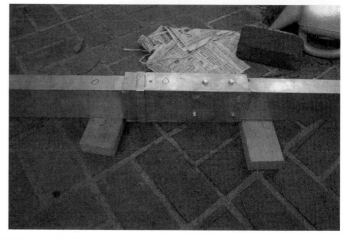

Try sliding it into one of the boxes (it might be a good idea to spray some WD-40 into the box first just in case). If it slides in without you forcing it, you're done. If not, you may notice some scratches or marks on the clean piece where it got hung up. If so, file down the piece on those marks. Just keep going until they slide together nicely.

Killer Camera Rigs That You Can Build

Now if you've slid them together and can't get them apart, here's a little trick: put clamps on either side of the connecting box and push the far clamp with your feet and pull the closer clamp with your hands. Then head back to the bench for more filing.

Let's take a reminder look at the finished pieces. See the shining ends on the right? That's what we are working on right now. The last piece of boom at the top of the photo doesn't have a shiny end because that's where the camera goes.

So finish up each of the ends that goes in a connecting box the same way.

16 Next we need a way to keep the pieces together once we've connected them. That's where our bolts and clamping knobs come in. There are only two: one in the top and one on the side. See the top knob? You want to place your hole as close to the metal band as you can without the knob actually touching the top of the band. It has to sit flush on the top of the box. The one on the side needs to sit 4" (100 mm) to 5" (12 cm) from the end of the box.

So we got the placement figured out. Now it needs to be at the halfway point across the top and the halfway point across the side. Use your prick punch to put a dimple in those two points. Once again, I'm using the long ¼" (7 mm) drill bit to go through the top, all the way through the bottom. Then making those holes larger with my ⁵⁄₁₆" (8 mm) bit, just as we did before when building the connecting box.

The side is no problem since my ⁵⁄₁₆" (8mm) bit can easily reach through the 2½" (63mm) it needs to go.

17 Once your holes are drilled in the box, insert a connecting piece of the boom. Think about this first though: Do you want all the bolt heads on the connecting boxes facing the same way once the entire crane is done? It doesn't matter in the way the crane operates, but it does look much nicer. So, is there a connecting box on the other end of the piece you just inserted? If so, are the bolts facing the same direction? If not, take it out and flip it around. Next draw a little symbol, number, whatever on the male side and the female side of each connecting piece. This way you'll know which piece fits into which later. As you can see, I've drawn little circles.

Since I don't have enough room to load this 10' (3 meters) section onto my drill press, I'm going to use a hand drill. It's easy because your guide hole in your connecting box is already there. So drill a ⁵⁄₁₆" (8mm) hole into the clean end that is inside the box. Flip the whole thing over and do the bottom hole.

Add a bolt and the clamping knob to this hole to hold everything in place. Then do the sides the same way.

Look! Strong like bull.

OK, pull them apart and check inside where the holes are. Are there little metal bits sticking up? If so, file them off.

Repeat for each joined section and you're done.

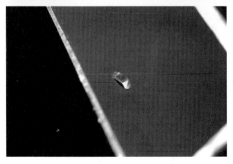

Killer Camera Rigs That You Can Build

Making the Counterweight Section

The 5′ long counterweight section has a lot going on. Not only does it hold the weights, but a fine-tuning bar, and this is the section your pivot hole goes on. There's a lot to do, so let's get started.

First, you've probably already filed down one end of this section to fit a connecting box. It may be obvious, but if you're tired and hungry you might get confused and think that this is the weight end. It's not. Let's put our pivot hole in first.

The pivot hole is what the entire crane booms up and down from. As I mentioned, I put two just in case I need a tiny bit more reach out of the crane. To be honest, I've never used that second hole, so I'm not sure how clever I was being in the end. If you want to save yourself a bit of work, just put one hole. You'll be fine.

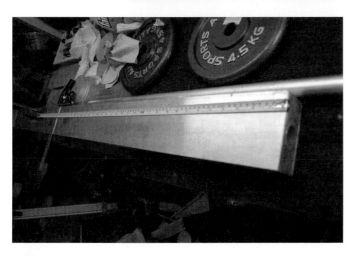

Halfway across your aluminum tube, put a mark across your first mark. Since my tube is 4″ (100 mm) wide, that's a mark at 2″ (50 mm). Do the same on the other mark if you have one. Use a prick punch to dimple the tube and drill a ½″ (14 mm) hole through the boom. Make very certain that the drill bit is going straight! It's so important here, so be very careful that the piece is level on your drill press platform.

1 Where to put it? The closer to the weights this hole is, the more weight you'll have to haul around. I know I've said this before a few times in this book, but on shoot day, it is a big deal. Do you really want to haul an extra hundred pounds for just another foot of camera height? With that in mind, start on the weight end and measure toward the camera end 40″ (1 meter) and mark it. If you want to drill two pivot holes, make a mark at 30″ (76 cm) as well.

A couple of things I know some of you will ask about: *Don't I need a bearing for the crane to pivot on?* No, you don't. I've made cranes with the bearing and without. I couldn't tell the difference in the operation of the crane. Plus, to inset a couple of bearings here is a lot of trouble without an advantage. And the second question: *Is a ½″ (14 mm) bolt big enough?* Yes; most steel bolts have about a 3,000 lb rating. That's plenty. But I know a ½″ (14 mm) bolt doesn't *look* awesome. But hey, if you want to go to the trouble of drilling 1″ (25 mm) holes in your cradle and your tube, who am I to stop you? Knock yourself out!

2 Next along our journey is to add holes for our weights. The thing to keep in mind is that if you put the holes too close together, the weights will get in each other's way, but you want them as close as possible too!

If you haven't bought your weights yet, off to the sporting goods shop you go. Don't worry. I'll wait. At a minimum for this part, you'll need two 10 lb weights. That's what is in the photo, because I like to work in minimums around here (I think there's a joke in there somewhere). Ideally, two 25 lb weights is, well, ideal. In the end, my 20' (6 meters) boom requires close to 170 lbs with my Panasonic HVX200 camera. Bigger camera? More weight. Be aware: There are two types of weights at your sporting goods store. One type has a huge "Olympic" size hole for the dumbbell. The ones we need have the smaller 1" (25 mm) hole (approximately). The smaller holes are much more common.

Anyway, back to building. Set the weights on the weight end (duh) of your boom. The back weight can go off the end of the aluminum tube a bit. The edge of the second weight needs to be about 3" (76 mm) from the edge of the first weight. Stagger them so that the back weight's hole is closer to the top of the tube, and the second weight's hole is closer to the bottom of the tube. Don't worry about being exact on that point yet.

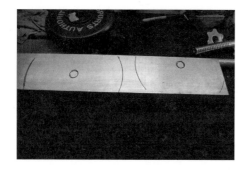

3 Use a marker to trace the edges of the weights and the holes. Set the weights aside.

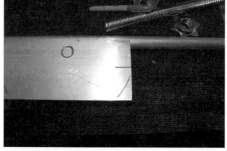

4 See that little line on the end of the tube in the photo? We need to run the counter weight aluminum bar up through the center of the square tube, so make a reference mark halfway across the tube. In my case, that's 2" since the tube is 4".

Get that 1" (25 mm) diameter by 36" (91 cm) long aluminum rod that will be used for fine adjustments. Lay it on that halfway mark, and make sure it's running straight along the center of the tube. Set one dumbbell bar next to the rod on the top near the traced hole of the weight, and a second dumbbell bar near the traced weight hole under the rod. The idea is that if you don't need the support cable, you can push this rod between the dumbbells. Even if you do end up needing the support cable, you can push this rod beyond the first dumbbell.

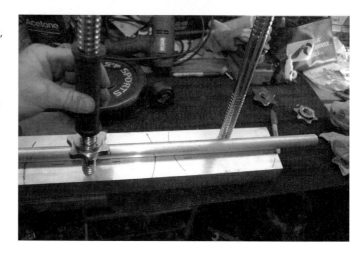

Killer Camera Rigs That You Can Build

Take a marker and trace around the end of the dumbbell. Surprisingly, these ended up in almost the exact same places as the trace of the weight hole. An accident, I assure you.

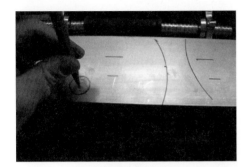

5 Take your prick punch and put a dimple in the middle of the circles you just traced.

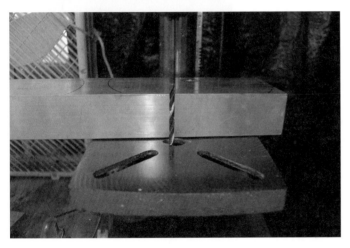

Use a long ¼" (7 mm) bit to drill a hole on your dimples, all the way through both sides of the tube.

Using the ¼" (7 mm) hole as a guide, use a 1" (25 mm) hole saw to drill a hole on the two ¼" (7 mm) holes. Flip the tube over, and do the same (the hole saw is not long enough to go through both sides in one pass).

Use acetone to clean off all of your marks.

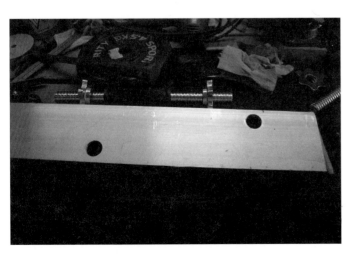

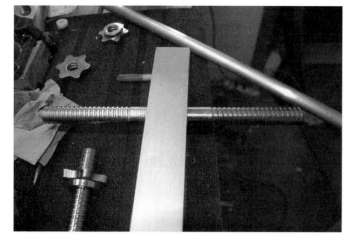

Remove the rubber handles from the dumbbells. I just twisted mine off. If they are troublesome, you can cut them off with a utility knife. Slide the clean bar through the holes. They will be loose, but that's ok. You want to be able to remove them easily. When you put weights and the big spindle nut on there, they will be nice and tight on the crane.

ADDING THE FINE-TUNING WEIGHT BAR

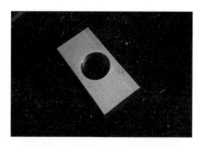

I talked about this chunk of 1" (25mm) thick aluminum in the materials section. It has to fit exactly inside the square aluminum tube. If you haven't cut that piece yet, get to it! Once it's cut, drill a 1" (25mm) hole in the middle of it.

Use 60 grit sandpaper to roughen up the first inch or so of the inside of the tube (weight end please!). Clean it with acetone.

Add some J-B Weld to the interior of the tube and slide the block of aluminum in so that it is flush with the edge of the tube. Clean up any J-B Weld that oozes out with a rag and some acetone. Let it dry overnight.

Killer Camera Rigs That You Can Build

8 We've tapped so many holes at this point that you should be an old hand at it by now. Using the bit that is the match for a ³⁄₈" (9.5 mm) tap, drill a hole through the top down into the 1" (25 mm) hole. Since the chunk of aluminum with the hole in it is 1" (25 mm) thick, measure back from the end of the tube ¹⁄₃" (14 mm), then halfway across the tube (in my case that's 1" [25 mm]) and dimple it. That's where your hole goes. Once your hole is drilled, use the ³⁄₈" (9.5 mm) tap to put threads in the hole.

9 You can adjust the rod by sliding it in or out, then tighten the threaded rod down onto it.

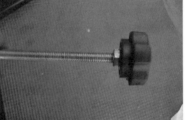

To add the ³⁄₈" (9.5 mm) rod, screw on a jam nut, then screw a female knob down to the jam nut and tighten the two together.

You have a couple of choices on how long to make the threaded rod. In this photo, it is long enough to extend above the weights so that it is easy to adjust the weighted rod when the crane is all put together. I like this way the best, because getting my big fat hands in between the weights is a pain. On the other hand, the shorter version is good for storing the crane when not in use. It's up to you.

10 To hold the fine-tuning weights in place, I'm using two shaft collars; one on each side of the group of weights. You simply push them against the weights and tighten down the set screw with an Allen wrench.

If for some reason you bought a 1" (25 mm) bore on your shaft collars and they don't fit the 1" (25 mm) aluminum rod (sometimes they fit, sometimes they don't), you can grind them out with a round metal file or with a round grinding stone that fits in a drill. It doesn't take much to grind them out; just clamp them into your vise and grind away. Make sure your grinding stone is smaller than 1" (25 mm) in diameter!

11 One last thing for the adjustment rod. Even though you've glued that chunk of aluminum inside the square tube, it's a good idea to make sure it never moves. Tap two ¼" (7 mm) holes in each side of the tube, into the chunk of aluminum that holds the rod. ½" (14 mm) deep holes are plenty. Screw some ½" (14 mm) screws in there, and it's never going to move.

The finished end should look something like this.

ADDING THE SUPPORT CABLE

12 If you've got a big long crane that requires a lot of counterweight, you'll need to add a support cable. You'll need those long eyebolts that go all the way through the boom from top to bottom.

Measure off about 6' of cable and cut it. There are a number of ways to cut this cable. The easiest and cheapest is to get a chisel, set the cable on your vise under the chisel, and give it a good thwack with a hammer.

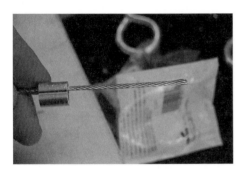

Run the cable through one of the ferrules.

Then through one of the eyebolts and back through the other channel on the ferrule.

Then pound the ferrule with a hammer until the cable is smashed inside.

13 Take the other end of the 6' piece of cable, and attach it to one of the eyebolts on the turnbuckle the same way.

Grab the long piece of cable that you cut the 6' piece from, and attach an eyebolt to one end.

Set your cable and eyebolts aside for a minute.

14 On the weight end of the boom, drill a ³⁄₈″ (9.5 mm) hole down through the top of the boom in between the two holes for the weights. Add an eyebolt with the cable attached and tighten it down well with a washer and nut at the bottom of the boom.

Grab the camera end section of the boom. Measure back about 6″ (15 cm) from the end and drill another ³⁄₈″ (9.5 mm) hole for another eyebolt. Attach this one as well. Make sure the eye of the bolt is facing the same way as it is in the photo.

15 Put all the sections of your boom together. You don't have to put the boom into the cradle at this point like I did. Just join all the sections. At this point you should have cable attached to the weight end through an eyebolt, then attached to the turnbuckle through one of its eyebolts. Then a long piece of cable traveling up from an eyebolt on the camera end.

Unscrew the eyebolts from the turnbuckle nearly all the way. Thread the piece of cable coming from the camera end through the second eyebolt on the turnbuckle and pull it tight with some locking pliers.

While holding it tight, mark the cable where it goes through the eyebolt on the turnbuckle. Now you can let go.

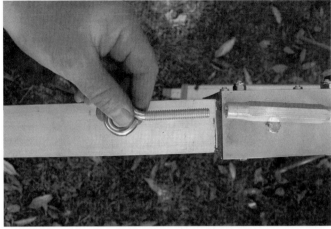

(16) Unscrew the eyebolt from the turnbuckle.

Find the mark on the cable, and attach the eyebolt at that mark with another ferrule. Cut off the extra cable.

You can coil the cable up and tape it to the boom for now. When you coil this cable, start at the eyebolt that is attached to the boom. If you start at the "free" end, it will start twisting in on itself.

TAKE THE CAMERA END SECTION OFF THE BOOM

 Measure in 1" (25 mm) from the end and mark it with a prick punch. Then measure halfway across (that's 2" (50 mm) for me), and make another mark across the first.

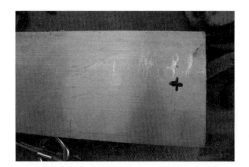

 Drill a ½" (14mm) hole through both sides of the tube. Make sure you are going straight and true!

 You want to put it together now? It's a good idea, 'cause we got some thinkin' to do. Make sure you have strengthened the surveyor's tripod before you put the boom on there!

Attach the cradle to the tripod.

Set the tripod up where you have plenty of room for the boom and the weights coming off the back. You *must* use a spreader and a sandbag on each leg of the tripod plus a sandbag in the middle of the spreader. Or...

Surveyor's tripods have these really long spiked feet. If you can shove the feet all the way up to the foot peg, you don't have to use sandbags. If you can't shove the feet into the ground that far, you simply must use sandbags. End of discussion. I'm not kidding. This is dangerous.

 Set a multilevel or bubble level on the base of the cradle. Release the clamps on all three legs.

Lift the cradle a bit until the legs are extended a few inches. Adjust the cradle until the level reads level. Hold the cradle and lock the legs in place.

Killer Camera Rigs That You Can Build

21 Start with the weight end section of the boom. Hold it in the cradle and thread a ½″ (14mm) bolt through one side of the cradle, through the ½″ (14mm) hole on the boom, then through the other side of the cradle. See that big space between the boom and the cradle sides? We're going to take care of that later.

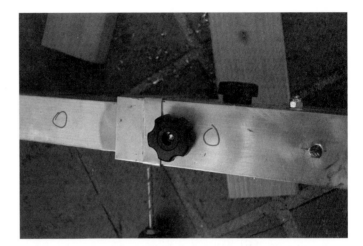

22 Keep adding your sections with the knobs, just like we did when it was on the ground. I sure hope you marked which sections join together like I told ya' to!

23 Uncoil the cables. Screw the eyebolt into the turnbuckle.

Use a screwdriver and pliers to tighten the eyebolts into the buckle.

Make sure the cable is really tight.

 24 Add the fine-tuning rod and the dumbbell bars.

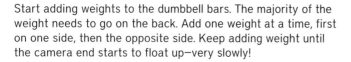

25 Add about 20 lbs to the fine-tuning rod.

Start adding weights to the dumbbell bars. The majority of the weight needs to go on the back. Add one weight at a time, first on one side, then the opposite side. Keep adding weight until the camera end starts to float up—very slowly!

Remember, since there is no camera and no tilt bar, you won't need as much weight now as you will when it's all finished.

Monkey around with it a bit. Take it all the way up. Turn it left and right. How does it feel? Has anything gone terribly, terribly wrong?

Put the camera end on the ground. Adjust the counterweight fine-tuning bar. See what a big difference an inch or two makes? Be careful. Are you sorry you didn't put the pivot hole closer to the camera end? If so, you can always drill another one. This is the time to be critical!

Killer Camera Rigs That You Can Build

Clamp a 5 or 10 lb weight on the camera end. *Now* how much weight do you have to add to the back end? Crazy, huh? It's a lot more than you thought, isn't it?

Next we'll be building the tilt bar and camera mount. Almost done!

Don't take the crane apart just yet.

Materials List for the *Double Indemnity* Crane Tilt Arm and Camera Mount

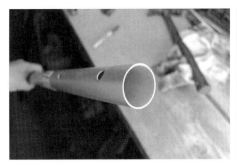

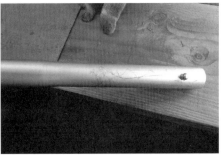

☐ Aluminum snap handles. You'll find this in the concrete supply section of most large home centers. They are a handle for a "float" to smooth out concrete. I've seen them in 5' and 6' sections that snap together. Not only are they cheaper than raw aluminum, but you don't have to build a way to connect them or break them down. I've also checked Web sites in Europe and Australia for these. Apparently they are available everywhere. So how long do you need? Measure your crane boom from the front of your cradle all the way to the camera end. Get enough snap together handles to cover this distance. As an alternative, you can use ¾" (19 mm) square tube aluminum. But you'll need to build the "boxes" to connect them. The handles are a much better way to go.

☐ Measure across the bottom of your camera and add 2" (50 mm). You'll need aluminum bar this long by ³⁄₄" (19 mm) to 1" (25 mm) thick × 2" (50 mm) wide.

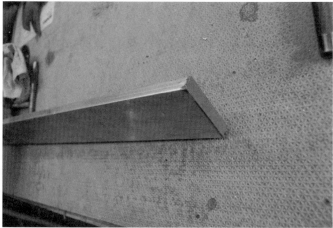

☐ (5) aluminum bars 1½" (38 mm) wide × 16" (40 cm) long × ¼" (7 mm) thick.

☐ (1) aluminum bar 2" (50 mm) wide × 26" (66 cm) to 36" [91 cm] long × ¼" (7 mm) thick. (26" is probably going to be plenty for most cameras. My supplier sells this stuff in 36" [91 cm] lengths, and it's much cheaper that way.)

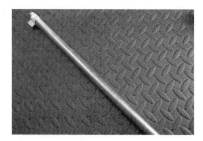

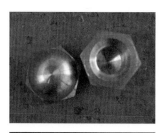

☐ ³⁄₈" (9.5 mm) threaded rod. You should have some left over if you bought the 36" (91 cm) long rod from before.

☐ (6) ³⁄₈" (9.5 mm) cap nuts. You can use regular nuts, but these look nicer.

☐ (1) ½" (14 mm) nut. The one shown is called a lock nut because it has that large grooved base. You can use a regular nut if you need to.

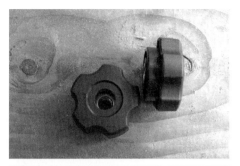

☐ (3) ⅜″ (9.5 mm) clamping knobs.

☐ (1) ¼″ (7 mm) male clamping knob. This attaches the camera to the plate. Most camera holes in America are ¼″. The knob bolt needs to be long enough to go up through the ¾″ (19 mm) or 1″ (25 mm) thick aluminum bar with enough left over to go into the hole at the base of your camera. If it's too long, your camera won't tighten down against the mount. If you're not sure how long you need, get something too long and cut the bolt with a hacksaw. You can also use a regular bolt for this.

☐ Handles for controlling the tilt. I'm using bicycle pegs. They just look cool and are pretty cheap. You can use just about anything for handles that you can figure out. Even a wood dowel with a hole drilled down the length of it. I've also used the handle that's in the stabilizer chapter. It's a little work to build, but operates really nicely.

☐ (4) nylon washers with a ½″ (14 mm) hole or larger. You'll also need nylon washers or spacers for the ⅜″ (9.5 mm) threaded rod. It's a little difficult to tell you exactly what you need here. You're going to need to put the tilt mount on the find that out. But, start with eight and we'll figure it out later.

☐ (2) ⅜″ (9.5 mm) wing nuts or two more ⅜″ (9.5 mm) female clamping knobs. Clamping knobs look nicer, but aren't a necessity. You will also need a ½″ (14 mm) wing nut.

☐ You'll also need something to act as a spacer to hold your boom in the center of the bolt on your cradle. You can use just about anything. A bunch of washers, that thick aluminum tube you used for the flange bearing if you have any left over, you get the idea. I'm using some thin aluminum tube I had left from the stabilizer.

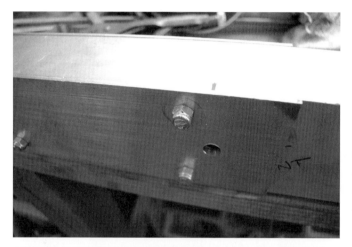

☐ If you want to strengthen the boom at its pivot hole you'll need two pieces of aluminum 12" (30 cm) long × ⅛" (3 mm) to ¼" (7 mm) thick, by however wide your square tube is. In my case, that's 4". I've really debated on whether you actually need this. I don't think you do, but a little more strength here wouldn't hurt, so I've included it. You'll need to keep the extra thickness in mind when you measure for the spacers above for the pivot bolt.

☐ Three or four different colors of electrical tape. I found a bunch of different colors in one package. This is so you can color code the sections that go together. It makes things so much easier! Feel free to come up with your own method. You also can use this to tape a bunch of metal washers together and use them as spacers instead of a bunch of nylon washers. And it's good for taping your support cable ends.

Killer Camera Rigs That You Can Build

Tools List for the *Double Indemnity* Tilt Mount

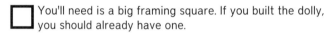

 You'll need is a big framing square. If you built the dolly, you should already have one.

A ⅜" (9.5mm) drill bit.

Let's Build It!

Is your crane still together? It will help later if it is. If not, that's OK, you can wait until you have all the metal tilt arms done.

1 Let's build the little camera mount first.

This is the ¾" (19mm) to 1" (25mm) thick aluminum bar that's 2" (50mm) by the width of your camera base plus 2" (50mm). We need to tap a ⅜" (9.5mm) hole that's at least 1" (25mm) deep. That's minimum!

Locate the exact center of one end of the aluminum bar.

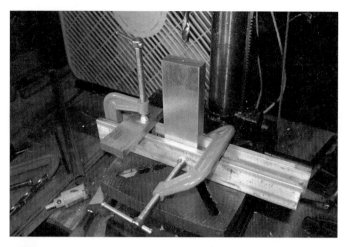

2 Load the drill bit that matches the ⅜" (9.5mm) tap. Mount this piece on your drill press platform so that the drill bit is going straight down through the dimple. I'm using a bunch of scrap metal clamped to the platform and the aluminum bar.

Use your multilevel or bubble level and set it on top of the bar. If it's not level in both directions, adjust it so that it is!

Drill the hole ½" (14mm) farther than you plan on tapping the hole.

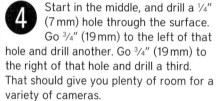

3 Tap the hole.

Pound it hard on the bench to knock out any metal chips. It's also a good idea to spray some water in there to wash out any stubborn pieces.

4 Start in the middle, and drill a ¼" (7mm) hole through the surface. Go ¾" (19mm) to the left of that hole and drill another. Go ¾" (19mm) to the right of that hole and drill a third. That should give you plenty of room for a variety of cameras.

5 Screw some threaded rod all the way into the hole on the edge. Set your clamping knob against the end, and mark the threaded rod on the outside of the knob. Remove the rod, and cut it on that mark with a hacksaw.

Killer Camera Rigs That You Can Build

6 Get that long aluminum bar that's 2″ (50 mm) wide and 26″ to 36″ (91 cm) long. Set the camera on the camera mount bar, then hold the long aluminum bar on edge against it. Use a marker to mark where the top of your camera is on that long bar.

7 Lay the long bar on your bench and measure up 3″ (76 mm) more inches from your top camera mark.

Dimple the center of the bar at that mark.

Go to the bottom of that bar and measure up from the edge half the thickness of your camera mount piece. So if your camera mount piece is 1″ (25 mm) thick, measure up ½″ (14 mm) from the base of the long bar.

Then measure 1″ (25 mm) across (halfway point), mark it, then dimple it.

8 Load a ³⁄₈″ (9.5 mm) bit into your drill press and drill a hole on the bottom dimple.

9 Load a ½″ (14 mm) bit into your press and drill out the dimple above that.

10 OK, stay with me here: Take a look at the photo. Off on the left side, out of frame is a ³⁄₈″ (9.5mm) hole on the bottom of the long bar. Moving to the right, you'll see the big ½″ (14mm) hole. From the middle of the ½″ (14mm) hole, measure 12″ more inches to the right and draw a line across the bar there, ½″ (30cm) above the ½″ (14mm) hole. Use your prick punch and combo square to actually scratch the lines into the metal.

Drill a ³⁄₈″ (9.5mm) hole at that 12″ (30cm) line in the middle of the 2″ (50mm) wide piece. Now you are free to cut the bar. I've measured 2″ (50mm) above from the center of the hole and cut it there.

11 Take your 1½″ (38mm) wide bars, all five of them, and line them up on your bench above the 2″ (50mm) wide bar you just did all that stuff to. Line them up so that they are even on the right edge.

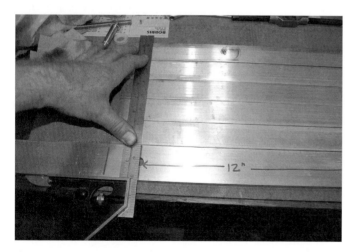

Line the combo square against the bottom 2″ (50mm) wide piece through the line you used to drill the ½″ (14mm) hole. Use your prick punch to scratch a line across all five pieces in exactly the same place.

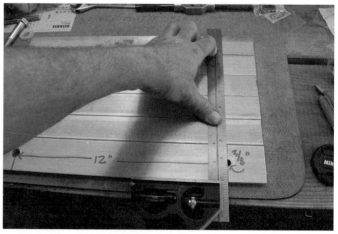

Do the same on the right-hand side running your combo square through the ³⁄₈″ (9.5mm) hole.

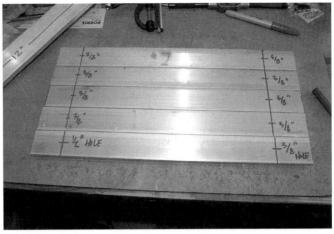

12 Set the 2″ (50 mm) wide piece aside. Set your combo square to half the width of the first 1½″ (38 mm) pieces. Mark a line across the first mark you made on both ends.

Now you'll need to drill some holes. On the first piece, the hole at the bottom (left-hand side) is ½″ (14 mm). All of the others are ⅜″ (9.5 mm). Go ahead and drill the ½″ (14 mm) hole now. Change out your drill bit and drill the ⅜″ (9.5 mm) hole on the opposite end of this first piece.

13 Use a prick punch to dimple the marks on one of the four pieces. Take the remaining four bars and clamp them together with the dimpled bar on top. Make sure that they are even!

Clamp the stack onto your drill press platform and drill out the ⅜″ (9.5 mm) holes on all the pieces at once. Flip them around and drill the hole on the opposite end.

14 Clean them up with the wire brush on a hand drill.

15 Grab one section of the snap-together handle that we'll be using as our tilt bar. As you've probably noticed, these snap together by inserting one end into another, and a little button snaps into one of two holes on the round tube. It just so happens that those holes are ³⁄₈″ (9.5 mm).

So half our work is done. On one of the round tube sections, find the snap hole that is nearest to the end of the tube. We need to drill out a hole that goes all the way through the tube. So use the existing hole as a guide, and drill a ³⁄₈″ (9.5 mm) hole all the way through the other side of the tube. We'll need to drill other holes later, but just this one for now.

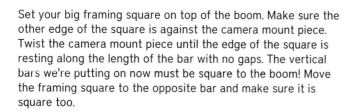

16 Gather up all of your bars, including the camera mount bar, the snap together round tube, three C-clamps, and head for the crane.

On the front of the crane, use a ½″ (14 mm) bolt and nut to attach the camera mount bar, then put the other bar with the ½″ (14 mm) hole in the bottom on the opposite side of the boom. Tighten it down really well. Don't worry about nylon washers or anything like that yet. Just bolt these pieces to the front of the boom.

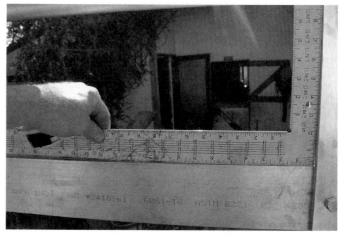

Set your big framing square on top of the boom. Make sure the other edge of the square is against the camera mount piece. Twist the camera mount piece until the edge of the square is resting along the length of the bar with no gaps. The vertical bars we're putting on now must be square to the boom! Move the framing square to the opposite bar and make sure it is square too.

On the top holes, put the round tube with the hole you just drilled in between the two upright bars. Slip a bolt through the bars and tube. Don't worry about bolt length, or adding nuts, or anything like that. We just need a way to hold the tube in place, so your bolt just needs to be long enough to span the gap between the two upright bars.

Killer Camera Rigs That You Can Build

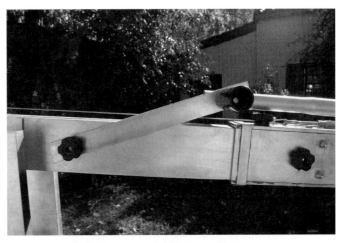

17 Move to the cradle. This is where we are headed: we need to figure out where we can put the two upright bars for tilting the camera. They have to go somewhere between the first joining box on the boom and the pivot hole.

There must be enough room for you to push the bar forward without it snagging on the connecting box.

And there must be enough room for you to pull it back before it hits the big bolt that is holding the boom in the cradle.

So take one of the bars and just hold it about midway between the connecting box and the cradle. Move it back and forth until you find a point on the boom where it doesn't run into anything on the boom. Once you've gotten it, clamp both bars onto the boom opposite each other. Make sure they are square with the boom using your framing square!

18 Now hold up your snap-together round tube in between the two upright pieces. Is it long enough? Is it too long? Too long is much easier to deal with. Too short... if it's just a tiny bit short, it's probably possible to move your upright pieces forward a bit without any problems in the tilt. And this long tube is probably sagging just a bit in the middle. If you support the middle with the help of a friend or a C-clamp and piece of lumber, you might get just enough more length out of it. If this is the case, try it. It would be a big drag to have to buy another section of round tube. If it's too long, great. We'll just cut it.

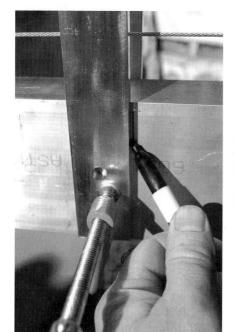

Once the uprights are in the right place and completely square, use a marker to draw a line on each side of one of the bars (you don't have to do this on the opposite bar).

Then hold the round tube in front of one of the holes on the bar, and mark where the hole meets the bar. Your round tube *is* still connected to the camera end bars, right?

It's best as this point to unsnap that section and go drill a 3/8" (9.5mm) hole through that little mark. Just leave everything else on the crane. But please make sure the mark is in the "middle" of the tube lined up with the hole in the upright piece. If it's closer to the top of the tube or the bottom you'll be drilling a hole straight through the wrong place. I know it's a circle, but the tube is snapped together lined up with the hole at the camera end. So you won't be able to twist the tube later if your hole is going through the wrong place! OK, enough jibber jabber. Go drill the ³⁄₈" (9.5mm) hole in the tube and come back. I'll wait here. Oh, bring a bolt back with you.

19 Snap the tube back on and slip a bolt through the tube and upright pieces just like you did on the camera end.

20 Now this round tube is sort of flimsy, so we need to support it in the middle. Go to the middle section of the boom, and find the halfway point between the two connecting boxes and mark it with a Sharpie.

Killer Camera Rigs That You Can Build

Clamp your last two bars at that point, again making sure they are square to the boom.

Again, trace along each outside edge of the upright bar.

Hold the round tube opposite the hole on the bar and mark the tube where the hole falls.

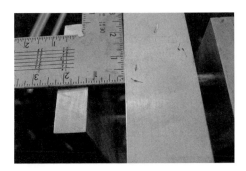

21 Now you can take the crane apart, but leave the cradle part of the boom in.

If you haven't done this yet, here's your best chance to find what size spacers you need on your boom pivot bolt. Adjust the boom on the ½" (14 mm) bolt that runs through the pivot hole so that you have an equal distance from the boom to the edges of the cradle on each side. Write down whatever that measurement happens to be.

Now you can remove the section of boom that's in the cradle.

22 You should have two outlines of the upright bars on two places along the boom. We're going to drill a ⅜" (9.5 mm) hole there.

Measure across the lines and find the halfway point.

Then measure across the width of the boom and find the halfway point there as well.

Dimple it, then drill a ⅜" (9.5 mm) hole all the way through the boom.

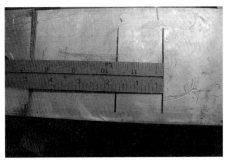

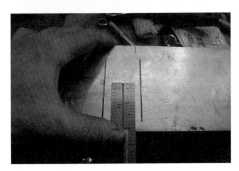

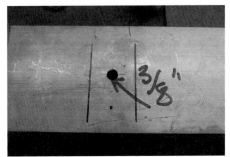

Repeat this on the other section of boom.

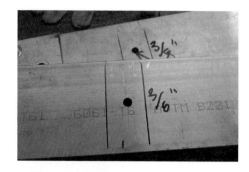

23 Take the center section of the round tube and find your mark for the hole. Drill a ³⁄₈″ (9.5 mm) hole through the tube.

24 Are you using the bicycle pegs as handles? On mine, the threaded hole is for is for a ³⁄₈″ (9.5 mm) bolt. But unfortunately, the threads are wrong for my threaded rod.

It's an easy fix. Just take your ³⁄₈″ (9.5 mm) tap, and tap new threads. I didn't even have to drill a new hole.

Try out the threaded rod in the new holes. Mine worked fine, but if yours is a bit wobbly, you can always use thread-locking goo or add a nut to the inside of the pegs onto the threaded rod on once you have determined the length of rod you'll need.

Killer Camera Rigs That You Can Build

 25 Cut your spacers for the pivot bolt in your cradle. Your spacers must be short enough to allow a nylon washer to rest against the boom on each side.

 26 Let's put the crane together... again.

Slide the pivot bolt in just far enough to add the spacer, then a nylon washer.

Hold the boom section in place and push the bolt through just beyond the opposite hole in the boom. Add a second nylon washer, then hold the spacer there and push the bolt through the spacer, then the rest of the way through the opposite cradle side.

Add a ½" (14 mm) wing nut. You don't have to tighten it down. Maybe just a tiny bit snug. This bolt is going nowhere, even without the wing nut.

Add the other sections of the boom. Connect and tighten the support cable.

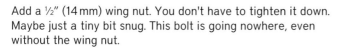

 27 Go to the camera end of the crane. On the camera mount bar, run a ½" (14 mm) bolt through the ½" (14 mm) hole. Then add a nylon washer.

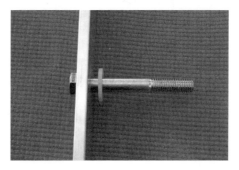

Then run the bolt through the ½" (14 mm) hole on front of the boom, add another nylon washer, then the upright bar, then a nut. These need to be able to move freely when in operation, but you can tighten that nut down for now to keep the upright bars pointing up.

28 Now we need to figure out a couple of things: how long our threaded rod needs to be and how thick our nylon spacers need to be.

Put the round tube in between the bars and slide the threaded rod in there.

I'm using these nice-looking cap nuts to give it a finished look. You can use any old nut. But with the cap nuts, they will only screw on so far, right? So the length of the threaded rod needs to be just long enough to span the two upright bars with enough left on each side to add a cap nut and no longer. You don't want the cap nut tight against the bar! Resting lightly against the bar, or a hairs' width between the bar and the nut, is perfect.

Figure that out, and cut your threaded rod to that length with a hacksaw. While you're at it, cut two more threaded bars the same length.

The second thing we need to figure out is what thickness of nylon spacer will keep the round tube in the middle of that bolt without shifting to one side or the other.

You can stack nylon washers, or get nylon spacers and cut them.

Or put a bunch of metal washers on a bolt and wrap them together with electrical tape.

Once you have all that figured out, attach the tube in between the bars.

29 Next, move the center of the boom. Slip one of the cut threaded rod bits through one of the upright bars, then add a nylon washer, then through the hole in the boom, then another nylon washer, then another bar.

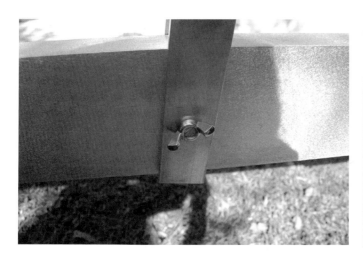

You can use a wing nut here on both sides of the threaded rod, or a couple of clamping knobs. Just remember that when you break the crane down for storage, these connectors come off. It's really best if you use something that can be removed by hand instead of a nut here. But a nut works too.

Then attach the round tube to the top of these upright bars just as you did on the camera end.

30 The reason I didn't have you cut another couple of lengths of threaded rod at the same length before was it will probably need to be longer on the handle end of the tilt. Take a close look at the photo. See where the tilt bar goes back and bumps into the aluminum plate that is there to strengthen the pivot hole? We can't have that. But it's an easy fix. Simply add another nylon washer or two between the tilt bar and the boom surface.

You may have also noticed I'm using female clamping knobs here: one on each side. These are to adjust the tension of the tilt, so you have to use these knobs! It's important. And it's a good idea to make your threaded rod long enough to be near the top of

the knobs when they are screwed on. To recap: You have thicker spacers, the width of the boom, and knobs. So figure out that measurement and cut your threaded rod.

For the top, screw on your handle to some threaded rod, run the rod through one upright, add a spacer (I'm using the electrical tape wrapped washers here) through the round tube, add another spacer through the second upright, then screw on the other handle. (In the photo, the handle isn't screwed on all the way yet. It should be against the bar when you're done.)

31 Leave the camera off for now, but try putting some weights on the back end until the crane floats, and try out the tilt by pushing forward or pulling back on the handle. Try different tensions on the clamping knobs too.

Does everything seem good? Great. Try putting your camera on.

Remember, it mounts on with that male clamping knob.

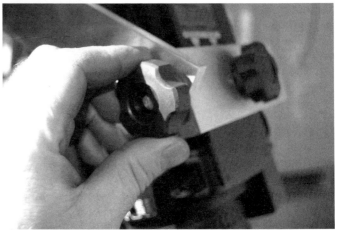

If you want an even more drastic tilt, you can adjust the camera mount to tilt even more.

Killer Camera Rigs That You Can Build

Some Final Touches

It might be a good idea to add some thread-locking goo to the threaded rod that screws into the camera mount.

Wrap some electrical tape around the ends of the cable and the cable ferrules.

If you're *not* going to paint your crane, now is a good time to add thread locking goo to the threads that hold the cap nuts.

If You Are Going to Paint Your Rig

Read Chapter 26, *Painting Your Rigs*. But specifically for this crane there are some things to keep in mind.

Keep the booms connected. You do *not* want to paint the section of the boom or the tilt tube where they join together.

After the paint dries, add color tape to the sections so that you know which section fits into which.

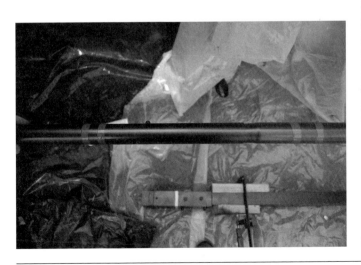

Remember to code the snap together tilt tube as well!

Breaking Down the Crane

Unscrew one of the eyebolts from the turnbuckle and coil the cable starting at the eyebolt in the boom. Use gaffer tape to tape the coil to the boom.

If you're using short threaded rod for the fine adjustment rod, simply screw it all the way into its hole. If you're using a long piece of threaded rod, unscrew it and tape it into the adjustment rod hole.

Leave your spacers for the cradle on the bolt.

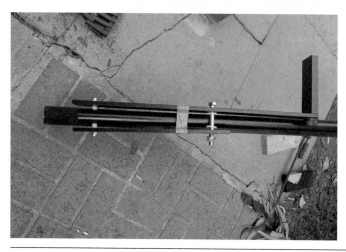

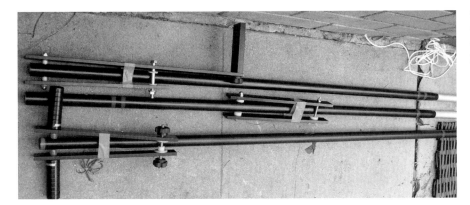

When breaking down the tilt tube, leave the tilt bars connected to the tube. Leave the bolts and knobs in the holes in the bars. Fold the bars to the tube and tape them.

Put the knobs and bolts back into the connecting boxes.

And there it is.

Make It Groovy!

For this section, let's add a monitor stand.

This is really simple. It's just an L-bracket attached to the cradle. It's a good idea to attach the monitor to the cradle, so that when you move the crane left or right, the monitor moves with you.

My monitor has a mounting bolt in the bottom that is ⅜" (9.5 mm). Most do. You'll need an L-bracket that's at least 10" (25 cm), a ¼" (7 mm) male clamping knob, and a female clamping knob or wing nut that is the same size as the mounting bolt on the monitor. You already have all the tools you'll need.

Let's Build It

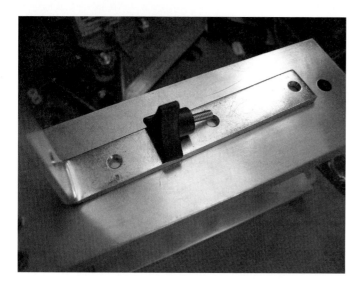

Find a good point on the side of the cradle to mount the bracket. You'll be using the middle hole on the L-bracket, so the bracket must clear the bolt holes on the bottom of the cradle, and the pivot bolt at the top of the cradle.

Put a dimple at that point halfway across the width of the cradle. Use the bit that matches the ¼" (7 mm) tap. Drill a hole all of the way through the cradle side bar, and tap that hole.

Screw the L-bracket to the cradle. Determine a good place for the monitor on the L-bracket. You want enough room between the edge of the monitor and the knob so that you can adjust the angle with the knob while the monitor is mounted. Mark the point on the bracket where the monitor mounting knob meets it.

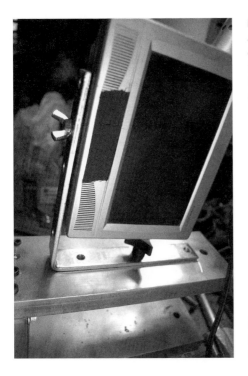

Drill a ³⁄₈" (9.5 mm) hole in the bracket at that point. Mount the bracket on the cradle. Slip the monitor bolt through the hole you just drilled, and tighten it down with a wing nut or female clamping knob.

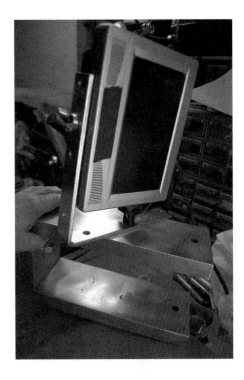

Now you can rotate the bracket to a good angle and tighten down the clamping knob to hold it there.

Working with The *Double Indemnity* Crane

Please read Chapter 18, *Working with a Crane*, but specifically for this one, you want to stand between the cradle and the weights. The left hand rests on or toward the weights, the right hand controls the tilt and boom movement right or left. Tilting the camera will shift the balance of the crane, so you'll need to use your left hand to give it slight pressure to keep the boom where you want it.

Really practice with this crane before the shoot. Keeping an actor framed with any crane is difficult, but if you add something like a tilt while booming up, well, it's a whole new world. There's a reason why crane operators are specific jobs on a film set and get paid appropriately!

Working with a Crane

What I'm about to tell you is common sense. Unfortunately, for some strange reason, people lose their common sense on a film set. I see it time and time again. I think the government is experimenting on Hollywood. It's the only logical explanation. So here are a few rules to use *always*.

1. Keep your tripod legs at the widest possible spread, within reason of course. There will be times that you'll have to balance safety and the needs of the shot.
2. Always weigh down the tripod legs—sandbags are perfect.
3. Make sure the tripod is level before you attach the crane.
4. Make sure the camera end is sitting on the ground and weighted before adding or removing (especially removing!) weights.

5. When blocking the shot, take the crane through its movements slowly and look for any potential hazard. I've seen the weight end of a crane crash through a window, and the camera end bonk an actor.
6. Cranes do take practice. Not nearly as much as the stabilizer, but I'd really recommend trying some moves before the shoot day. The tilt mount *does* take a lot of practice. Try following an actor and tilting at the same time. It truly is difficult keeping your composition, and that's why crane guys get the big bucks.

Attaching a Monitor

If you want to see what you're shooting, attaching a TV or one of those small LCD monitors is a piece of cake. You know that cable that came with your camera that allows you to go out of the video mini plug on the camera and into a VCR via RCA plugs? Just get a long video cable that has RCA connectors. Use an RCA barrel to plug the short cable coming from your camera into the long video cable. Then plug that into a TV or LCD monitor. No need to plug in the audio cables! Give the camera end of the cable a little slack so the camera can move freely without pulling on the cable. Tape the cable to the bottom boom of the crane in a few places. Set your monitor where you can keep an eye on it as you pan the boom, and plug the cable into the "Video In" on the monitor. Easy.

I'm using an HD camera here, so I've got a *component out* adapter.

Tape the monitor cable along the bottom boom. It there are connectors along the line, make sure to tape the cable down on each side of the connections.

When it's on the static mount, you don't have to worry too much about cable slack. Just enough so you can move the fluid head about.

Tape it near the center column on the boom as well.

DOI: 10.1016/B978-0-240-81337-0.00018-5

Killer Camera Rigs That You Can Build

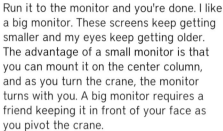

Run it to the monitor and you're done. I like a big monitor. These screens keep getting smaller and my eyes keep getting older. The advantage of a small monitor is that you can mount it on the center column, and as you turn the crane, the monitor turns with you. A big monitor requires a friend keeping it in front of your face as you pivot the crane.

On the tilt mount, make sure there's enough slack cable so your camera has room to move!

One Last Word

Let's say you've gone to all the trouble to build a crane, and it wobbles a tiny bit. This is a result of the aluminum not being heavy enough, the pivot hole too far back, or a camera too heavy for the crane—or possibly all three. *Don't panic!* E-mail me at Dan@DVcameraRigs.com and I'll give you an easy fix.

The *T-Men* Crane Weight Holder

These babies are a drag to haul around, but haul them you must. Here's a cheap and easy weight holder. You don't even need any tools!

Materials List for the *T-Men* Weight Holder

☐ A 12" (30 cm) long, ½" (14 mm) diameter plumber's pipe threaded at both ends.

☐ A ½" (14 mm) floor flange.

☐ A ½" (14 mm) T fitting.

Let's Build It!

Screw the floor flange tightly to one end of the pipe.

Set it upright, and stack your weights on the pipe.

Twist the T fitting on top.

There. You're good to go. Doesn't get much easier than that, does it?

Killer Camera Rigs That You Can Build

DOI: 10.1016/B978-0-240-81337-0.00019-7

SECTION 4: FILMMAKING TOOLS YOU JUST GOTTA HAVE

The *They Drive by Night* Car Mount

This car mount works really great. At least it hasn't flown off the hood of my car yet! As you can see, it uses four suction cups to keep it where you put it, and uses two ball joints to position the camera platform in just about any configuration.

Please read the "Mounting the *They Drive by Night* Car Mount" section carefully. This rig isn't meant to go traveling down the freeway unless you're in a slow-moving traffic jam (which is pretty much all the time now in Los Angeles).

Before you buy materials, I'm going to show you how to make a ball and socket joint out of commonly found materials here in America. You can just as easily buy a heavy duty ball and socket joint and skip building one, but good ones are expensive. Having said that, the price has gone way down since I wrote the first edition of this book, so look around. You might find a good one for cheap. If that's the case, of course you won't need the materials for building your own ball and socket joint.

Before starting this project please read the appendix, *Working with Metal*.

Materials List for the *They Drive By Night* Car Mount

☐ You'll need four, 4" (100 mm) or larger suction cups. You can find these at bigger automotive shops in the body repair section. You don't need the big expensive ones. These run about $5 each, and are also the easiest to find.

☐ (4) bolts 1¼" (32 mm) long × ³⁄₁₆" (4.7 mm) or so, with nuts.

DOI: 10.1016/B978-0-240-81337-0.00020-3

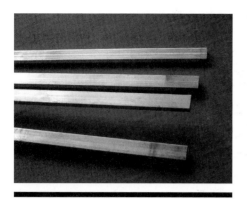

☐ (4) aluminum bars. Mine are ½" (14 mm) tall × ¼" (7 mm) thick by 18" (45 cm) long. Try to find something close to this. *Do not* use steel bars as a replacement. They are too heavy!

☐ (1) A standard clip board. *Note*: If you are going to use a commercially available ball and socket joint, replace the clip board with a ¼" to ½" thick piece of plywood.

The Ball and Socket Materials (skip this if you are buying a ball and socket joint)

☐ (4) ½" (14 mm) insulating bushing. You might be able to get by with just two, but they're so cheap, you might get four to save yourself a trip back to the hardware store. These are in the electrical section.

☐ (2) drawer pulls. Take a look at "Finding the Right Drawer Pulls" later in the chapter.

☐ (1) Threaded rod. This needs to be able to screw into the drawer pulls.

☐ (1) Nylon spacer. See later in the chapter for the size you'll need.

☐ (2) 1" (25 mm) electrical compression connector for electrical conduit.

☐ (1) 1" (25 mm) floor flange. The above connector needs to be able to screw into this flange. You'll find the flange in the plumbing department.

☐ (4) ¾" (19 mm) long screws for the flange.

The following marine adhesive, glue spreader, and tool box liner are optional. They simply help cut down on car mount vibration from a car engine that isn't running at its best.

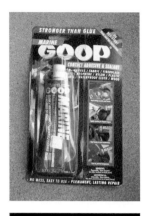

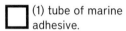

☐ (1) tube of marine adhesive.

☐ (1) spreader for smearing glue.

☐ (1) roll of tool box drawer liner. This is a rubbery material for the camera tray and car mount base. It's best to use this instead of cork because it helps cut down on vibration from the car. If you're foregoing this stuff, you'll still need some kind of padding for the camera mount. You can use a mouse pad, cork, rubber... there are lots of different materials I've used in these pages. If this is the first rig you're building, flip through the other rigs for padding ideas.

☐ Some yellow carpenter's glue.

☐ (2) female clamping knobs with ¼" (7 mm) threads. Don't get knobs that sit too tall. These are an inch, and that's about the limit. Also, you'll save yourself some work if you get knobs that allow the bolt to screw all the way through as opposed to stopping at the top of the knob.

☐ (2) bolts 1½" (38 mm) long × ¼" (7 mm). These need to fit the thread on the knobs.

☐ (2) steel mending braces, 10" (25 cm) long × 1" (25 mm) wide.

☐ (1) can of polyshield. This puts a rubber coating of whatever you dip into it. Not totally necessary, but it will help cut down on car vibration.

☐ (4) bolts ½" (14 mm) long × ³⁄₁₆" (4.7 mm) with nuts.

☐ (4) nylon spacers, ½" (14 mm) diameter × ¼" (7 mm) deep. Make sure the bolt can fit through the hole.

☐ (12) fender washers, 1¼" to 1½" (32–38 mm) in diameter. (Fender washers have a smaller hole than regular washers.)

☐ (4) ¼" (7 mm) bolts × ¾" (19 mm) long with nuts. Make sure this bolt can go through the hole in the fender washer without falling out.

☐ (1) ¾" (19 mm) block of plywood around 6½" × 9" (165 mm × 23 cm).

☐ ¼" (7 mm) block of oak. You'll find this in its own little section of the hardware store. It might read something like "Hobby Lumber." It doesn't have to be oak, but it does need to be a hard wood. You'll need two pieces around 6½" (165 mm) long and between 3" and 3½" (76 mm and 89 mm) wide. I bought a 24" (61 cm) long piece and cut it with a back saw and mitre box.

Tools List for the *They Drive By Night* Car Mount

☐ A mitre box with saw. This is for cutting the bit of oak. You don't have to have it, but it does help keep your cut straight and clean.

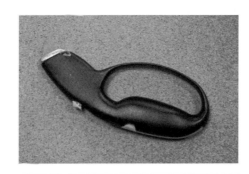

☐ Some kind of blade or scissors to cut the tool box liner with.

☐ Drill.

Killer Camera Rigs That You Can Build

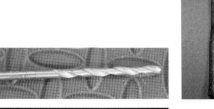

☐ Drill bits, ¹³⁄₆₄" (5 mm), ¼" (7 mm), 1¼" (32 mm).

☐ Hammer.

☐ Cutting oil.

☐ Hacksaw. The blades should have between 14 to 16 teeth per inch.

☐ File or grinding stone, for taking the burrs off the cut metal.

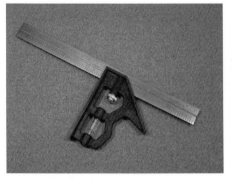

☐ Combination square.

☐ Locking pliers.

☐ Prick punch and/or center punch. If you've made the crane, you know about these.

☐ Vise.

Let's Build It!

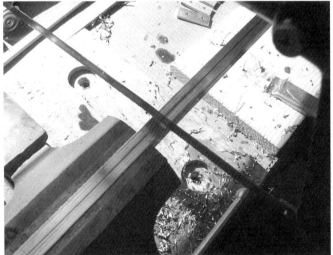

1 Line up two of the aluminum bars and lock them in to your vise. Measure off 18" using your combo square and prick punch.

2 Cut the bars at that mark. Pair off your other two bars and do the same thing. If you're feeling adventurous, you can do all four at once.

Take your metal file or grinding stone and file the rough bits off the freshly cut aluminum ends.

3 On two of the bars on each end, measure down ½" (14 mm) from the end and draw a line. Then at that line measure halfway across the width of the bar and draw another line. Take your center punch and a hammer and thwack a dimple where the two marks cross. Remember, do this on each end.

4 Put the dimpled bar on top of the other three and clamp them into your vise. You are going to be drilling all four at once. The idea is that the dimpled bar is your guide so you need easy access to it with your drill when you clamp it into the vise. Use your combination square to make sure all the ends are even.

5 Put a ¹³⁄₆₄" (5 mm) bit into your drill. Dip the bit in the drill oil. Set the tip of the bit in the dimple, make sure your drill is level, and drill a hole through all four bars at once.

Put a bolt through the hole and add a nut. This will keep your bars even. Take them out of the vice, flip them around, and drill a hole at the other end of the bars. File off the burrs and set them aside.

6 Now we're going to remove the clip from the clip board. Turn it over. See the little rivets that hold it on? Take a pair of pliers or vice grips and squish the rivet.

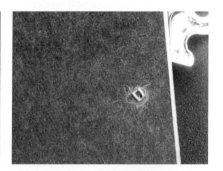

See, like this. Do both rivets and pull the clip off the front.

7 Find the center of the clip board by setting a straight edge from corner to corner. Draw a line near the center of the board.

Do the same from the opposite corners and draw another line.

Killer Camera Rigs That You Can Build

Where the lines intersect is dead center of the board.

8 Now we need to drill a hole on that X for the electrical pressure coupling. I'm using a 1¼" (32 mm) bit.

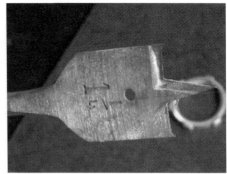

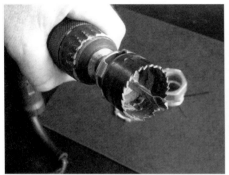

A hole saw will work too.

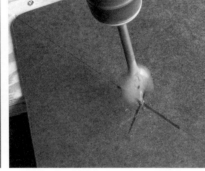

Drill a hole in the middle of your board.

9 Slide the coupling up through the hole to make sure it fits. It should be snug.

Take the coupling's retaining ring and screw it on the opposite side of the board, so that it holds the pressure coupling in the hole.

Once you've made sure everything is hunky-dory with the pressure coupling and its hole, you can either remove it or leave it in there. Doesn't much matter at this point.

10 Next measure down the length of your board and mark the halfway point about 1½" (38 mm) from the edge of the board. In the case of my clip board, the halfway point is 6¼" (158 mm). Do this on the opposite side as well.

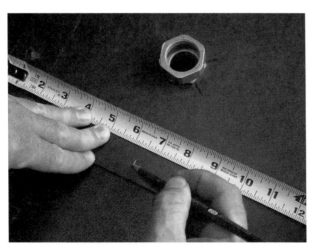

Once you have your halfway marks, measure in 1½" (38 mm) from the edge and make another mark. Now you should have a little cross where the two measurements intersect. Do this on the opposite side as well. This is where we'll be drilling a hole for the knob bolt.

Can you make out the two crosses, one above and one below the coupling?

11 Drill a hole on the crosses just big enough to accommodate your bolt. I'm using a ¼" (7 mm) bolt, so I'm going to use a ¼" (7 mm) bit. It will be a little snug, and I'll have to screw the bolt in, but that's what we want.

Here are the bolts screwed in. These are 1½" (38 mm) long. Go ahead and screw them in.

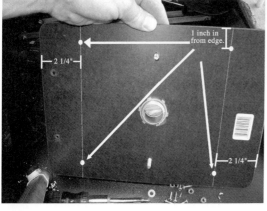

12 Now we're going to mark the board for four more holes. Take a close look at the photo. Draw a straight line across the width of the board, 2¼" (57 mm) from the edge on each end. Then on that line, measure in 1" (25 mm) from the edge and make another mark. This is where we'll drill some holes (see the white dots?).

13 Set your marked-up board aside for a minute and grab your four big suction cups. We're going to attach the aluminum bars to the suction cups by drilling a little hole in the suction cup handle.

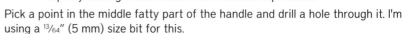

Pick a point in the middle fatty part of the handle and drill a hole through it. I'm using a ¹³⁄₆₄" (5 mm) size bit for this.

Do all four suction cups in the same spot. This is the same size bit I used on the aluminum bar holes.

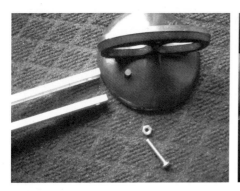

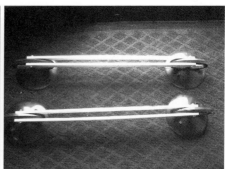

14 Take your suction cup, two bars, and a nut and bolt. My bolt is 1¼" (32 mm) long. Yours may be different depending on the thickness of your aluminum bars. The holes may also be a different diameter depending on your bolt.

Place the bars on each side of the suction cup handle and line up the holes. Slip the bolt through and screw on the nut.

Do this on the remaining suction cups.

Killer Camera Rigs That You Can Build

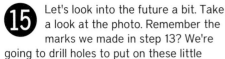 Let's look into the future a bit. Take a look at the photo. Remember the marks we made in step 13? We're going to drill holes to put on these little nylon spacers.

These spacers come in a huge variety of sizes. Here's what we want:

The spacer needs to be small enough in diameter to fit between the two aluminum rods that are attached to the suction cups. They can even touch the bars, but not so big as to bend the bars out. The spacer also needs to be bigger than the nut that is holding it on.

The spacer and the nut should not be any higher than the top of the bar. As you can see, this one goes about halfway. And of course, the hole in the spacer needs to be large enough to take the bolt you're using.

So, to put all that together: Because of the bars and suction cups I'm using, my nylon spacer can not be more than ½″ (14 mm) in diameter, ½″ (14 mm) tall, and the hole needs to be big enough to take a ³⁄₁₆″ (4.7 mm) bolt. Yours may be different.

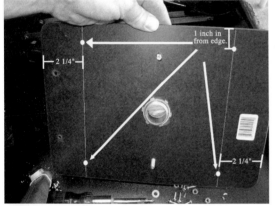

 Next, drill holes for the spacers where you put the marks in step 13. I'm using a ³⁄₁₆″ (4.7 mm) drill bit.

Attach your spacers with a bolt just long enough to go through the spacer and take a nut on the end. In this case, my bolt is ³⁄₁₆″ (4.7 mm) by ½″ (14 mm) long. Do this on all four holes.

(18) Now we need to drill a hole in the center of the two steel braces.

The braces are 10" (25 cm) long, so in the middle of the brace at 5" (12.5 cm) I'm going to make a dimple with my prick punch.

Just give the punch a couple of good thwacks with a hammer.

Clamp the brace down on your bench on top of a scrap bit of lumber. Add a little drilling oil to the dimple.

If the oil dries up while you're drilling, just add a little more.

When you're finished, clean up the metal with a little acetone or hot water and a good grease cutting soap.

Repeat for the other bar.

(19) This next step isn't absolutely necessary, but recommended. We're going to "rubberize" the metal brace. This does a couple of things: it helps hold the mount to the rails, and it helps to cut down on vibration coming from the car.

Take the braces and simply dip them in the polyshield.

Hang it from a wire over the polyshield for a few minutes to let the excess run off.

Close up the polyshield can and let the rubber on the brace dry. Once dry, flip it around and repeat the steps for the other side. Feel free to give it two or three coats. Repeat the steps on your second bar. Let the polyshield dry completely before going on to the next step.

We are almost finished with the base. While you're letting the rubber dry, you can set the base aside and skip up to making the camera platform. Frankly, I'd take a break and finish up tomorrow. For the next step you'll need all the pieces that you've built so far, plus the threaded knobs.

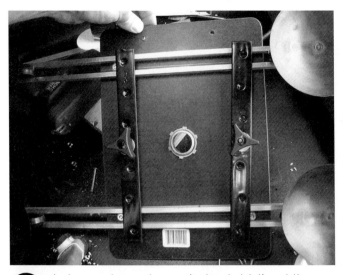

 Just so you know where we're headed, let's put the base together.

Take your suction cups with the rods attached and place them on the base as shown in the photo. The nylon spacers you put on ride in between the two bars. Take the metal braces and slide the holes you drilled in them earlier over the ¼" (7 mm) bolts. Take your threaded knob and screw them onto the ¼" (7 mm) bolt.

They should be placed so that the ends of each metal strap clamps down on the suction cup bars.

 Here are the parts for the ball joint. These are simply two solid metal drawer pulls along with a 1" (25 mm) long nylon spacer and a threaded rod that fits the drawer pull threads.

FINDING THE RIGHT DRAWER PULLS

First, they have to be round. Second, they have to be metal. And third, they have to fit the electrical pressure coupling. So while you're at the hardware store, go get your 1" (25 mm) electrical pressure coupling first. Then head over to the drawer knob department and start sticking round knobs into the coupling.

We still have a little work to do on the base that requires stiffening up the former clip board, but that requires some glue, and so does the top of our base and the camera platform. We'll just do all the gluing at once. So first, let's build the ball and socket joint and the camera platform.

The largest part of the ball needs to fit, just barely, into the part of the coupling that applies the pressure. So experiment around with different size knobs until you find one that doesn't move once you tighten down the big nut on the pressure coupling. Make sure that the largest circumference of the knob is against the pressure ring. If the ball is too far in or too far out, it will never tighten properly.

See the little metal ring just inside the top of the coupling? This is the part that tightens down on the ball, and believe me, once you tighten it down with a wrench, it's not going anywhere.

Take a look at the following photos to make sure you get a good fit before leaving the hardware store.

Loosen up the big nut that tightens the pressure ring.

Find a knob that fits in the opening. Oops. I put it too far in.

Dang. Not far enough.

Just right. Now tighten the nut down.

There. That's not going anywhere.

Now that you have the right drawer pull, head over to the part of the hardware store where they keep the threaded rod. Find the correct size for screwing into the threads on the knob. You only need a couple of inches, but the least you'll probably be able to buy is 12" (30 cm). The knob I found takes an ⁸⁄₃₂" (6.3 mm) rod. Yours may be different.

Wait! Don't leave the hardware store yet. Take that threaded rod over to the nylon spacers. You need one about 1" (25 mm) long. The hole should be just big enough to take the size of the rod. The picture on the right is the spacer and the rod cut to the proper length.

BUILDING THE BALL AND SOCKET JOINT

So let's say you're able to screw the rod into the knob ¼", double that. So now we have ½". Add the length of your spacer. In this case, 1". So that's 1½" (38 mm) total. Measure off 1½" (38 mm) on the rod and cut it there. It's better to cut the rod a little shorter than a little longer. If it's too long, the knobs won't tighten against the spacer.

22 Find out how much threaded rod you need by screwing one end of the rod as far as you can into the drawer pull. Mark the rod where it meets the base of the drawer pull and unscrew it. Measure from that mark to the end of the threaded rod. It will probably be under a half inch. Now double that measurement then add the length of the spacer.

23 Take some pliers or vice grips and grab the rod somewhere in the middle. You can tear up these threads in the middle all you want. Next tighten the pa-jeezus out of that rod into the drawer pull.

348

Killer Camera Rigs That You Can Build

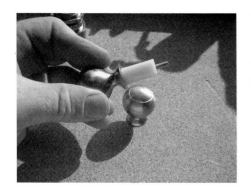

Slip the spacer on.

And add the second drawer pull to the other end. Tighten the whole thing down with some locking pliers.

BUILDING THE CAMERA PLATFORM

 Get a ¾" (19 mm) thick piece of plywood that measures around 6½" (165 mm) × 9" (23 cm). Find the middle as you did with the clip board: take a straight edge from corner to corner and draw a line. Do the opposite corners so you end up with an X. That's your center point.

Take the 1" (25 mm) floor flange and center it over the X. Mark where the four screw holes are on the plywood, and drill pilot holes for the screws. Use a bit that is much smaller than the screws you're using.

Use a ¾" (19 mm) long flat head wood screw to attach the flange. Get screws that are pretty fat.

Careful not to get them too big, they still have to fit through the holes on the flange!

Draw a line down the middle of the platform and drill five or six ¼" (7 mm) holes along the line. Obviously, it is pointless to drill where the flange is, but get a hole right next to the edge of it. As you use this mount, you might find weird and beautiful ways to use it, so feel free to drill more holes anywhere on the platform. You can also do this later, as the need arises on a shoot.

 Grab your second electrical pressure fitting and screw it tightly into the flange. Use a big wrench and really muscle that thing in there.

Remember the ½" (14 mm) insulating bushing (whatever the heck that is!) you picked up at the electrical department? Here's what they're for.

Drop one or two of them inside the pressure conduit, the larger open end up. This keeps the ball joint at the proper height so you don't have to monkey around with the thing every time you want to adjust the ball joint. You don't have to use these, it just makes life easier. Put one or two (you'll just have to experiment to see what works for your pressure conduit) in the clip board base conduit as well.

Put your ball joint in the pressure fittings and tighten them down. Monkey around with this ball and socket joint to get a feel for it. This baby can tilt every-which way. Pure Genius!

26 So we're almost done. Just a few finishing touches. Take the camera tray and the ball mechanism off and set it aside.

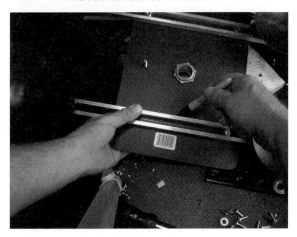

Flip the clip board base over and remove the steel braces. On the inside edge of where the suction cup bars lay, draw a line the width of the board. Do this on the inside of both bars.

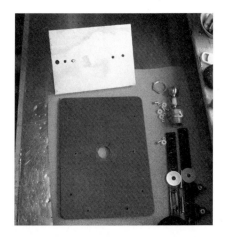

Now take the rest of the hardware off the clip board.

27 Measure the distance between the two lines. My measurement ended up being 6¾" (171 mm). If your bars are thicker or thinner than mine... you get the idea.

We're measuring this distance to strengthen the clip board, because it will bow if you tighten the threaded knobs too tight. So I'm going to add a couple pieces of ¼" (7 mm) oak to the bottom.

The oak I'm using is 3½" (89 mm) wide. Do not go wider than this or you won't be able to put the pressure conduit back in. Fact is, the reason we are using a clip board in the first place is that it is thin enough to take the pressure conduit, so we can't start with a thick piece of wood without a lot of trouble getting the conduit to fit.

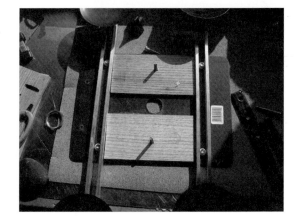

Cut your oak or other hardwood to the correct length. Again, in my case that's 6¾" (171 mm). Now, you could try using ¼" (7 mm) plywood here, but the oak is much stronger and doesn't give as easily.

If you want to drill the holes now for the screw knobs, you can line up the oak on the clip board, then mark the oak where the screw knob bolt hole falls. Frankly, I'd wait until you've glued the thing on the clip board and it'll be easier. I don't know what I was thinking.

350

Take the former clip board and glob on the marine adhesive. Do this in a well ventilated area. Mine wasn't and I swear I saw little garden elves in my fridge. But that's a story for another day.

28 Collect the things you'll need for all the gluing. I'm using a marine adhesive to glue the padding on the mount and a yellow carpenter's glue to attach the oak pieces. I like the marine stuff because it stays flexible and works well with rubber. You'll also need something to smooth on the glue with.

Do the same thing on the top of the camera platform. (If you want to use a different glue and padding for the camera platform, feel free to do so!)

Roll out the tool drawer liner and slap the two pieces down there, or you can cut the rubber in two pieces; but make them larger than the clip board and the camera plate. We'll trim them later.

Smooth out some carpenter's glue on the oak pieces and center them between the lines you drew earlier on the clip board.

Slap some weights on the whole shebang and let them dry overnight.

29 Trim off the excess tool drawer liner with some kind of blade. Don't forget the big hole in the center too.

Take a drill bit and poke holes through the top pad where all of your holes are in the clip board.

On the larger ¼" (7 mm) hole that holds the bolt for the threaded knob, you'll just have to feel around through the pad until you find it. When you do, load up a ¼" (7 mm) bit and drill straight through the pad and oak.

Put on a fender washer and screw the bolt into the hole.

Do the same on the bottom and add a nut. Remember, if the bolt goes beyond the nut, cut it off.

30 Once you have all the holes poked in the pad, flip the thing over. Pick a point somewhere near the middle and each end of the oak and drill a ¼" (7 mm) hole. So that's four new holes in all, right?

For each new hole you'll need two fender washers, a bolt, and nut. The bolt should only be long enough to be flush with the top of the nut when you screw it down. If the bolt protrudes beyond the nut, take a hacksaw and cut it off. My bolt is ¾" (19 mm) long.

Put all your spacers and nuts back on and the pressure coupling back in the center hole.

Add a fender washer to the bolts that holds the threaded knobs.

It's starting to look sexy, baby, yeah!

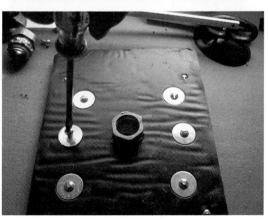

When you put the steel straps on, add a fender washer before you put on the screw knobs.
Flip the whole business over, add the camera tray, and you're done.
One car mount ready to test.

Killer Camera Rigs That You Can Build

Make It Groovy

There might be times when you use this car mount, that the camera tray will be upside-down, and you'll need to mount the camera on the bottom of the tray. Because of the large floor flange most cameras won't quite fit. So in this section we'll be making a little platform that extends off the bottom of the camera tray. You won't need any different tools, but you will need an old mouse pad and a ¼" (7 mm) thick piece of plywood that measures around 6" × 6½" (152 × 165 mm).

Take your plywood and center it on one side of the camera tray.

Keep the board in place and flip everything over.

Take a nail or some other long thin thing with a point (I'm using the prick punch) and push it through the existing holes on the camera tray, marking the plywood underneath.

I have three holes on the camera tray, so I'm going to drill three holes on the extension. Use a ¼" (7 mm) or a little larger bit to drill these holes.

Line the holes on the extension up with the holes on the camera tray...

...and draw a line across the extension using the edge of the camera tray as a guide.

Use a ¼" (7 mm) bit to drill a bunch of holes between that line and the outside edge. Placement is not critical, but do drill a hole or two near the line you drew. These are for your camera screw.

I'm using a mouse pad for padding. Anything like that will do.

Set the extension on the pad and cut off the excess mouse pad. Then cut the pad where the line on the plywood lays.

That's the ticket!

Now we need to put some holes in the pad to allow for the camera screw. For this, I'm going to use a fabric punch from a grommet kit. A razor blade or hobby knife works well too.

A really easy way to mark the mouse pad for the holes is to use chalk or baby powder. Just line the pad up on the board and flip the whole thing over. Take some baby powder and sprinkle it in the holes.

And when you remove the board, the chalk or baby powder marks the places for the holes.

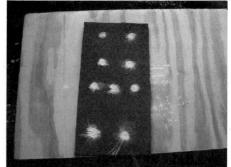

I'm using a hole punch from a grommet kit to punch the holes in the pad.

And there it is.

Clean off the powder and glue it to the board and you're done.

Killer Camera Rigs That You Can Build

Mounting the *They Drive By Night* Car Mount

Pay close attention to the mounting instructions and follow them! I'm fairly certain the last thing you want to see is your very costly camera go flying under the wheels of a cement truck.

Even though I tested this mount with only the suction cups holding it on (even after a couple of hours, they held tight) it's important to have a back-up and strap the camera down.

Before sticking the suction cups to your car, loosen the nuts on the cups so that they can move back and forth. This allows the cup to conform to the angles of the car.

Like every other suction cup you've used, adding some spit to the edge of the cup will keep it where you stick it. Make darn sure the car is clean. If there is a lot of dirt, the suction cups won't hold.

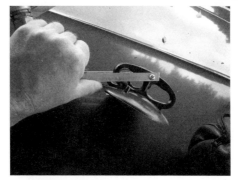

Push each cup down firmly, forcing out the air for a good grip.

Make sure the cup rests on a flat spot!

Once you have a good grip, tighten down each bolt that holds the cup to the bars.

Mount the camera to the tray with a camera screw—usually ¼" (7 mm). You need one long enough to reach through the ¾" (19 mm) plywood and hold the camera tight with no play.

Loosen up the compression couplings and adjust the camera to the angle you want it, then tighten them down tight with a wrench. Don't use a bubble level to level the camera tray. The car may be out of level! Use the edge of the windshield for a framing reference.

If you look underneath the mount, you'll see that you have very little room between the threaded knob and the surface of the car. This is why you need to buy knobs as short as you can. You can flip the knobs and bolts around so that the knobs are on top. It's up to you. I always had enough room. I can honestly say, I don't know why I designed it so that the knobs are on the bottom. Usually, I have a really good reason to do things the way I do.

Even though I've never had a problem with the cups coming loose, why tempt fate? Use at least one strap across the base. I'm using a strap with a ratchet for tightening and coated hooks on each end. In this case I've hooked the ends onto the fender above the wheel.

I'm also using an elastic cord across the top of the camera and hooking each end onto the aluminum bars.

And that's the basic mounting. Use your head with this rig because it is potentially very dangerous. Don't block the driver's view, stick to side streets, and go slow.

Warning! Do not go flying down the street with this on the outside of your car! Maximum speed is 35 MPH; 25 MPH or slower is recommended.

Here are some other places I've mounted this rig:

Looking forward on the hood.

Looking backward on the trunk.

Looking through the back window.

Killer Camera Rigs That You Can Build

Mounting on the Car Interior

This is where the extension tray comes into play. In this photo, the mount is rigged to the inside of the front windshield.

Take the extension tray and bolt it to the mount tray. Use a wing nut so you can easily remove and attach the extension tray.

Screw the camera onto the extension tray and adjust the ball and socket joint to level the camera.

Here it is mounted on the back window looking forward.

Unlike most of the rigs in this book, the car mount takes no skill to use! Just some common sense. Use that and go make a road movie!

The *Third Man* Tripod

Oh, sure, it looks like a lightweight surveyor's tripod, but it is so much more. In this section, I'm going to show you how to butch this baby up so you can throw a crane on it. (And if you're never going to use a crane, this tripod is plenty heavy duty for DV camera work.)

I found this tripod at a big home center for about $80. It sure beats $500 for a "cinema" tripod, doesn't it? In the next section we'll be building a tripod spreader for this and any other cinema-style tripod.

By the way, when I say "cinema-style" tripod, I'm talking about double legs that have the ability to fold all the way out to get the camera as low as possible, as in the picture above. You must use a spreader with this style of tripod!

And as always, read through the instructions before heading off to the hardware store because your tripod may be different from mine and you must adjust things accordingly!

Please read the appendix, *Working with Metal*, before starting this project!

Materials List for the *Third Man* Tripod

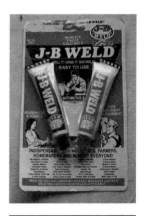

☐ Aluminum tube. See step 2 about removing the legs from the surveyor's tripod. Once you get the tubes separated from the rest of the leg unit, take one of the tubes to the hardware store or metal supply and find another aluminum tube that will slide right inside the tripod tube. You don't want any wiggle room between the two tubes. Measure the length of the tripod tubes to find out how much you'll need in all. And if your tripod is like mine, you'll need enough tubing for six. In this photo, the original tripod tube (the one with the hole in it) is on the left. The tube going into it on the right is what you'll be buying.

☐ ¼" (7 mm) diameter steel rod. To figure out how much steel rod you'll need, measure the length of the top of the leg assembly. This one measures 4" (100 mm). Since there are three of these, I'll need 12" (30 cm) of steel rod.

☐ (2) J-B Weld. You'll need two packages for this project.

DOI: 10.1016/B978-0-240-81337-0.00021-5

Killer Camera Rigs That You Can Build

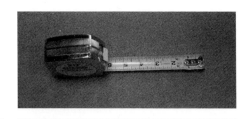

☐ Tube cutter. Like the vise, think ahead to future projects. For this project, you can get by with a smaller one. But if you plan on making the stabilizer, for example, make sure you get one that can open wide enough to go around a 1¼" (32 mm) diameter pipe. As an alternative, you can cut the pipe with a hacksaw.

☐ Tape measure.

☐ A hammer.

☐ Vise. For this job, you can get by with three or four good clamps to act as a vise. But if this is your first project and you're going to build anything else in this book, go get a vise.

☐ A screwdriver. My surveyor's tripod has Phillips head screws. Yours probably does too.

☐ ¼"(7 mm) drill bit and a ⅛" (3 mm) drill bit.

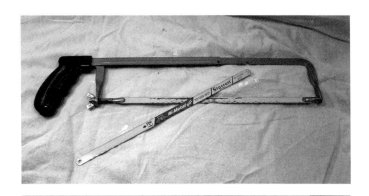

☐ A drill.

☐ A hacksaw.

☐ Drill cutting oil.

☐ A center punch or a prick punch. This puts a dimple in metal to keep your drill bit from "walking." This is very important!

☐ Pliers or socket wrench.

Let's Build It!

1 First, remove the leg units from the head of the tripod. And while you're at it, lose that knob with the treads on it. You can hold on to that paperclip-looking thing—it can be used to run the crane bolt through on the smaller crane. A good alternative is to remove it, and use a large washer (check out attaching the *Double Indemnity* Crane to this tripod in Chapter 17).

This is the head of mine with two of the leg sets removed. (I painted the top part of the leg set black so you could see it a little better.)

Your leg set will look a little something like this once you've taken it off the head.

2 Take a screwdriver and remove the screws that hold the legs to the top.

Make sure you keep track of all the little pieces and where they came from. I threw all of mine in a big bowl.

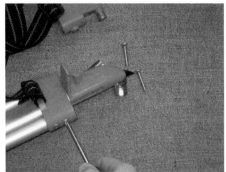

3 Now take off the feet. Repeat the steps on the other two legs.

Remove the tubes that are on either side of the center leg column.

These are the tubes you'll want to take to the hardware store to find a good match to slide inside.

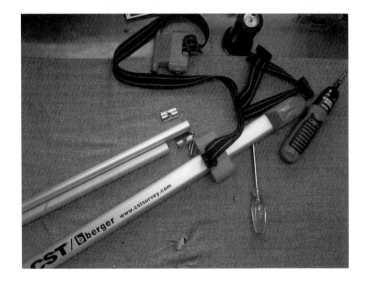

4 Take the top unit that held the legs and clamp it in to your vise as shown. Make sure it is vertically straight. I've also put some scrap wood under the bottom part to support the piece so it doesn't move around, because we're going to drill into it.

Take your center punch and place it in the middle of the piece in the vise (I just eye-balled it), and give it a good thwack with the hammer to make a dimple. You *must* do this. It is critical that your drill not drift from the center. I'm using a ¼" (7 mm) bit. Yours will depend on your tripod and rod size.

Put some cutting oil on the dimple and drill straight down. Make sure your bit travels straight! This is also why it is important to take your time putting this piece into the vise, making sure it is straight.

This is a view of the inside as I drill down through. I'm going all the way through the little support piece in the center (see the little shelf with all the metal shavings on it?).

There she is. Next, flip the unit over, and drill through the other side. Then do the same on the remaining two units.

Clean these units really well to get all the oil and metal shavings out. Dish soap and hot water works.

5 Measure the width of the part you just drilled through. In my case, 4". This is how long the steel rod needs to be for each piece.

Clamp the rod in the vise, and cut three 4" lengths with your hacksaw.

Killer Camera Rigs That You Can Build

Again, these rods need to be as long as the top of the leg head.

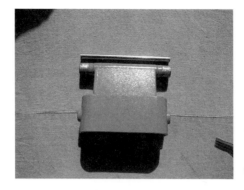 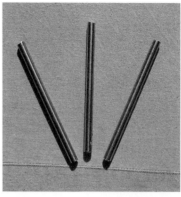

Clean these really well.

Mix the entire tubes of J-B Weld together.

6 Take a steel rod section, and coat it with J-B Weld. Shove it into the hole you drilled all the way through to the other side. You may have to tap it in with a hammer. Do this to the other two.

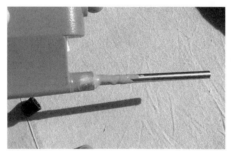 

This is why you needed the whole tube of J-B Weld: You want to completely cover the steel rod inside the tripod piece. This is not the time to be cheap with the Weld. If you need to mix another tube, do it! Finish up the other two like this, and set them aside to dry for at least 24 hours.

7 Next, take the tube you took off the tripod, and slide the aluminum tube from the metal supply shop inside all the way, so that the ends match up.

Mark the inner tube where it meets the top of the tripod tube.

Trim off the excess with the tube cutter or a hacksaw. You'll need to make six of these.

8 Mix up another batch of J-B Weld. (And no, I'm not being paid by the J-B people. Not yet anyway!) Take a long stick of some sort (I'm using a little spatula) and glop some Weld down in the tripod tube from the top to about 6" (152 mm) in or so. Make sure to get it on all sides as best you can. Do this on both ends of the tube.

Slide your cut tube all the way in, rotating it at the same time to coat the J-B Weld as much as you can on the inside.

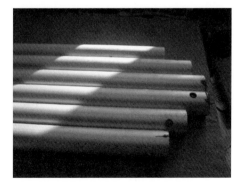

Set the tube aside and do the other five.

Let them dry 24 hours before moving on.

Killer Camera Rigs That You Can Build

9 OK, here's the thing: The tripod legs that you modified yesterday (you *did* let them dry 24 hours, *right*?) have holes in them for the screws that hold the whole tripod together. But we, in essence, put a core in those legs. So now we have to drill holes in the core that match the existing holes from the manufacturer. I can't tell you what size drill bit to use, because I don't know what tripod you're working with. So take a few bits, and place the end in the hole to try and find a match. A little smaller is OK, a little bigger is not!

Once you've determined the size of drill bit you need, add some oil and drill away. The holes on my tripod don't go all the way through, so I only need to drill a hole in one side of my core.

On the bottom of the manufacture's tube are these two little holes. I'm going to find a drill bit to match, and drill these out as well. Do this on all your tubes, and it's downhill from here!

10 If you want to paint your tripod cinema black, now is a good time before you put it all back together.

11 Put the whole tripod back together. I hope you were paying attention when you took it apart!

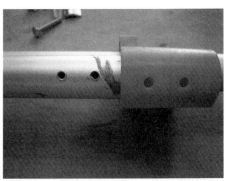

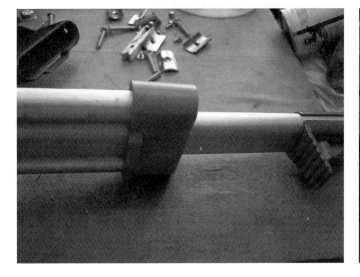

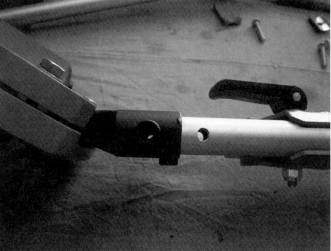

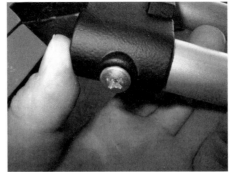

If you want to mount a camera instead of a crane on this tripod, we'll do that in the next chapter, *The* Guilty Bystander *Camera Mount for the* Third Man *Tripod.*

Then you'll need a tripod spreader. That's in Chapter 23, *The* Steel Trap *Spreader*. This rig is a piece of cake to build, and a good thing too, because you *must* have a spreader for this tripod in most situations. Don't go throwing a crane on this tripod until after you've built the spreader!

The *Guilty Bystander* Camera Mount for the *Third Man* Tripod

This is a really simple way to mount a fluid head on your surveyor's tripod. That's Hollywood cameraman, Mike Ferris, using the *Third Man* tripod with *The Guilty Bystander* mount. Just in case you were wondering, yes, I really do use the rigs in this book on actual shoots!

This is simply a block of wood with thin padding to keep the fluid head from slipping. I've had some people make this out of a block of aluminum too. There's really no advantage to making this out of aluminum, except it looks meaner.

Materials List for The *Guilty Bystander* Camera Mount for the *Third Man* Tripod

☐ A ¾" (19 mm) thick piece of plywood as big as the mounting plate on the surveyor's tripod. I've cut mine into the same shape as the mounting plate, but you can leave it square.

☐ You'll need some thin padding, enough for both sides of the plywood. I found mine at a hobby store, and love this stuff because it has a sticky side. No glue! Yeah!

DOI: 10.1016/B978-0-240-81337-0.00022-7

☐ A bolt and a washer or two. This bolt goes into the bolt hole on the bottom of your fluid head. Most fluid heads of this size require a ⅜" bolt, coarse thread. (If you live in the metric world, keep in mind that the drill bit below needs to be as big or a little bigger than the size bolt you need.) It's best to take the fluid head to the hardware store to find one that fits. As far as length goes, it has to be long enough to go up through the tripod plate, through the thickness of the wood or aluminum, and into the hole on the base of the fluid head. If the bolt is too long, you will never be able to tighten the fluid head down. Of course, you can always add washers until you can really tighten the bolt into the head. Read these plans fully before buying the bolt, and all will be clear!

Tools List for The *Guilty Bystander* Camera Mount for the *Third Man* Tripod

☐ A ⅜" (9 mm) drill bit. A little larger is just fine too.

☐ A utility knife to cut the padding.

☐ A drill.

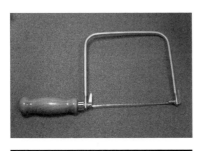

☐ A jigsaw or coping saw if you want to cut the wood the same as the plate.

☐ A sander with a fine sandpaper—120 grit is good. Sanding the thing is completely optional. It's only for looks.

Let's Build It!

1 Cut the plywood in the same shape as the plate on the surveyor's tripod with a jigsaw or coping saw. (I've taken the plate off to make it easier for you to see. You do not have to go to the trouble!)

2 Drill a ³⁄₈" (9mm) hole through the center of the wood. You can sand the edges so that it looks nice if you want.

3 Lay the plywood on top of your padding and cut around the shape. Remember, you need enough padding to do this twice: one for the top of the plywood and one for the bottom.

There it is. Now do one more.

4 Peel and stick a pad on each side of the plywood. Of course, you can reverse steps 3 and 4, and stick it on before you cut it.

5 To mount it, set it on the tripod plate, and run the fluid head bolt through a washer, through the big paperclip-looking thing, up through the hole in the plywood, and into the fluid head hole.

As an alternative, if you removed the paperclip-looking thing because you are going to use a big crane on this tripod (like I do), you'll need a big washer to replace the paperclip thing. I use a big steel washer. It obviously has to be big enough to rest against the collar of the big hole in the tripod plate. In the photo, this is how the crane mounts. Your fluid head bolt will be going up instead of down.

Anyway, tighten the bolt down tight into the fluid head bolt hole, and that's it. Easy! The padding will keep everything in place. I've never had the fluid head slip even a tiny bit.

Hey, Mike! Thanks for being the DP on my film! YOU ROCK!

Next we'll build a spreader for the tripod.

Killer Camera Rigs That You Can Build

The *Steel Trap* Spreader

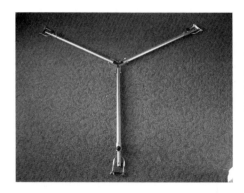

What the heck is a spreader, anyway? Basically, a spreader keeps the tripod's feet where you want them, strengthening the whole shebang in the process. If you were going to buy a spreader it would run you anywhere from $50 up (more toward the up; cheap spreaders aren't that great). You can make this one for less than $25. This spreader is designed for any tripod with spike feet, and is a perfect, if not necessary, companion to the *Third Man* tripod. Read the section, "Make It Groovy" at the end of this chapter.

Materials List for the *Steel Trap* Spreader

☐ (3) nuts and bolts, ¼" × 1½" (7 mm × 38 mm) long.

☐ (3) L-brackets. The length of one side of the L should be 2½" (63 mm) long.

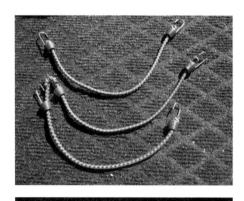

☐ (3) mini bungee cords.

DOI: 10.1016/B978-0-240-81337-0.00023-9

371

Filmmaking Tools You Just Gotta Have

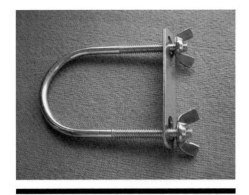

☐ (3) U-bolts, ¼" × 3" (7 mm × 76 mm) or longer. If you can find ¼" U-bolts that run 6" (152 mm), even better (I couldn't find 'em anywhere). Also, I've replaced the nuts that came with the bolt with wing nuts.

☐ (6) ¼" (7 mm) wing nuts.

☐ (3) knobs (male). You don't *have* to have these, but it makes setting up your spreader much easier. The threads must be able to screw into the conduit coupling (next on the list), and long enough to reach the ½" (14 mm) conduit that slides inside the coupling. Take a look at the picture above on the right. A ½" (14 mm) long thread will do it.

☐ (3) ¾" (19 mm) conduit couplings. Go to the electrical section and pick these up before the knobs. These have two set screws in the top. Take one out and try screwing different sized knobs or bolts until you find the correct for the set screw hole.

☐ Electrical conduit. This comes in 8' (2.4 meter) lengths or longer; 8' is plenty. You need (1) ¾" (19 mm) and (1) ½" (14 mm).

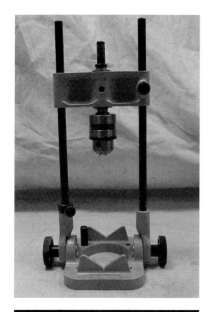

☐ If you don't have a drill press, I really encourage you to get one of these. It's a handy drill guide, and will keep your holes straight and true—very important in this type of work. It also has a V in its base to hold a round piece of pipe for perfect center drilling (something we do a lot around here). It runs about $35. A good investment if you build more than one project in this book.

☐ Tube cutter. As I mentioned on the tripod plans, on this project you can get by with a smaller one. But if you plan on making the Stabilizer, for example, make sure you get one that can open wide enough to go around a 1¼" (32 mm) diameter pipe.

☐ A drill.

☐ Locking pliers, pliers, a screwdriver, wrench... any ol' thing that will grab a nut.

☐ A center punch or prick punch. This puts a dimple in metal so your drill bit doesn't "walk."

☐ Drill bits, ¼" (7 mm) and ⁵⁄₁₆" (8 mm).

☐ A tape measure.

☐ A felt tip marker.

☐ A combination square.

Let's Build It!

1 Take that long piece of ¾″ (19 mm) electrical conduit and measure off 22″ (55 cm).

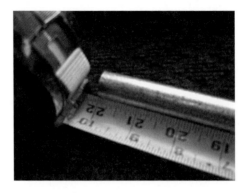

Take the pipe cutter and cut it at the 22″ (55 cm) mark.

Measure off and cut two more 22″ (55 cm) pieces.

2 Now take your ½″ (14 mm) pipe and cut three 22″ (55 cm) pieces.

3 On the three ½" (14 mm) pieces of conduit, measure in a ½" (14 mm) from the end and make a mark. Then take your center punch and carefully make a dimple on the marks.

4 I truly hope you took my advice and bought this little drill jig. It makes life very easy when cutting round things. Put a ⁵⁄₁₆" (8 mm) drill bit in. Line up the dimple on your tube at the tip of the drill bit. See how the tube rests in the V on the drill jig? I'm also using a bit of scrap lumber (it's under my hand) to support the long end of the conduit. When drilling in metal like this, go about half the speed as you would through wood. Also, just get the hole started, then put some drilling oil in the hole. Add more oil if you have to as you drill. The idea is to keep the bit wet. Once you've got this one done, do the other two.

Do not drill through both sides of the tube! Just drill through the top and stop!

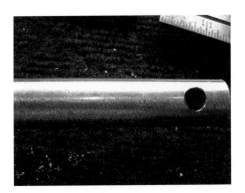

5 OK, read this carefully. Set the tube with the hole you just drilled on your work bench. Adjust the conduit tube until the hole is on top (facing the ceiling). Now, carefully roll the tube a quarter turn until the hole is on the side of the tube. Next measure down 2" on the top of the tube and make a mark. We'll be drilling straight through the tube on this mark, so go ahead and make your dimple with the center punch. Take a look at the next photo to clarify things.

Load a ¼" (7 mm) bit into the drill. Take a look at the photo. See the larger hole on the side? And now we're going to drill through the top. This time go through both sides of the conduit. Do this on the remaining two pieces.

6 Leave the ¼" (7 mm) bit in the drill. Take your ¾" (19 mm) conduit pieces. Measure 1" (25 mm) from the end and put a mark, then pound a dimple on that mark like we did on the ½" (14 mm) conduit. Again, using the ¼" (7 mm) bit, drill down through both sides of the pipe on all three.

7 Grab your three L-brackets and nuts and bolts. Use the nuts and bolts to attach the L-bracket to the ¾" (19 mm) conduit. Use the outside holes on the L-bracket. Tighten these babies tight.

Set up your tripod. We'll be using it for reference. Now we're going to bend the L-bracket so the angle of the conduit matches the angle on the tripod legs. Grab one piece of conduit in your left hand and one in your right. Line up one of the pipes over a tripod leg, and bend the two outward until they match the same angle as the legs. Because the pipe gives you plenty of torque, that L-bracket will bend like butter.

See how they match the legs now?

8 Leave the first L-bracket on, and attach a second bracket to one of the pieces of conduit that holds the now bent bracket. Then attach the third pipe to the unbent bracket. Confused? Just take a look at the picture.

Line the two pieces of conduit over the tripod legs.

Bend the third piece until it is over the third leg. See, piece of cake.

9 Next, remove the pipe from the bent L-brackets. Then take the third unbent L-bracket and attach it to the pipes you just removed. Does that make sense? Yeah, I know, just look at the photo from step 8. We are simply bending that last L-bracket like the others.

Take these last two, and bend away just like you did on the first two.

10 Now bolt everything together so it looks like the picture on the left.

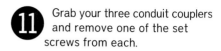

11 Grab your three conduit couplers and remove one of the set screws from each.

Replace the set screw with the screw knob on all three.

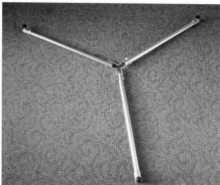

12 Put the new connector on each ¾″ (19 mm) pipe on your spreader and tighten down the set screw super tight.

Make sure the top of each knob is pointing up.

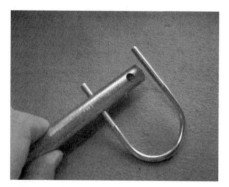
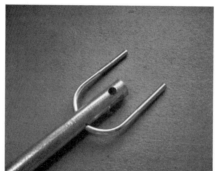
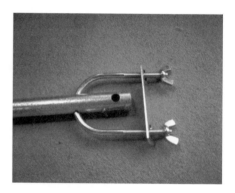

13 Take the ½″ (14 mm) conduit and run the U-bolt through the ¼″ (7 mm) hole. Add the U-bolt plate and wing nuts.

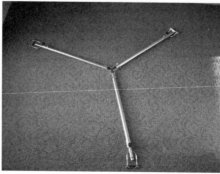

14 Slide the new ½″ (14 mm) units into the ¾″ (19 mm) tubes and tighten down the knob.

It's starting to look like something, isn't it?

15 Lay out the spreader on the ground and slip the spike feet of the tripod into the hole at the end of the spreader. (Remember, this spreader is for tripods with spike feet.)

On the three mini bungee cords, you'll need to tie a little loop in the middle to take up the slack you're going to have.

Loop the hook ends of the bungee into the holes on the U-bolt plate.

Squeeze them down with a pair of pliers.

16 On the base of the tripod legs, you'll find a little foot mantel that is used for pushing the tripod into soft ground with your foot. Loop the bungee over this mantel, then tighten down the wing nuts all the way.

The bungees keep the tripod leg from popping out of the hole on the spreader. Very important!

Let me confess that my original idea was to have the plate on the U-bolt tighten against the mantel, and not use a bungee at all. The problem was that any U-bolt I found that was long enough to reach the mantel also had a huge diameter. So if you can find a ¼" (7 mm) U-bolt out there that is long enough to reach the mantel, that's an option for you. There is one drawback to this method: if you want to adjust the legs you'll have to loosen the plate that rests on the mantel each time. A real pain.

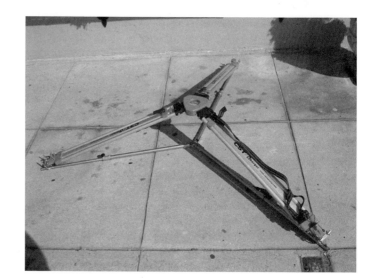

OK, that does it for the Steel Trap spreader. Its use is pretty straightforward. Simply slide the ½" (14 mm) tube in or out to where you want it and tighten down the knob. Remember, the wider the legs, the more stable.

And look, it folds up when not in use!

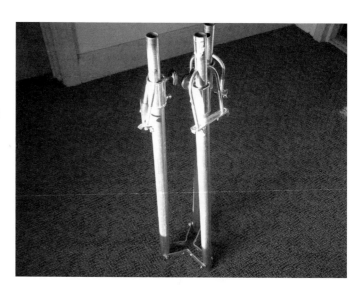

There is something to be aware of with this spreader: eventually, the threads in the conduit coupling with the knob in it will wear out. These couplings are so inexpensive that it is a very good idea to have two or three extras in your filmmaking tool kit. Make sure you bring them on any shoot you have. If you can't tighten down the knob, the leg won't stay in place. If this happens, just switch it out with a new conduit connector and you're good to go.

Killer Camera Rigs That You Can Build

Make It Groovy!

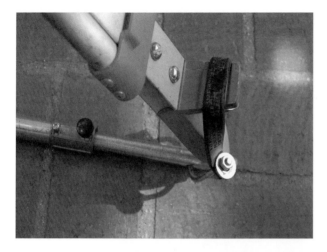

Well, I don't know how groovy this is, but it is an option. You can use a piece of rubber instead of the mini-bungee cords. There are a couple of advantages: they just don't wear out, and they hold the legs like The Terminator. The disadvantage is that you'll have to use pliers to slip them up over the feet pegs.

If you built the tripod holes on the dolly, you may be familiar with these rubber straps. Get yourself a really long one, like 24" or more.

Each end hooks onto the U-bolt and goes over the foot peg. Determine how long your rubber strap needs to be by measuring this distance and subtracting a bit so that you have to stretch the rubber strap up and over the peg.

Once you've determined the length, cut your long strap to that length. You'll need three of these.

Drill a ¼" hole in each end of these three straps. Shove them onto the U-bolt. Add a washer, then a nut.

That's all there is to it. With these straps on, there is no way the legs are ever going to leave the spreader.

You're going to need a ton of sandbags. *Please* make these. You really need them.

The *Harder They Fall* Sandbag

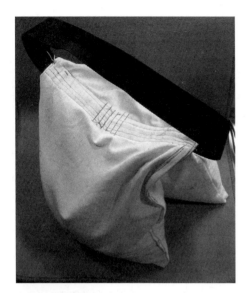

Sandbags. Not very sexy, are they? Yet, if you were going to make only one rig in this book, I'd want it to be this one. I've seen a lot of injuries and equipment damage on sets because someone didn't bother to throw a couple of sandbags on a light stand, tripod, or C-stand. Sandbags are also handy supporting a camera where a tripod won't do. The bag in the next chapter is even easier to make. Want to keep that PVC dolly track in place? Throw a sandbag on each end. Sandbags—a thousand uses and counting. Make a bunch of these and use them.

I said a bunch!

Would it be easier to go to the rental house and get all you need? Yep, it would. But do you live near such a place? Most of America doesn't, so you'll have to buy or make them. Even a tiny shoot uses a ton of sandbags. Think about it—two lights, three C-stands, and a crane on a tripod... that's eight *minimum!* Time to get busy.

Note: In the materials section, you'll see I'm making this sandbag out of canvas. Years ago I received an e-mail from a filmmaker who had bought the book. His wife said, "I can do better than that" when he showed her the plans for this sandbag. And she did do better. She used Cordura® Nylon instead of canvas. A completely better way to go. Even with the extra expense of the Cordura, she was able to make seven or eight bags for the price of one commercially available bag, and this material holds up so much better than canvas. Especially if the bag gets wet. That sand will never dry, and the canvas will

rot eventually. Even though you'll see I'm using a gallon freezer bag inside the canvas, this is more for ease of building the bag, and not so much for keeping the sand dry. Cordura Nylon is pretty water resistant and super strong. If I could remember this couple's names, I'd certainly give them credit, but I lost that e-mail in a hard drive crash (and yes, I do back up my stuff, but got lazy—let this be a lesson to you!). So thank you, unknown couple!

A couple more things: Over the years, manufacturers have started to make different styles of bags. Mostly, the lifting straps are in various configurations. Take a look at the commercial bags and see if you'd like your lifting strap to be different. Personally, I've never cared as long as there is a strap to haul the things with. Once you throw them on a C-stand, they all act the same.

You might also find bags called *shot bags*. These use some kind of heavy pellet instead of sand. This shot is usually *lead*! This may be harmless once it's inside the bag (I'm not so sure), but handling and breathing lead is just not a good idea when building your own bag. If you insist on exposing yourself to lead, use gloves and a respirator. Here's a quick story I hope will discourage you: Not so many years ago, certain cranes would use lead counterweights (and there are still plenty of them around, so be careful if you get a job on a show where these are still in use). I knew this crane grip who always laughed when I used gloves before loading these counterweights onto the crane. I bumped into him about 10 years later. "*Dan, you were right about those lead weights. My blood is full of lead.*" I haven't seen him in 20 years now, but I hope he's doing well. Sure, lead shot is much heavier than sand, so you don't have to use as much, but is it worth it?

DOI: 10.1016/B978-0-240-81337-0.00024-0

☐ Canvas. I'm just cutting up a paint drop cloth. This is minimum. The thicker your canvas, the longer it will last, so don't skimp. You can use denim, or of course, Cordura too.

☐ A big funnel. You can also just cut the bottom off a bleach bottle to make a funnel.

☐ 1½" to 2" (38 mm–50 mm) wide nylon webbing. You'll need about 2' (61 cm) per sandbag.

☐ Sand. A 50 lb (that's about 20 kilos, right?) bag will do a little over two large sandbags.

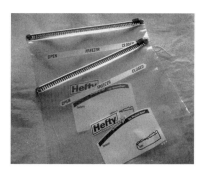

☐ (2) Heavy duty zipper-lock plastic bags, gallon size. If you get a brand with the zipper on the bag, you'll save yourself some trouble.

Tools List for the *Harder They Fall* Sandbag

☐ Scissors.

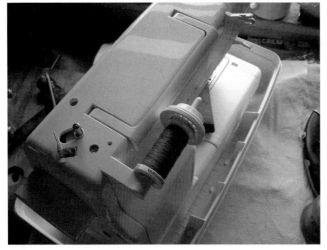
☐ A sewing machine.

☐ Measuring tape.

☐ Pins.

☐ Pencil or Taylor's chalk.

Let's Make It

1 Cut a piece of canvas 48" (122 cm) long × 11" (28 cm) wide.

2 Mark the center of the canvas lengthwise at 24" (61 cm).

Take each end and fold the canvas so the two ends meet at the center line.

Killer Camera Rigs That You Can Build

3 Pin the canvas in place along the open edges. You don't want the pins so close to the edge that they'll get in the way of the foot of the sewing machine.

4 Sew one side, the length of the canvas. Once you have a stitch running the length of the bag, do two more. We need a lot of strength here.

I know, it's not very pretty, but I never said I could sew!

On the corners of the bag, do a few forward and reverse stitches to reinforce it.

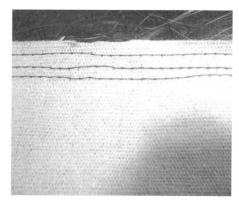

5 On the opposite edge of the bag, where the top edge of the canvas meets the middle, draw a line about 3" (76mm) long. Do this on both pieces that you folded to the center.

Stitch this side as you did on the other, but stop at the pencil line on each side! We need to leave this bit open for now.

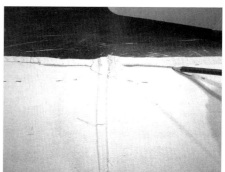

6 Flip both sides of the bag inside-out, so your stitch is hidden.

Take a freezer bag, and close it except for the last 2" or 3" (50–76 mm).

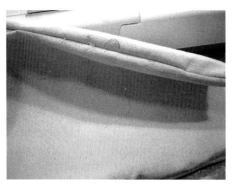
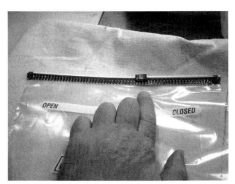

7 Slide the plastic bag inside the pocket of the canvas. Do this on the other pocket of your sandbag. *Note*: The bags will hold the sand without using the freezer bags, but putting the sand in the plastic bags keeps everything neat while you're sewing up the little holes.

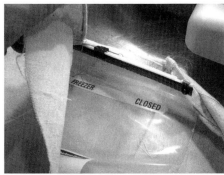

8 With your plastic bags safely inside the pockets, sew up the middle seam. Don't sew up the 3" (76 mm) opening from the pencil mark yet, and be careful not to sew into the plastic bag.

Here's the right side finished. Now I'll sew up the left side.

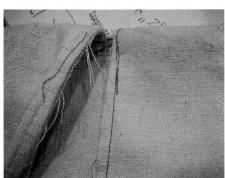

9 Now take some webbing and center it so that is overlaps the seams you just sewed, starting about halfway across the bag.

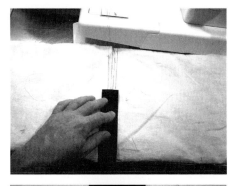

Stitch the webbing on, sewing all the way down the edge of the webbing to the side of the bag. Do this on each side of the webbing. You'll be sewing through two layers of canvas plus the webbing, so make sure you have a machine that is up to the task.

Take a close look at the photo. We'll be cutting the strap now. Remember, this is the handle, so leave it a little slack before you cut it (in step 10).

10 Loop the rest of the webbing under the bag and around until it meets up with the end you just sewed down. Cut the webbing at this point. Make sure that you use a match to melt the end of the webbing where you cut it. This will keep it from fraying.

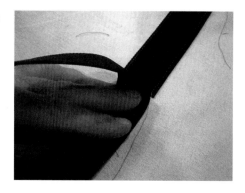

11 Run the webbing under your machine so that you don't sew the handle to the top side of your sandbag.

Bring this end around to meet the attached end, and sew the strap down as you did with the other end.

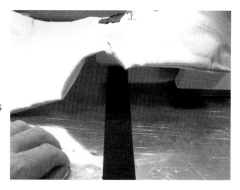

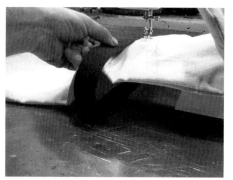

12 Once the edges are sewn down, come back and do three or four stitches across the webbing. Feel free to reverse stitch a few times. Do this on each of the ends.

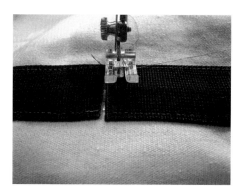

There. Not very pretty, but strong like bull.

Here's what it should look like so far.

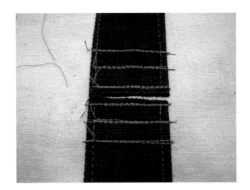

13 OK, have your sand handy and locate the little opening.

Stick the funnel down into the plastic bag and fill that baby with sand. Lots and lots of sand.

Once the bag is full, you might want to tape down the edge of the zipper on the plastic bag.

14 Sew that little opening closed, and you're done with this side. Do it all again for the other side.

And you're finished. Make at least a couple more. You'll need three just for the tripod holding the crane.

If you used canvas, it might be a good idea to put a good coat of Scotch Guard™ on the entire surface of the bag to keep it water resistant.

If this bag seems like too much trouble, check out the super-easy-to-make sandbag on the following pages.

The *Harder They Fall* Sandbag, Jr.

Things just don't get much easier than this. See that sandbag in the lower left corner holding down the dolly track in the photo? That's what we're making. I use a ton of these all the time.

Check out the Tools list for the *Harder They Fall* sandbag in the last chapter. You'll need the same stuff minus the measuring tape. For materials, you won't need the canvas.

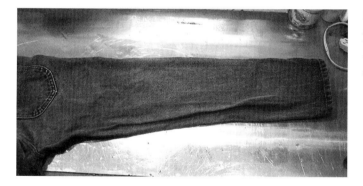

Head for your closet or a thrift store and get an old pair of jeans. If you're going to the thrift shop, you can get the jeans in the kid's section. They're even cheaper and plenty big enough for most stuff. You can get some adult-sized jeans for heavier sandbags.

Let's Build It

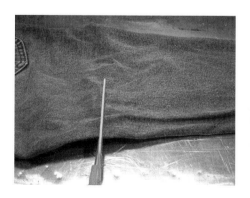 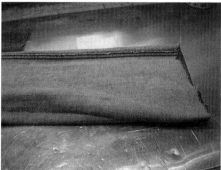

1 Start by cutting the leg off.

Then turn it inside out.

DOI: 10.1016/B978-0-240-81337-0.00025-2

2 Sew up the freshly cut end. As with the pro-looking sandbag, make at least three rows of stitches.

3 Turn the bag so that your hem is on the inside.

4 Grab about 10" (25 cm) of webbing.

Loop the ends over each side of the pant leg. Sew across the pant leg and webbing, but stop about 2" (50 mm) from the opposite edge.

5 Once you've gone across the pant leg (and left a small opening), sew the strap down with five or six rows of stitches across its width.

6 Stick the funnel in the hole and fill the bag about three-quarters of the way full with sand.

7 Sew up the hole very tightly, please. We're not using a plastic bag on this one, remember.

And there she is. I'm sure you'll find a ton of uses for these. It's a good idea to spray these with Scotch Guard™ to help resist water.

Painting Your Rigs

Where do I start? Seems a simple thing to take a can of spray paint to these rigs, right? But metal is its own sort of beast. No matter what you do, you will end up with scratches. There seems to be only one way to make a color permanent and that's powder coating. You can't do powder coating by your lonesome. It has to be done at a special facility because it requires special equipment for "painting" and then gets cured under heat. The good news is that most cities have a place where you can have your rigs powder coated.

I've never gone through the expense myself. I'm probably too cheap, and I just don't care what a rig looks like. It *is* good to paint larger rigs like a crane for practical reasons; you don't want that bright aluminum reflecting any light that might spoil your shot or distract your actors. A few scratches in the paint simply won't matter in this case.

I have tried, I think, everything in the paint department in a desperate attempt to find something that will work well. I've tried metal etch, and different primers before painting with OK results. I've tried every type of paint: metal paint, car paint, high heat paint, you name it. In this chapter, you'll find the best result of all of these trials and experiments. Feel free to try your own way, but chances are, I've already made that mistake for you.

Here's What You'll Need

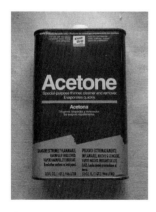

Our old friend acetone.

A palm sander with 60 grit sandpaper.

Shop towels.

A car engine paint. Yep, this seems to work best. You can find it at any automotive supply store. Use flat or semi-gloss black. I painted the *Double Indemnity Crane* with semi-gloss, and the finish is quite beautiful. Buy twice as much as you think you'll need. My 20 *Double Indemnity Crane* took five cans of spray paint.

Some rubber gloves.

DOI: 10.1016/B978-0-240-81337-0.00026-4

Let's Do It!

1 Start by taking your rig apart. (This is the last time, I promise!) Use 60 grit sandpaper to sand all the metal parts that you plan on painting. This gives the metal a little teeth for the paint to grab onto. If you're painting the *Killer's Kiss* crane, you don't need to sand the pipe or take the rig apart. Just clean it well with acetone, and paint it while it's all in one piece.

2 Pour some acetone on a towel and clean every surface really well.

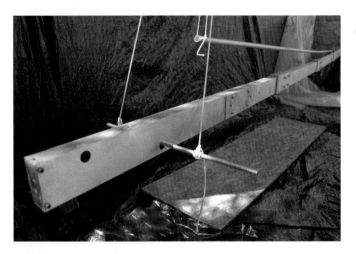

3 If you can, hang your parts so that they are easy to spray paint without having to rotate them. One good way is to hang the parts under a couple of sawhorses if they are big like a crane. These are the parts to the *Double Indemnity* crane. You'll notice that the boom sections are put together. If you have *any* parts that fit into other parts, don't paint the bits that fit into one another. Another example are the threads that need to turn like the *Killer's Kiss* crane.

Here I've hung the tilt bars for the crane on a bit of rope.

4 Have at it! It's best if you start at bolts that are permanent (of course, you took out all the bolts that *aren't* permanent, right?) Do a light spray on each side. *Very light, please!* You don't want drips. You're so close to the end, you don't want to rush this! Do this on edges that are raised too, like the connecting boxes on the crane.

5 Do a light first coat on all the pieces. You do not want any drips! Do a second and third coat. Read the directions on the paint can. Some paints say to wait an hour between coats, some say go for it as soon as it's dry to the touch. Follow these directions!

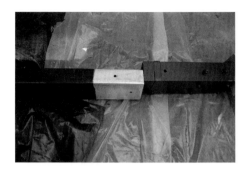

6 If your spray paint directions say to wait 24 hours for the paint to dry, not so fast! Whatever the can says to wait, double it before touching the rig! Cure time is really important. Trust me, I've made the mistake of waiting the recommended time. Longer is better.

7 I mentioned this in Chapter 17, *The* Double Indemnity *Crane*, but repeating it doesn't hurt: If you have pieces that go together a specific way like the boom sections of a crane, code them with color tape or paint before you take them apart after the paint has cured.

8 Admire your handiwork!

Working with Metal

Working with metal isn't difficult, especially aluminum. What it does take is patience. Drilling a hole in a chunk of aluminum isn't much different than drilling a hole in wood, but it does take a bit longer and requires a bit more care.

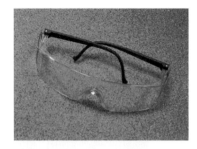

There is one thing you simply must have when working with metal that is nonnegotiable: safety glasses. I'm deadly serious about the safety glasses! I can't tell you how many times I've heard the sound of a chip of metal tap against the glasses I was wearing. Every time I think, *ah, good. I've not gone blind once again!* Don't fool around with this! Buy the glasses and wear them. They are cheap, and can be found at any hardware store. You can't make movies if you're blind.

Drilling Metal: Things You'll Need

A lot of the rigs in this book can be made with a hand drill. Some require a drill press. I would encourage you to look into a drill press. They are fairly inexpensive. You can probably find one for less than $150 that is plenty good enough to get all the projects in this book finished, so you don't have to spend a fortune. And considering the thousands of dollars you'll save by building this stuff yourself as opposed to buying it, an extra couple of hundred on tools is a good investment. You'll find that some of the rigs in this vastly expanded third edition simply require a drill press. No way around that. Sorry.

If you want to use a hand drill, get one that plugs in. Battery powered drills just don't have what it takes. There are quite a few drills out there that have a level on them so that you can be sure you are drilling a straight hole. Very handy indeed! A drill guide like the one shown can be a big help as well in getting those straight holes that are so important.

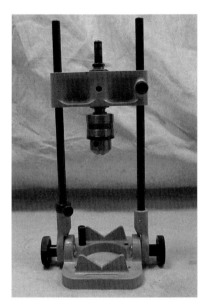

A center punch and/or a prick punch is something you can't do without. Officially, a prick punch is used for marking metal (like a pencil is for wood). A center punch is used for pounding a dimple into metal where you want to drill a hole. I use them interchangeably. So if you want to save a few dollars, a ¼" (7 mm) or slightly larger prick or center punch is fine.

A bench vise. This is invaluable! Just gotta have it. Normally these are bolted to a workbench. But if you don't have a lot of working room like myself (the rigs for the first two editions of this book were built in my apartment kitchen!), it's a good idea to take two ¾" (19 mm) thick pieces of plywood about 12" square and glue them together with wood glue. Bolt your vise to this. Then you can move the vise around and use a clamp to clamp it to your bench.

DOI: 10.1016/B978-0-240-81337-0.00040-9

Clamps. Lots of them. You'll find that you'll need clamps when making a movie too, so don't worry about buying too many. Like sandbags, there never seem to be enough. I use the 3" (76mm) C-clamp the most, but there are times when you need something bigger. Please read through the plans of the rig you intend to build before heading off to the hardware store. If a piece of aluminum is 4" (100mm) thick and your bench is 1" (25mm) thick, you'll need a clamp or two, or three, that can open at least 5" (125mm). When drilling into metal *always* clamp down the metal! If your drill bit jams, the metal will spin into your body and you will get injured. And it happens in the blink of an eye. One second you're happy. The next, the hole in your stomach is bleeding like a waterfall.

A lubricant. You have to use oil to keep your drill bit "wet." There are a few different types you can use. The lubricants that are specifically designed for metal drilling are amazingly expensive. Other oils like 3-in-1 or WD-40 are great for lubricating a hinge, but aren't butch enough for drilling into metal. I use a compromise oil called *cutting oil*. It's generally used for machines that cut threads into pipe, for example. But it's also pretty good for drilling, and really affordable. Make sure you get a little oil can with a long spout to put the oil in.

A drill bit sharpener. This is completely optional. But metal wears down a bit fairly quickly, so you have two choices: buy a new bit or sharpen the old one. Since I build this stuff all the time, I love my *Drill Doctor* bit sharpener. It has saved me a fortune in new bits. But if you're only building one or two projects, in the end it's cheaper to buy a new bit.

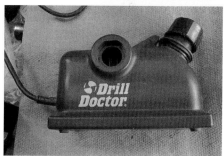

How to Drill a Hole in Metal

1 Always wear safety glasses.

2 Mark your metal with a prick or center punch. Why not use a felt marker? A few reasons: one, marker can rub off. There will be times that you'll need to use a marked measurement on a piece of metal again a few pages later. A prick punch scratches that mark into the metal, so it will always be there. Two, if you need to find the center of a piece, you'll have two marks—one horizontal and one vertical. When you get ready to dimple that metal, the point of the prick punch finds where those two lines intersect very easily, so you'll be putting your dimple exactly where you need it.

3 Dimple the metal. Before you drill a hole, you need to use a prick punch or center punch to pound a dimple into the metal. Simply put the tip of the punch where you want to drill a hole. Give it a good thwack or two with a hammer.

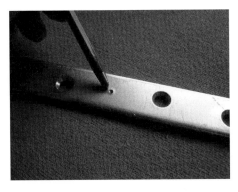

See that little dimple? That's what you want.

4 Clamp down the metal. This is very important. Always clamp the work you'll be drilling!

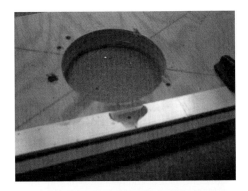

If you're using a hand drill and drilling all the way through a piece, put a scrap piece of lumber under the piece before you clamp it down. This gives your drill bit a place to go besides your bench!

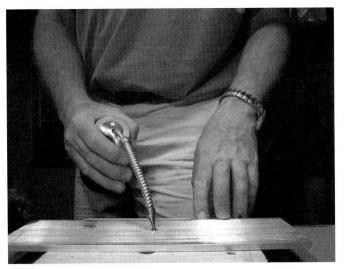

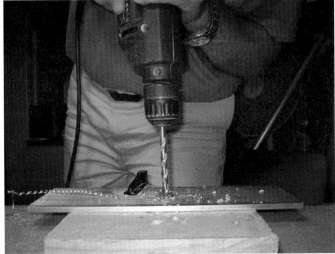

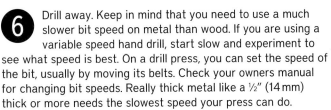

5 Add some drilling oil to the dimple. If you're drilling through a thick piece, you'll need to pull the bit out, add more oil to the hole, drill a bit more, add more oil. The idea is to keep your drill bit wet.

6 Drill away. Keep in mind that you need to use a much slower bit speed on metal than wood. If you are using a variable speed hand drill, start slow and experiment to see what speed is best. On a drill press, you can set the speed of the bit, usually by moving its belts. Check your owners manual for changing bit speeds. Really thick metal like a ½" (14 mm) thick or more needs the slowest speed your press can do.

Place the tip of the bit into the dimple. This is important. This dimple keeps your drill bit from "walking" across the metal.

Killer Camera Rigs That You Can Build

Using the Drill Guide

Sometimes positioning and clamping down the drill guide requires it to be mounted to a piece of plywood. Just drill a bit hole in a ¾″ (19 mm) thick bit of plywood and center the guide over the hole and screw it into the plywood. There are holes on the base of the drill guide for this purpose.

Using a Drill Press

Everything is the same here, including clamping your work! You can clamp it directly to the work plate on the press.

Here, I'm using a special drill press vise. This has a lower profile than a bench vise. Once the material is in the vise, you'll need to clamp the vise to the press working platform.

If your working platform and crank are low enough, you can even use a bench top vise to hold your work.

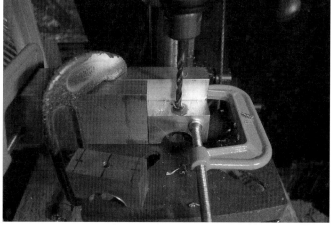

Or you can use scrap metal to form a way to clamp pieces below the bit. This is good if you have several pieces that need a hole in exactly the same place. You just leave the scrap piece in place, then hold each new piece in exactly the spot.

Using a Hole Saw

There are various ways to get a big hole (over a ½") into a piece of metal: all of them outrageously expensive! There are a few projects in this book where you'll need a big hole. There is really only one way to do this yourself without spending a fortune: a hole saw and a drill press.

A hole saw is just a big drill bit. Whenever you buy one of these, make sure it has a guide bit in the middle. Some just have the larger hole part of the bit. You need the guide bit to place it in the dimple so that the larger part of the bit is perfectly centered.

When using a hole saw, you need a very slow drill bit speed. Too fast, and the metal chips will actually weld themselves to the teeth of the bit. And for thick pieces, this will take forever! So be prepared for that. Trying to force it will get you absolutely nowhere. Every ⅛" (3 mm) or so, you'll have to stop the bit, clean the metal off the teeth and out of the center of the hole saw, add more drill oil, then go another ⅛" (3 mm), repeating the process until you're all the way through.

When you are getting near the end, you'll be tempted to put all of your weight behind the bit, and force it through. Don't. Keep adding more oil. You want the big plug of metal to fall out the bottom. If you force it, the plug will get stuck in the hole saw. You'll need to force it out with a screwdriver, and sometimes it just doesn't want to budge!

What to Do If Your Drill Jams in the Metal

The minute you feel the bit jam (you'll feel the drill turning instead of the bit) *immediately* release the trigger on your drill.

Put the drill in reverse and back the bit out.

Put the bit in forward motion again, position the bit slightly above the hole you started. Start the bit spinning at a good clip before lowering it back into the hole. If you start the bit in the hole it will just jam again. Lower it back and finish the hole.

Beware: If your bit jams and your work is not clamped down, you *will* get hurt by a big hunk of spinning metal. *Clamp your work!!*

If the bit jams in a drill press (this is pretty rare, but is does happen), turn off the press, and use your hand to twist the chuck backward until the bit pops out of the hole.

To sum up:
1. Always wear safety glasses. It only takes one metal chip to end your career.
2. Always clamp your work.
3. Make sure your drill bit stays "wet" with drill oil.

Cutting Metal

There are quite a few ways to cut metal—most of them expensive. One of the best ways is a metal band saw. Way out of reach, and frankly it's silly to spend the small fortune they cost to build a few rigs! The other option is to have your metal supplier cut the parts for you. I don't like this way for a couple of reasons; it's way too easy to make a mistake if you are using different sizes and thickness of materials than in this book, but if you are cutting this stuff yourself, it's quite easy to figure stuff out as you go. Second, metal suppliers charge a lot for cutting. My supplier charges $8 a cut. At that rate, I could buy a couple of chop saws before I'm done building everything in this book. And I promise, once you start building this stuff and see how truly easy it is, you'll be hooked. You might even come up with your own designs for new stuff. It's nice to have an easy way to cut metal in your own shop.

Having said that, you can accomplish every cut in this book with a hacksaw. When you get to thick blocks of aluminum, you may curse me for having said that, because you might spend 15 minutes sawing through that 1" thick bar that's only 4" wide. But everything in here is aluminum, a very soft metal, so it is possible. You just need patience, a lot of hacksaw blades, and to cancel that gym membership, because you won't need it any more.

When cutting metal, *always* wear protective glasses!

Things You'll Need

A vise. Nonnegotiable. You just gotta have a bench vise.

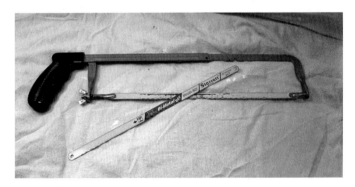

A hacksaw and a package of blades. Get blades that have 14 to 20 teeth per inch. The blade will have something like "14T" stamped on it, meaning 14 teeth per inch. The more teeth you have, the slower going it will be. You'll need a hacksaw regardless of other cutting tools you have.

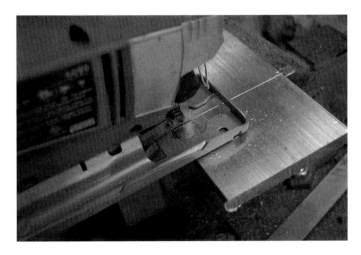

A jigsaw with a metal cutting blade. This is *optional*. I never use a jigsaw. But you can cut aluminum *thinner* than ⅛" (3 mm). You can't cut thicker stuff with a jigsaw. Knowing that some of you will ignore that advice, I tried an experiment with a ¼" (7 mm) thick piece shown in this photo. I got about an 1" (25 mm) in before the blade was useless. A hacksaw would have been much faster! But if you've got a ¹⁄₁₆" thick tube aluminum and a jigsaw, give it a try. But don't go spending money on one just for the projects in this book.

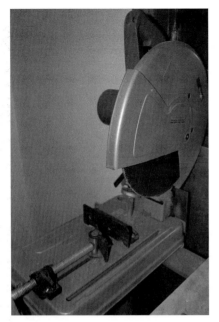

A chop saw. Let me say this right off the bat: you are not supposed to cut aluminum with an abrasive blade chop saw. But I do. Things like aluminum tube or channel are really no problem. But a thick bar is madness, yet I still do it. The reason is a balance of price and the ease of cutting a bar of aluminum. To do it right is expensive. (There are blades especially designed to cut aluminum that you can get for your table saw if you have one. A 12" blade can cost well over $100. If you go this route, make sure it is rated to cut at least a 1" thick bar. Plus you'll need some kind of costly lubricant for this. I don't have the room or the money for a table saw, so this option was out for me from the beginning.)

Cutting an aluminum bar with a chop saw can be done, but the bar will get extremely hot (proper saws use a coolant) and generate a lot of metal dust, so be prepared for this. Also, let me say this: if I were making a ton of cranes or shoulder mounts or stabilizers, there is *no way* I'd use a chop saw. But to get through the projects in this book, it seemed the only alternative to a hacksaw that was affordable. If I had around $500 to spend, Medford tools makes a great cut off saw for any type of metal, called *Raptor*, that is amazing (www. Medfordtools.com). A decent abrasive blade chop saw will run you about $200. Muscling a $10 hacksaw is looking pretty good right now, isn't it? Yes, I am trying to talk you out of doing things "wrong" with an abrasive blade chop saw, even though I've done it that way. Fact is, if you're only going to be buying this stuff for the rigs and nothing else, just use a hacksaw and know from the beginning that you're going to be very tired in the evenings.

Using a Hacksaw

There are two ways to put a blade in a hacksaw: teeth pointing forward or pointing back. If they are pointing forward, you will be cutting on the *push stroke*. If they are pointing back, you'll be cutting on the *pull stroke*. I like the *pull stroke,* but it's up to you. Some hacksaws are designed for the blade to go in one way or the other. If that's the case, follow the manufacturer's direction! Since aluminum is a soft metal, you can go a bit faster than if you were cutting steel. But you still want to keep the strokes down to about one a second. If you go faster, you might heat and break the blade. It's also a really good idea to put a couple of drops of cutting oil on the blade. This will keep the heat down, and your blade will last longer.

Always secure the metal you are cutting. The vise is the absolutely best way! Make sure that you mark the cut before you start with a prick or center punch. The deeper the "scratch" you make with the punch, the easier it will be for the blade to follow the cut. And finally, use the entire length of the blade.

Using a Chop Saw

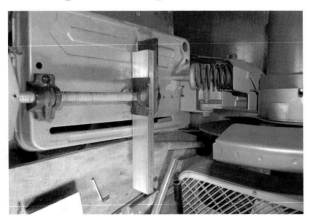

Really? You bought one, huh? OK. First let's talk about the abrasive blade. These will make a thick cut in your aluminum, so make sure you line the edge of the blade against your cut line. If you center the blade *on* the cut line, your piece will come up short. The aluminum must be flat against the base of the saw, or your cut will not be square. Chop saws have a good clamp to hold the material. If yours doesn't, return it to the store and get one that does. On thick aluminum, it's better to stand it on edge, rather than flat.

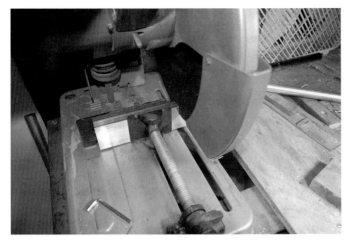

Do *not* force the blade! It will take a while for an abrasive blade to cut through a bar of aluminum. The weight of your hand on the chop saw handle is plenty of pressure. The blade will cause a lot of chips and dust. If you're not wearing your safety glasses while doing this—I'm sorry to say this—you're an idiot.

When your cut is done, do *not* pick it up with your bare hands. It is so hot, you can't believe it. Have a garden hose of bucket of cold water to drop the piece into to cool it down.

You'll have to file the piece to get rid of some metal burrs, so this seems like a good time to talk about filing metal.

About Metal Files

All files remove metal, it's just how they do it that we're concerned with. Typically for our needs, I'd get a *coarse* or *rough* file. A rough file removes the most metal in the shortest time. A diamond pattern rough file will remove stuff even faster. Files are a lot like sandpaper; the rougher grits remove lots of wood, but leave it a bit rough, while a fine grit sandpaper makes wood baby smooth. If you'd like, you can get a range of files from rough to smooth. You start with the rough file and work your way to smooth and you could get a mirror finish on aluminum. For me, I just use a rough file because we are concerned mostly with removing aluminum in the shortest time. The wider and longer the file, the faster your work will go. If you need to file out a hole, you'll need a round file.

How to Use a Metal File

Files work by pushing the file away from you. Don't saw it back and forth. I use two hands: one on the handle and one on the end. Push down while moving the file forward, release the pressure, and bring the file back for another push forward. That's really about it. It's a good idea to use a wire brush to clean all the metal chips out of the file teeth every now and again. Always clamp the work down! Always!

You'll mostly be concerned with cleaning up a piece after you've cut it.

Tapping a Hole in Metal

Tapping a hole creates threads in that hole so that you can screw a bolt or screw into it. This is really easy to do, and the tools to do it are very inexpensive. There are quite a few rigs that require tapped holes.

A tap. These come in various sizes that match bolt sizes. For example, if you want to screw a ¼" bolt into a hole, you need a ¼" tap.

A drill bit that matches a specific tap. A drill bit for a tap is slightly smaller than the tap itself. A tap will either come with a matching drill bit, or the tap will have a number on it that says something like *use #24 drill bit*. Head for the drill bit section of the hardware store where you'll find numbered bits. Pick the right one for your tap. It's that easy.

A tap wrench. This is a special tool that you use to screw the tap into the drilled hole to make the threads.

Cutting oil.

How to Tap a Hole

Use the drill bit that matches the tap. Drill a hole in your metal. Clean all the metal chips out of the hole. This is easy if the hole goes all the way through, but if it doesn't, use a hose or faucet to force the chips out. If your hole does not go all the way through the metal, drill at least ½" deeper than your tap will eventually go.

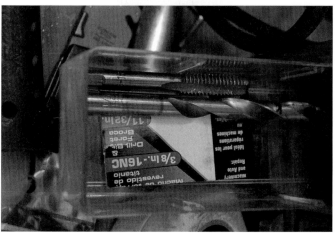

When you're finished drilling the hole, immediately remove the bit from the drill and put it back with its matching tap. I keep all of my taps and matching drill bits in separate little drawers. It's a drag if you use the wrong drill bit for a tap!

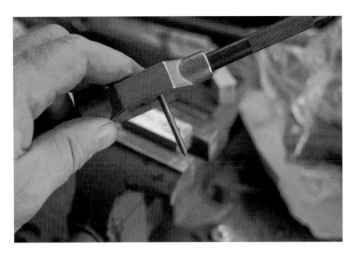

Insert the tap into the tap wrench and tighten the handle down to clamp the tap into the wrench.

Add oil to the tap or if the hole doesn't go all the way through the metal, you can add oil to the hole instead.

Clamp your work in a vise, and insert the tap into the hole. Turn the tap like you turn a screw: clockwise. For every two or three turns, back the tap out a half turn, then proceed. If you're tapping a deep hole that doesn't go all the way through the metal, you'll have to unscrew the tap all the way out and clean it off a couple of times as you go.

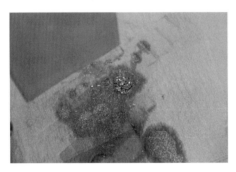

Clean the newly tapped hole really well. There are a lot of metal chips in there. Again, use a hose or sink to get the hole cleaned well.

Make sure to put the tap back with its matching bit.

That's all there is to it. It's pretty cool.

A Final Word

Thanks a million for purchasing this book. Since the first edition, there have been tons of DIYers out there realizing it actually is possible to build the tools of filmmaking yourself. Plans have spread across the Internet since those early editions, but you'll not find anything else like this book anywhere. I've gone to a lot of effort to make these plans easy to follow, with parts easy to find. I've made every effort to keep the information in this book correct, but this is one monster project you hold in your hands, so some errors might have fallen through the cracks (though after nearly 10 years and three editions, I think I've gotten things

down). With that in mind, please let me know if you have any trouble building the rigs or finding materials. I really am here to help. Just shoot me an e-mail at Dan@DVcameraRigs.com.

And *please* let me see the films you make with these rigs! Not only do I love making films, I love watching them, too.

Sincerely,

Dan Selakovich
Los Angeles, CA

The Films the Rigs Are Named For

I love film noir. There's something about the underbelly of American life that I find very appealing. Though the term is French, *film noir* is an American invention. Imagine that for a second—inventing a *genre* of story telling. When is the last time that came around?

The other reason I love this genre is that it is one of the most inventive. These films started out as "B" movies with "B" list directors—amazing directors who wanted to be "A" list under their studio contracts. To move up the studio ladder, what better way than to be creative and daring in story, character, lighting, and editing? Sometimes it works, sometimes it doesn't, but what guts it took to *try*.

Although this isn't necessarily a list of my favorite film noir (I picked many of them simply because the title sounded good with the rig), they are all worth watching!

THE DARK PASSAGE (1947)

Director: Delmar Daves
Screenplay: Delmar Daves
Editor: David Weisbart
Director of Photography: Sid Hickox
Starring: Humphrey Bogart, Lauren Bacall

THE KILLERS (1946)

Director: Robert Siodmak
Screenplay: Anthony Veiller
Editor: Arthur Hilton
Director of Photography: Woody Bredell
Starring: Edmond O'Brien, Ava Gardner

GUN CRAZY (1950)

Director: Joseph H. Lewis
Screenplay: MacKinlay Kantor and Millard Kaufman
Editor: Harry Gerstad
Director of Photography: Russell Harlan
Starring: Peggy Cummins, John Dall

THE NAKED KISS (1964)

Director: Samuel Fuller
Screenplay: Samuel Fuller
Editor: Jerome Thoms
Director of Photography: Stanley Cortez
Starring: Constance Towers, Anthony Eisley

If you've ever wondered where that movie cliché of "a prostitute with a heart of gold" started, this is it.

THE DARK CORNER (1946)

Director: Henry Hathaway
Screenplay: Jay Dratler and Bernard Schoenfeld
Editor: J. Watson Webb
Director of Photography: Joe MacDonald
Starring: Mark Stevens, Lucille Ball (yes, *that* Lucille Ball)

CRY VENGEANCE (1954)

Director: Mark Stevens
Screenplay: Warren Douglas and George Bricker
Editor: Elmo Veron
Director of Photography: William Sickner
Starring: Mark Stevens, Martha Hyer

THIEVES' HIGHWAY (1949)

Director: Jules Dassin
Screenplay: A.I. Bezzerides
Editor: Nick De Maggio
Director of Photography: Norbert Brodine
Starring: Richard Conte, Valentina Cortesa

THE GLASS KEY (1942)

Director: Stuart Heisler
Screenplay: Jonathan Latimer
Editor: Archie Marshek
Director of Photography: Theodor Sparkuhl
Starring: Brian Donlevy, Veronica Lake

SHOCK CORRIDOR (1963)

Director: Samuel Fuller
Screenplay: Samuel Fuller
Editor: Jerome Thoms
Director of Photography: Stanley Cortez
Starring: Constance Towers, Peter Breck

THE SWEET SMELL OF SUCCESS (1957)

Director: Alexander MacKendrick
Screenplay: Clifford Odets, Ernest Lehman
Editor: Alan Crosland, Jr.
Director of Photography: James Wong Howe
Starring: Burt Lancaster, Tony Curtis

As I mentioned, this isn't a list of my favorite film noir movies, but *Sweet Smell* truly is my favorite movie of all time.

THE CITY STREETS (1931)

Director: Rouben Mamoulian
Screenplay: Dashiell Hammett, Max Marcin
Editor: William Shea
Director of Photography: Lee Garmes
Starring: Gary Cooper, Sylvia Sidney

STORM FEAR (1956)

Director: Cornel Wilde
Screenplay: Horton Foote
Editor: Otto Ludwig
Director of Photography: Joseph La Shelle
Starring: Cornel Wilde, Jean Wallace

KILLER'S KISS (1946)

Director: Stanley Kubrick
Screenplay: Stanley Kubrick
Editor: Stanley Kubrick
Director of Photography: Stanley Kubrick
Starring: Frank Silvera, Jamie Smith

If you ever wondered what a film noir directed by John Cassavetes would look like, *Killer's Kiss* is it. Not at all what you're used to from Stanley Kubrick!

THE BIG COMBO (1955)

Director: Joseph Lewis
Screenplay: Philip Yordan
Editor: Robert Eisen
Director of Photography: John Alton
Starring: Cornel Wilde, Richard Conte

DOUBLE INDEMNITY (1944)

Director: Billy Wilder
Screenplay: Raymond Chandler and Billy Wilder
Editor: Doane Harrison
Director of Photography: John F. Seitz
Starring: Fred MacMurray, Barbara Stanwyck

Double Indemnity is widely considered the best film noir of all time. I feel it's also a purely noir film in every way. (You'll find no sentimentality in this movie!)

T-MEN (1948)

Director: Anthony Mann
Screenplay: John C. Higgins
Editor: Fred Allen
Director of Photography: John Alton
Starring: Dennis O'Keefe, Alfred Ryder

T-Men was a small film made by a small studio (Eagle-Lion Films), but so well noticed that both the director and cinematographer were signed by MGM.

THEY DRIVE BY NIGHT (1940)

Director: Raoul Walsh
Screenplay: Jerry Wald, Richard Macaulay
Editor: Thomas Richards
Director of Photography: Arthur Edeson
Starring: George Raft, Humphrey Bogart, Ann Sheridan

THE THIRD MAN (1949)

Director: Carol Reed
Screenplay: Graham Greene
Editor: Thomas Richards
Director of Photography: Arthur Edeson
Starring: Joseph Cotten, Anna Schmidt, Orson Welles

Technically, *The Third Man* isn't film noir. But Orson Welles' *Harry Lime* is so lacking in humanity that I just couldn't ignore its noir flavor.

THE GUILTY BYSTANDER (1950)

Director: Joseph Lerner
Screenplay: Don Ettlinger
Editor: Geraldine Lerner
Director of Photography: Gerald Hirschfeld
Starring: Zachary Scott, Faye Emerson

Definitely not great, but if you'd like to learn how *not* to use exposition, this is the movie for you. Every character in this thing is a despicable one. That alone makes it worth seeing.

THE STEEL TRAP (1952)

Director: Andrew L. Stone
Screenplay: Andrew L. Stone
Editor: Otto Ludwig
Director of Photography: Ernest Laszlo
Starring: Joseph Cotten, Teresa Wright

THE HARDER THEY FALL (1956)

Director: Mark Robson
Screenplay: Philip Yordan
Editor: Jerome Thoms
Director of Photography: Burnett Guffey
Starring: Humphrey Bogart, Rod Steiger, Jan Sterling

About the Author

Photograph by Adam Reynolds

Prior to 1986, Dan Selakovich worked professionally on almost every position on a variety of film and video projects: cinematographer, assistant camera, camera operator, loader, gaffer, grip, and even boom operator. In 1986 he moved to postproduction as an editor. On his first feature as editor, he acquired the reputation of someone that could "fix" a film in trouble by directing additional scenes and reediting. Since the film world is quick to pigeonhole a skill, Mr. Selakovich has worked uncredited for years trying to make terrible films a little less terrible.

When not editing, he is writing, making, and teaching film. He has taught his rig-building techniques and their use at the University of Southern California Summer Film Program as well as at seminars at the NAB conventions in Las Vegas and New York City. He also teaches the wildly popular film seminar *Finding the Right Shot*, which teaches filmmakers how to capture emotion and character through camera placement, movement, art direction, and editing. He is often told, *"I went to four years of film school, and we didn't learn any of this stuff!"*

He lives in Los Angeles with his dog, Silvie.

Index

Note: Page numbers followed by *f* indicates figures.